Educational Leadership:
Ambiguity, Professionals and Managerialism

Author details

Eric Hoyle is Emeritus Professor and Senior Fellow in the Graduate School of Education, University of Bristol. His major interests are in organization theory, the professions and professional development. He is author of *The Politics of School Management* and (with Peter John) *Professional Knowledge and Professional Practice*.

Mike Wallace is a Professor of Education in the Department of Education, University of Bath. His research interest is in the management of change in education and other public services. He is author (with Keith Pocklington) of *Managing Complex Educational Change* and editor (with Louise Poulson) of the teaching text *Learning to Read Critically in Educational Leadership and Management*.

Education Leadership:
Ambiguity, Professionals and
Managerialism

Eric Hoyle and Mike Wallace

⑨SAGE Publications

London ● Thousand Oaks ● New Delhi

First published 2005
Reprinted 2006

SAGE Publications Ltd
I Oliver's Yard
55 City Road
London EC1Y 1SP

SAGE Publications Inc.
2455 Teller Road
Thousand Oaks, California 91320

SAGE Publications India Pvt Ltd
B-42, Panchsheel Enclave
Post Box 4109
New Delhi 110 017

British Library Cataloguing in Publication data

A catalog record for this book is available from the British Library

ISBN-10 0-7619-6742-7 (cased)
ISBN-10 0-7619-6743-5 (paperback)
ISBN-13 978-0-7619-6742-2 (hbk)
ISBN-13 978-0-7619-6743-9 (pbk)

Library of Congress Control Number: 2005904555

Typeset by Pantek Arts Ltd, Maidstone, Kent
Printed on paper from sustainable resources
Printed and bound by Athenaeum Press Ltd., Gateshead Tyne & Wear

Contents

List of Tables

Preface

We have selected *irony* as the organizing concept of this book because it offers a link between our five main concerns.

Our first concern is to bring to the fore a perspective on organizations that has existed for some time but has remained marginal to the prescriptive leadership and management literature. This perspective acknowledges that organizations are characterized by ambiguities, dilemmas and incommensurable values. It recognizes that such characteristics are endemic. This is particularly so in educational organizations, on which we focus. The goals of educational organizations are both diverse and diffuse. They lead inevitably to the irony of unintended (as well as intended) consequences of well-intentioned actions. In the past, leaders and managers in state-funded schools have been content to live with the ironies of organizational life. They now have less of an option since the underlying purpose of educational reforms has been to eliminate ambiguity through tightly specifying the work of headteachers and teachers, coupled with equally tight surveillance and punitive measures for failure to meet this specification.

Our second concern is to engage with the unintended consequences of the prevailing approach to the management of change: policy initiatives promulgated by central government coupled with the expectation that they will be efficiently implemented through strengthened leadership and management at the school level. Policies may be designed to improve learning and teaching, or to strengthen organizational leadership and management as a means of improving the educational activity that leadership and management support. While the raft of policies has brought considerable changes in structures and procedures in the education system, the core of the educational enterprise – learning and teaching – has remained relatively untouched. The irony here lies in the fact that, as each successive policy initiative comes to be seen as having brought unintended consequences, the response has been to develop corrective policies – which have themselves generated further unintended consequences.

Our third concern is to suggest that the rhetoric currently dominating the discourse of policy and of leadership and management, encapsulated in the term 'transformation', is largely a myth. The irony here is that school staff are being urged to be 'transformational', implying the achievement of radical change, under conditions that actually constrain their opportunities for achieving change. Transformation at the school level means, in practice, finding more efficient ways of implementing government policy.

Our fourth concern is to suggest that most headteachers and teachers have not wholly rejected recent educational reforms nor offered overt resistance, but have mediated government policies to render them congruent with the needs of students in individual schools in particular contexts. The irony here is that headteachers and teachers, through a stance of principled infidelity, are implementing policies that would not have worked if their prescriptions had been faithfully followed. In the interests of their students, headteachers and teachers are moderating the negative unintended consequences of central government policies.

Our fifth concern is to suggest that perhaps a majority of headteachers and teachers are bringing to their work a scepticism towards government policies, a pragmatic approach towards their implementation, a sense of contingency in their relevance, and a constructivist approach to learning and teaching collaboratively pursued. These are some of the manifestations of what we have termed an 'ironic orientation', an approach that we endorse.

Having briefly set out our purposes, it is necessary to indicate some of the considerations that have gone into writing what is unapologetically a 'position' book. In no way do we pretend to offer a detached account of the contemporary educational scene. For this reason we have written in the first person plural throughout.

Our stance is sceptical but not cynical. There are no villains in the book. We believe that politicians, government advisers, inspectors, administrators, headteachers and teachers generally act in good faith and with a genuine desire to improve educational quality. However, it will be clear that our sympathies lie with those headteachers and teachers who persist, despite the power of external forces, in doing their best for their students as far as circumstances allow. We want to celebrate their efforts and to rescue these from their *samizdat* status.

The term 'leadership' has only recently overtaken the term 'management' in political and practitioner discourse as the main descriptor for what is entailed in running and improving public service organizations. We recognize the distinction between leadership (making new things happen) and management (keeping new and existing things on track). However, because of the ambiguity in meanings of leadership and management we have throughout used the two terms in conjunction except where we are specifically dealing with differences. The conjoined terms equate to the single term 'administration' as used in North America over a long period.

We are not advancing a theory, constructing a model, reviewing a literature, presenting a body of research data, or offering a set of procedural recommendations. We are simply offering an invitation to engage in a discussion. Hence we draw on an eclectic range of data and on a range of personal experiences in telling our story. Our approach is one of informed speculation.

It must be stressed that we believe in the importance of school leadership and management. Schools need positive leadership and it is vital that they are effectively managed. We are concerned that school leaders and managers should have a suitable preparation for their difficult roles. But while we have no reservations about the importance of effective leadership and management, we do have reservations about managerialism – leadership and management to excess – because it is more likely to create problems for headteachers and teachers than to solve them.

We fully recognize both that central government has a mandate to improve state funded education, and that attempting to bring about the necessary large-scale change is highly complex. But in our view the prevailing strategy is flawed because it underestimates the importance of headteacher and teacher agency and limits room for manoeuvre in school settings.

Our approach is somewhat downbeat in that we do not prescribe what should be done. We offer no 'magic bullet' in the mode of many books to be found on airport bookstalls – most of which are probably abandoned by their purchasers on the arrival of the drinks trolley. In fact, our underlying argument is that the idea that there could be a 'magic bullet' for solving educational problems is wishful thinking. It follows that there is a need for a massive scaling down of the number and frequency of policy initiatives designed to eradicate ambiguity, and a complementary need to search for ways of reducing the press of leadership and management in schools.

We are very conscious of the forces that would have to be overcome in reducing managerialism. We identify two in particular. One is the decline of trust within society. What might be called 'the tragedy of the professions' is that they have clung to their self-interested practices for so long that politicians have over-reacted in their mistrust of professions, and clients have become over-ready to turn to litigation. Yet we do not abandon the possibility of sustaining a principled professionalism. The other barrier is the effect of career patterns favouring those who can display managerial credentials and fluency in the managerial discourse, which understandably makes it difficult for many to deviate from managerialist expectations.

Our 'case' is state funded schooling within the educational system of England and Wales, the source of most of our examples. But our account could equally apply to other public – and perhaps private – services in Britain and in other countries. Ambiguity is endemic in all organizations. Out of ambiguity arises irony. Overzealous attempts to remove ambiguities make life more difficult for front-line practitioners. An ironic orientation allows them to live with the external pressures imposed upon them. They continue to obtain job satisfaction, not from attending the ever-increasing number of committee meetings or completing ever-growing amounts of paperwork, but from doing their best for the people they serve in their contingent circumstances. We hope to contribute to the growing discussion of these issues.

The book is timely. There are signs of a growing recognition of the dysfunctions of managerialism, particularly in terms of its impact on the workload of teachers, growing work-dissatisfaction, and the consequent problems of teacher recruitment and retention. Some politicians are coming to realize that the huge expenditure on accountability is having at best only a marginal impact on learning and teaching. It is thus highly cost ineffective, since the investment is largely in structural change and in accountability procedures. On the other hand, we accept that many politicians may find it difficult to abandon the belief that yet another policy initiative will put matters right. We aspire therefore to offer reassurance to those headteachers and teachers whose method of coping with current pressures is through what we term an ironic orientation.

Our concerns are addressed in the book through a four-part structure. Part One introduces our approach to irony and demonstrates its generic applicability to education. Chapter 1 conceives irony in terms of unintended consequences and defines the key concepts of our ironic perspective. Chapter 2 explores diverse sources of endemic ambiguity, and their exacerbation by change, constituting preconditions of irony in schools as organizations. Chapter 3 adopts a complementary focus, showing how parallel sources of ambiguity stimulate equivalent ironies in the implementation of improvement policies across administrative system levels in education.

Part Two introduces the notion of managerialism as excessive leadership and management. It traces ironies generated unwittingly by the implementation of central government managerialist policies that militate against educational improvement, especially those connected with reforms. Chapter 4 looks historically at the early and more recent rise of managerialism in school education, portraying how its promise radically to reduce ambiguity has been belied by the resultant ironic consequences. Chapter 5 critically examines how managerialism threatens to produce self-serving leadership and management at the expense of educational activity.

Part Three takes our critique of managerialism further by deconstructing the rhetoric of educational crisis and the urgency of system transformation which underpins managerialist reforms. Chapter 6 reveals ambiguities and associated ironies engendered by the gap between aspects of the mythical discourse of transformation and externally imposed constraints which leave school staff with little scope for transforming learning and teaching. Chapter 7 similarly scrutinizes the discourse of organizational leadership as a means of promoting educational transformation and the ambiguities and ironies that in reality restrict leadership to the transmission of centrally specified reforms.

Part Four examines the ironies of school staff responses to managerialism and builds the case for more temperate approaches to educational administration. Chapter 8 looks at evidence that many, perhaps most, school staff are mediating reforms rather than endorsing them. Chapter 9 hypothesizes that most school staff have adopted an ironic orientation towards managerialism, which is actually highly appropriate for professional practice in relatively ambiguous circumstances. Chapter 10 sketches out what temperate educational administration and incremental improvement efforts might look like, supported by wise policies that are accepting of ambiguities and return professional practice in leading, managing and teaching to the heart of the service of education.

Eric Hoyle
Mike Wallace

Acknowledgements

We owe a considerable intellectual debt to Professor James March, whose writings and conversations have strongly influenced our thinking. Mike Wallace was awarded a Senior Fellowship within the AIM (Advanced Institute of Management Research) initiative during 2003–05, funded by the Economic and Social Research Council (award number RES-331-25-0011). His fellowship was focused on managing complex and programmatic change in the public services, and included exploring ambiguity in the change process and implications for coping effectively with it. Ideas and opinions expressed in this book are those of the authors and do not represent the view of the ESRC.

PART ONE: THE NATURE OF IRONY

1

Introducing the ironic perspective

Why do efforts to improve the quality of education via organizational leadership and management make matters worse in some respects as well as better? In what ways are education professionals responding to such efforts? Could the endeavour to improve education through organizational leadership and management be rendered more effective by accepting certain limitations in practice on what is desirable in principle? These questions are of considerable significance for education now and in the future, yet they are also contentious. Implicit in the first question is the assumption that contemporary efforts are producing negative as well as positive impacts. The second question raises the possibility that not all educational professionals are responding as would-be improvers might wish. The third question suggests that there are perhaps limits to the potential for improvement at the level of practice that need to be taken into account. These reservations rarely surface in current policy discourse – at least in its public expression, though we suspect that some might be acknowledged privately. For alongside the gains of reform, there is plentiful evidence of problems.

Here is just one indicative example. Heralded by the passing of the Education Reform Act in 1988, successive British governments have generated an extensive series of policies aimed at transforming English state school education as part of a wider strategy to reform, or to 'modernize', all the public services (e.g. OPSR, 2002). An unintended negative consequence has been to overload chronically the headteachers and teachers charged with responsibility for implementing the multiplicity of innovations entailed in these policies. Government-sponsored surveys between 1994 and 2000 revealed a steady increase in working hours of those employed in schools (Table 1.1). As a result of pressure from representatives of teachers and headteachers, at the end of the 1990s central government instituted an initiative to reduce the level of bureaucracy in schools that had mostly resulted from its own reforms. However, subsequent surveys showed that the initiative had done little to stem the tide of paper and computer files. One comparative study showed that the annual working hours of headteachers – even after taking the length of school holidays into account – were still above the average for managers across a range of occupations. Weekly term-time hours of headteachers were much higher (PWC, 2001).

Table 1.1: *Evidence from PriceWaterhouseCoopers teachers' workload study*

Data from previous diary studies

School and teacher type	Hours worked in a 'typical' week		
	1994	1996	2000
Primary			
Headteacher	55	55	58
Deputy head	51	54	55
Class teacher	49	51	52
Secondary			
Headteacher	60	61	60
Deputy head	56	56	58
Head of department	50	52	52
Class teacher	48	50	51
Special			
Class teacher	46	49	50

Data from PwC study, 2001

Teacher type	Hours' work per week	Primary school	Secondary school	Special school
Headteacher	total hours	59	64	58
	hours spent teaching	5	1	3
Other teaching staff	total hours	54	55	51
	hours spent teaching	22	19	18

Table 1.1: *Cont.*

Hours worked according to different salary and associated responsibility levels (all schools)

Hours of work per week	Salary and responsibility level of teacher or headteacher				
	Newly qualified teacher	Main pay scale	Management points	Upper	Leadership
Total hours	53	54	54	53	58
Hours spent teaching	19	21	20	20	16

Hours worked during the school holidays

Annual hours worked during the school holidays in different types of school				
Primary school		Secondary school		Special school
Teacher	Headteacher	Teacher	Headteacher	Teacher
116	100	121	196	107

Source: Based on extracts from the interim report of the PriceWaterhouseCoopers teacher workload study (PwC, 2001)

In late 2002, another major survey of the responses of teachers to the demands of their work, sponsored by the General Teaching Council for England and the *Guardian* newspaper (GTC, 2003), found that:

- approximately one-third (35 per cent) of teachers planned to leave teaching in the next five years, just over half expecting to retire. But the remainder of those planning to leave (including 15 per cent of all newly qualified teachers) expected to secure jobs elsewhere;
- more than half (56 per cent) stated that their morale was lower than when they joined the profession;
- the longer teachers had been in the profession, the worse their morale. However, there was also a sharp dip in morale immediately after the first year of teaching;
- in nominating three factors which demotivated them as teachers, over half (56 per cent) identified 'workload' (including unnecessary paperwork), over a third (39 per cent) referred to 'initiative overload', about a third (35 per cent) the 'target-driven culture' (connected with central government-imposed improvement targets), and almost a third (31 per cent) blamed poor student behaviour and discipline;

- four-fifths (78 per cent) of teachers perceived that the government accorded them little or no respect.

An enduring staff recruitment and retention problem had emerged, created in large part by the heavy workload that was being experienced. Carol Adams, the chief executive of the GTC, commented (GTC, 2003):

Teachers in the 45+ age range constitute half the workforce and represent a significant and valuable resource of experience and expertise. Often, however, their potential contribution is overlooked for a variety of reasons:

- workload has increased to the point that they feel a proper work–life balance is impossible to achieve and some start to look at the option of early retirement or a change of occupation;
- seniority in the profession still tends to be associated with taking managerial responsibility, whereas some would prefer to remain in a teaching post;
- for women returners promotion involving an even heavier workload may not be attractive.

As a result of undervaluing the over-45s, we are not only seeing many experienced teachers go early, we are also failing to tap into their valuable experience of change management, behaviour management and as potential mentors for new recruits. Many of this group of teachers were involved in the school-based innovations which preceded the Education Reform Act of 1988 and they have been instrumental in managing substantial change through the past decade. But instead of valuing what they can offer – we are watching them go.

She noted that according to government statistics one-third of teachers retiring in 2000–2001 had retired prematurely.

If government reforms had produced such consequences for the morale and aspirations of teachers, one can assume that the impact on headteachers was even greater. However, notwithstanding all the reform efforts of policy-makers, and the increased workload of teachers and headteachers, educational outcomes based on qualifications across the UK as a whole have not kept pace with all of its international economic competitors. A recent league table published by the Organization for Economic Cooperation and Development (2003) compared the proportion of students achieving good qualifications at the end of secondary school in 30 developed countries between 1991 and 2001. The UK had dropped from 13th to 20th in the league because improvement in the UK since 1991 was more modest than elsewhere.

We recognize that survey data are contestable and open to different interpretations. Nevertheless there is strong evidence from a variety of sources that two decades of reform have not led to anticipated levels of educational improvement, and certainly not commensurate with levels of investment in education, but have led to widespread teacher and headteacher dissatisfaction. We regard the gap as ironic. For this reason we have taken *irony* as our key analytical concept. However, although one side of the coin of irony reveals the gap between intention and outcome in government policy, the other side of the coin reveals how headteachers and teachers have adopted an ironic orientation as a means of coping with the pressures which this gap has generated.

Taking irony seriously

Irony has no canonical meaning. It is a term with a long history in the English language and has diverse connotations. Some are intentionally playful, mocking or cynical, as in Mark Twain's dictum: 'To succeed in life, you need two things: ignorance and confidence.' We realize that taking this term as the centrepiece of our perspective risks us being interpreted as frivolous, and so not to be taken seriously. But we are very serious about improving education. We have chosen to employ this term as the basis for a new perspective because no alternative concept so incisively illuminates the phenomenon we believe needs exploring if government and organization-based improvement efforts are to become more effective. To minimize the risk of being misunderstood, we will below unpack the connotations that we have attached to *irony* for the purpose of our argument. However, before considering the concept itself, we offer two illustrations of irony by way of setting the scene.

The first is far from education. We have selected it as the most extreme of cases to show how irony is a concept that can direct attention both to coincidences and to unintended cause and effect linkages, including those of the most shocking kind. Perutz (1998) recounts the story of the 'ambiguous personality and career' of the German chemist Fritz Haber (1868–1934), a Jew by birth. In 1909 he became the first scientist to synthesize the gas ammonia from nitrogen in the air, paving the way for industrial production of nitrogen fertilizers that dramatically increased worldwide agricultural production, producing the very positive long-term consequence of improving life chances for millions of people.

However, Haber's discovery also enabled the German manufacture of nitrates for explosives to be continued throughout World War I, after the British naval blockade in 1914 halted supplies of Chilean saltpetre from which explosives had traditionally been manufactured. According to Perutz, without Haber's invention the Germans would have soon been forced to sue for peace. This invention thus generated the negative consequence of prolonging the war, robbing millions of people of their life chances.

Haber, fervently patriotic, was instrumental in developing poison gas for trench warfare. He helped to mount the first chlorine gas attack which caused some 15,000 allied casualties, a third of them fatal. That night Haber's wife committed suicide, shooting herself with her husband's service pistol. Her act was widely interpreted as a protest against his chemical warfare activities.

In recognition of his pioneering synthesis of ammonia, Haber received the Nobel Prize for Chemistry in 1918. He continued advising Germany's government on the secret production of chemical weapons until 1933, when the Nazis seized power. They forced him from his official position because he was Jewish, and he soon fled abroad, dying a year later. He never lived to witness the longer-term consequences of another of his inventions, in 1919: the poisonous gas Zyklon B, originally intended for use against agricultural pests. Nine years after Haber's death, the Nazi SS chose this gas for deployment at Auschwitz and other Nazi death camps, and among the millions of Jews who were killed in the Holocaust were Haber's own relatives.

But as Perutz (1998: 16) reflects:

> By a terrible irony of fate, it was his apparently most beneficent invention, the synthesis of ammonia, which has also harmed the world immeasurably. Without it, Germany would have run out of explosives once its long-planned blitzkrieg against France failed. The war would have come to an early end and millions of young men would not have been slaughtered. In these circumstances, Lenin might never have got to Russia, Hitler might never have come to power, the Holocaust might not have happened, and European civilization from Gibraltar to the Urals might have been spared.

There is a horrific mixture in this story of the ironies of coincidence and the ironies of unintended consequences, often far removed in time from the actions that led directly or indirectly to them. We move on to a second example, of a very different order from such an utterly appalling case, but which could have serious enough implications for education.

Our second illustration is nearer to home: on 28 April 2003 it was announced that Jarvis, an engineering company, had been awarded a three-year contract from the British government to advise the 700 worst performing secondary schools in England and Wales, through its subsidiary Jarvis Educational Services Ltd. The *Guardian* (2003) newspaper reported that the announcement was condemned as 'shocking', 'extraordinary' and 'a joke' by teachers' leaders. Their angry reaction was provoked by the fact that Jarvis had been notably unsuccessful as the main contractor for the privatized national railway network infrastructure. The parent company was at that time under police investigation in connection with the possibility of negligence in the Jarvis railway line maintenance work that might have caused a fatal train crash. It was thus deemed highly inappropriate for Jarvis to be commissioned by the government to 're-engineer' failing schools.

By July 2004 the *Guardian* was reporting the Jarvis group to be close to bankruptcy. Its Accommodation Services Division was the biggest contractor in the country within the central government private finance initiative for refurbishing schools and universities. Underbidding to win new business had brought the dire unintended consequence of cost over-runs. Jarvis was forced to write them off, plunging the group into debt and threatening to delay much-needed improvement in the education building stock. In the same month, the parent company was heavily fined for negligence over a second rail repair incident described by a judge as 'breaking basic rules known to every child with a train set'. A freight train had been diverted onto a line with a missing stretch of track.

The award of the advisory contract to Jarvis is emblematic of the ironies of unintended consequences besetting state education in the UK. We contend that such ironies have been generated by unintentionally inappropriate responses to alleged problems. Although greatly increased levels of funding have been allocated to education, it is not evident that members of the public perceive corresponding improvement. There is some evidence to the contrary – witness the OECD international league table mentioned earlier. Although government policy is to give schools greater freedom through policies of devolution and 'cutting red-tape', many headteachers and teachers perceive only greater bureaucracy. Although a policy of equality of opportunity is proclaimed, another government policy to create 'specialist' schools is creating new forms of selection, and although government ministers have confirmed their intention to recruit and retain high quality teachers, we have already noted evidence of a decline in the job satisfaction of teachers and a drift away from the profession.

These discrepancies appear to stem in part from a lack of understanding among policy-makers about the daily realities of schooling and how the multiple changes they introduce impact on what is already a difficult job. They arise especially from a misguided faith in leadership and management as a panacea. The discrepancy between intention and outcome in relation to policy has been widely discussed in the policy literature. But here we seek to explore the significance of this discrepancy in terms of the experience of headteachers and teachers and its implication for professional work.

The ironic perspective will help us to sustain the argument that the latent function of much recent policy has been to eliminate prevailing ambiguity from educational organizations even though, in our view, much of that ambiguity is endemic. This strategy has entailed the pursuit of greater uniformity over the process and outcomes of education, to be achieved by establishing a much tighter link between official goals, school leadership and management, school structures, school cultures, the technology of learning and teaching, and measured learning outcomes. It is a strategy based on the optimistic Taylorist assumption (to be discussed further below) that the tighter the coupling the greater the efficiency. We accept that there are compelling reasons for reducing ambiguity in schools in order to provide a consistent and incremental education – but only up to a point. We consider that policy-makers have unwittingly tried to reduce ambiguity beyond that point, bringing the ironic consequence of generating increased ambiguity. We also accept that there exist in schools as organizations endemic ambiguities that can neither be 'managed away' nor 'dissolved' through a 'shared culture'. Headteachers and teachers live with these ambiguities and cope with them on a daily basis. Over-reliance on managerialism, which seeks to resolve ambiguities in the interests of accountability and on the enforcement of 'national standards', has made life difficult for teachers and headteachers. Managerialism diverts teachers from their core task of promoting learning into an expanding range of managerial roles. Some are at best pseudo-managerial, and at worst, could be merely self-serving for their incumbents. Too much leadership and management could be constraining the very educational activity they are there to facilitate.

Despite the unacceptable pressures on headteachers and teachers, a majority remain committed to their vocation. By selectively reinterpreting policy they are continuing to do their best for their students in their immediate circumstances. In this way they are offsetting to some degree the unintended, and potentially deleterious, consequences of managerialism. Ironically this response often ensures that the intention of policy-makers is fulfilled to a degree that would not be possible if specified procedures had been followed to the letter.

An approach to irony

Our approach, then, is to adopt the notion of irony as affording a profitable perspective upon contemporary leadership and management in education. It is a modest approach. Our perspective has neither the rigour of a theory nor the neatness of a model. It has no pretensions to be more than one lens for bringing into focus the implications of the gap between policies and their effects. In using the term we seek to encourage reflection, provoke thought, generate discussion and thereby enhance understanding. Normal academic protocol would require us to define our key term of irony at the outset. Yet no single definition meets our needs. In fact, many who have written on irony have noted the problem of defining the term. Enright (1984), in *The Alluring Problem: An Essay on Irony*, questioningly heads his first chapter: 'Definitions?' Here he cites a remark by Muecke (1969) that 'getting to grips with irony seems to have something in common with gathering mist, there is plenty to take hold of if we could'. Since there appears to be no canonical definition of irony, we feel at liberty to propose connotations which are appropriate to our purposes. In this spirit we draw an initial distinction between what we will call *situational irony* and *semantic irony*.

Situational irony refers to those ironies that are part of the reality of social life. The major manifestation of situational irony is the unintended consequence: when good intentions lead to unfortunate consequences and also where apparently unfortunate occurrences have a happy outcome. The term 'ironic' is often applied to a coincidence. But some writers on English usage warn against this: 'Recently all seriousness seems to have departed from the word. The slightest and most banal consequence or point of resemblance or even just-perceptible absence of one, unworthy of a single grunt of interest, gets called ironical' (Amis, 1997: 113). Two close friends, both professors of politics in different universities, dropped dead within a relatively short space of time of each other within the precincts of the Houses of Parliament. Some would interpret this unusual circumstance as irony, but presumably Amis and others would regard it as simply coincidence.

We are concerned with the serious aspects of irony. In the next chapter we will discuss how situational irony is endemic in all organizations, and members have to live with it through making repeated adjustments and negotiating frequent compromises. However, policies embodied in the educational reform movement of the past two decades have brooked little compromise, relying on the excessive resort to leadership and management that we will term 'managerialism' to ensure implementation. This reliance, coupled with the increase in ambiguity intrinsic to change connected with reforms, has considerably increased the potential for situational irony. We write in support of headteachers and teachers as they find ways of coping with the high level of ambiguity. But we also argue that managerialist attempts to remove ambiguity can have deleterious consequences. Many could be avoided if there was a greater recognition of the endemic nature of irony and a consequent refocusing on effective leadership and management – which may mean *less* leadership and management than are demanded of headteachers and teachers today.

Semantic irony we use to connote the ironic use of language, which comprises a variety of linguistic and literary forms. We suggest that semantic irony may be either intended by a speaker or writer, or unintended but still detectable by an observer. A common *intentional* strategy was noted by Samuel Johnson in his dictionary definition of irony: 'A mode of speech of which the meaning is contradictory to the words.' There are many forms of wordplay which are ironic. When the late Daniel Moynihan allegedly observed that 'there's money in poverty' he was presumably using irony intentionally to indicate that poverty was becoming a well-funded area of research. In response to the news that Jarvis, the railway engineering company, had been offered the contract referred to above, The *Guardian* newspaper reported that the Liberal Democratic Party spokesperson on education derided the fact that Jarvis 'had no track-record' in education. Was this intentional or unintentional semantic irony? On hearing of the coincidence that two professors of politics had died in the Houses of Parliament, a colleague responded: 'No professor of education would be found dead in a school.' Irony was thus expressed through multi-level ambiguity.

We suspect that ironic humour has a considerable role to play in schools whose staff members are confronted by managerialism. But little of the banter we hear in school staffrooms has reached the public domain, for obvious reasons. A rare example of published ironic humour is the spoof account by Davison and Kemshall (1998) of a school inspection under the auspices of the central government Office for Standards in Education (OFSTED).

Ironic humour is widely recognized as a defence mechanism for those who find themselves in difficult circumstances. The Soviet logician Alexander Zinoviev (1979) wrote a novel poking fun at the ironies entailed in the unintended consequences of Soviet bureaucracy – before wisely escaping to the West, and Powell and Paton (1988) have discussed the role of humour in relation to conflict and resistance. We suspect that it is a common response to the current pressures of school life, but we cannot document this.

It is usually clear when a writer or speaker is being consciously ironic. However, we are intrigued by the possibility that there also exists, in the context of educational leadership and management, a form of indiscernible 'inward' or unarticulated irony. Careers in educational leadership and management are now dependent on having mastered what is usually dubbed *managementspeak*. Today's everyday discourse of school leadership and management simply did not exist 30 years ago. Consider terms like 'curriculum delivery', 'mission statement', 'development priorities', 'achievement targets', 'budget-setting', 'incentivizing' or 'deliverables'. Managementspeak is an international phenomenon. Fullan reports a North American school principal as saying: 'If I had said twenty years ago that I had a vision, I would have been put in an institution. Now I can't get a job without one!'

Many users of managementspeak may well be secret ironists smiling inwardly even as they use managerialist language in conformity with current expectations. We entertain the possibility that there exist, alongside the straight-faced conscious ironists, those who are in this respect bilingual and would not dream of using managementspeak outside work, and those who unreflectively use managementspeak but are capable of appreciating its ironic aspects when events force this realization upon them. There are also, undoubtedly, those who have internalized the managerialist discourse to such a degree that they are oblivious to its irony, however great the discrepancy between the comfort of language and the harsh reality of events. As Auden put it: 'He lectured on navigation as the ship was going down.'

Visionary rhetoric is a form of managementspeak that has increased very noticeably in schools since the advent of educational reforms. Much is designed for public consumption, and it has even become a commonplace official expectation that staff in senior posts will be visionaries. Under the OFSTED (2003a: 41) framework for school inspection, criteria for assessing leadership quality include the extent to which 'leadership shows clear vision, a sense of purpose and high aspirations for the school, with a relentless focus on pupils' achievement', and 'leaders inspire, motivate and influence staff and pupils'. Advertisements placed by school governors for headteacher posts make frequent reference to vision, as in this illustration: 'The governing body will require and expect the new headteacher to: be a transformational leader, inspiring staff and students; develop the vision of a high quality fully inclusive community secondary school – the natural choice for local parents ...' Or this list of ingredients:

> What's needed:
> 1 part passion
> 1 part vision
> 1 part sheer hard graft ...

Or even this example, linking humour with serious expectation:

> Can you walk on water? Or leap tall buildings? Have you got the strength to lead by example? ... We are looking for a professional with experience and vision to build on ... [an already strong] foundation. We have high expectations that you will be able to demonstrate your excellent strategic planning and management of resources, while maintaining a good sense of humour as you guide the children to reach their full potential.

The semantic irony of the visionary discourse that senior staff are required to produce lies in the more or less conscious or unconscious gap between the hubris of the rhetoric and the more prosaic reality as actually experienced by teaching staff, students and parents alike. If all the visionary rhetoric corresponded with reality, would a third of teachers be seeking to leave the profession?

Visionary rhetoric may create situational irony if those who are to be inspired find the discourse unrealistic. One of us recalls working as a teacher in a school where the headteacher was referred to by most of his colleague teachers (but not to his face) as a 'vision-a-day' person. The unrelenting effusiveness of his visionary rhetoric and enthusiasm for myriad initiatives to realize this vision did not square well with the classroom experience of his colleagues. He unilaterally decided one day to have an unbreakable mirror installed in each of the student toilets, since he wanted students to take more pride in their appearance as part of their social development. He announced as much in morning assembly and, by the end of the day, the students had succeeded in proving experimentally that the mirrors were in fact not unbreakable.

Another form of semantic irony can occur through *reification,* where a collectivity such as a school is referred to as if it is a corporate entity capable of corporate action independent of the people who constitute it. Attention is thus diverted from the possibility that there may be significant differences among members. Reification is defined by Berger and Luckmann (1967: 106) as 'apprehension of the products of human activity *as if* they were something other than human products – such as facts of nature'. Collective nouns are inescapable, but reification in such phrases as 'the school has decided on an improvement plan' or 'this school has a passion for learning' can blind users to the existence of competing positions.

The difficulty is well illustrated by the notion of 'organizational capacity'. A school staff and others in the community may be regarded as having more or less capacity for the learning needed for effective educational innovation. Stoll (1999: 506) defines internal capacity for school improvement as: 'the power to engage in and sustain continuous learning of teachers and the school itself for the purpose of enhancing student learning'. But how can 'the school itself' learn, as opposed to the staff and other community members? She states further that 'a school with internal capacity can take charge of change because it is adaptive'. This definition implies that schools – rather than the people who work in them – are capable of taking charge of change. It belies the impact of people beyond the school gates who may also wish to take charge of change inside them, including central government policy-makers.

Reification is even starker in metaphors such as 'the self-managing school' (Caldwell and Spinks, 1988), 'the intelligent school' (MacGilchrist et al., 1997), or 'the learning organization', to be discussed in more detail below. Those who use such terms in academic texts are aware that the reification is shorthand. Most readers will also be well aware from their experience that this is the case. But there will be eager managerialists who take it that such entitiness is both desirable and achievable and may, with unintended consequences, pursue the chimera.

Let us return to our saga of the unbreakable mirrors. Suppose the headteacher had announced that the school vision included students possessing high self-esteem and so taking pride in their appearance. Such a statement would have glossed over the fact that neither the other staff nor the students actually shared this vision. It was the headteacher's vision and he failed to achieve its widespread adoption, leading to the situational irony entailing the negative unintended consequence (from his perspective) of the students testing the indestructible mirrors to destruction. Reification is often allied with the visionary rhetoric now widely expected of school leaders. Vision is usually expressed as the property of an entity rather than the property of such of those individual members of the school who have internalized it.

To the distinction between situational irony and semantic irony we add two further distinctions. The term *responsive irony* refers to the coping strategies adopted by headteachers and teachers when confronted with irreconcilable demands in matters of curriculum, pedagogy and organization. We here use the term *mediation* – to be discussed at greater length below – as a category of ironic response which seeks to meet the accountability requirements embedded in national policies while adapting those policies to the perceived needs of particular students and classes, and the circumstances of particular schools. *Responsive irony* thus relates to the *actions* of headteachers and teachers. We have inferred its existence from a variety of case studies, and from the typologies that some ethnographers have generated of how headteachers and teachers have coped in practice with the policy demands of the reform movement.

An illustrative form of responsive irony in English schools is 'teaching to the test'. The reputation of teachers and, ultimately, the jobs of headteachers depend on comparative performance of their students as represented in public league tables of national assessment and examination results. National tests therefore impinge significantly on the circumstances of every state-funded school in the primary and secondary sectors. Yet the 1996 Education Act also requires that school staff should provide a 'broad and balanced curriculum' which 'promotes the spiritual, moral, cultural, mental and physical development of pupils at the school and of society', reaching way beyond what is tested. The assessment policies were designed by government policy-makers to promote the educational goals of raising standards of achievement and informing parental choice of school. But a widespread ironic response has been to focus on teaching what stands to be measured and published, at the expense of other government-sponsored educational goals. It is notable that a cycle of ameliorative policy-making has been stimulated. For example, legislation under the 2002 Education Act allows applications to the Secretary of State for Education and Skills to exempt a school in England from specific educational legislation, for up to three years, where such action is judged to be likely to raise standards. (What might constitute sufficient grounds for a positive judgement in advance of the improvement action seems inevitably ambiguous.)

We use the term *ironic orientation* to refer to the disposition that allows many headteachers and teachers not merely to cope, but to flourish in circumstances of value conflict and irreconcilable external demands. Let us offer an illustrative anecdote. An experienced supply teacher had worked regularly in a particular school which was due shortly to receive an OFSTED inspection. This supply teacher volunteered to come into the school during the inspection, masquerading as a parent helper. The supply teacher then supported a class teacher with maintaining student discipline during lessons observed by an OFSTED inspector, enabling the class teacher to give the best possible performance.

Subsequent conversation hinted at the supply teacher's disposition leading to this ironic response. What had been done was justified partly on the grounds of having complied with the letter of the law: the inspectors had not been obstructed in any way from observing the learning and teaching process they had come to evaluate. But the justification was also moral, on two counts of the end justifying the means. First, it had been right to take action to protect the staff and students from disruption that would ensue if the class teacher was negatively judged. Second, it had been right to offer covert resistance to a policy deemed unfair because of the massive pressure it placed on staff, and the distorted picture of practice to which it gave rise. We neither condone nor condemn this person's rationale behind the ironic response to an external inspection regime. We cite it in support of our claim that a more or less intuitive or consciously held disposition may lie behind the actions constituting ironic responses.

Hypothesizing an 'ironic orientation' is the 'high wire' part of our argument for three reasons. First, we have no empirical evidence from attitude scales or other measures that such an orientation exists. Second, there is the problem of whether we can legitimately attribute an ironic orientation to people who would not use the term in their daily language – the general problem of 'first order' and 'second order' concepts in the social sciences. Closer to our concerns we note that Alexander (1995) criticizes Berlack and

Berlack's (1981) conception of teachers' 'dilemmas' on the grounds that they do not demonstrate that teachers are aware of these dilemmas. Third, the notion of an ironic orientation may appear too playful to constitute a moral approach. It is true that the scepticism (in the sense of 'reasonable doubt'), pragmatism (complying with external demands while attempting to sustain valued practice where possible), and contingency (what will work in specific circumstances) that we will associate with the ironic orientation run counter to current approaches to educational leadership and management. The latter emphasize the transformative power of values (to be discussed in Chapter 7). We will simply state at this point that we believe the ironic orientation to be genuinely but realistically moral.

Gathering mist: getting to grips with irony

It is self-evident that the questions asked in any field of enquiry determine the answers that are found. We opened this chapter with the questions:

1 Why do efforts to improve the quality of education via organizational leadership and management make matters worse in some respects as well as better?
2 In what ways are educational professionals responding to such efforts?
3 Could the endeavour to improve education through organizational leadership and management be rendered more effective by accepting certain limitations in practice on what is desirable in principle?

They reflect our 'intellectual project': our scheme of enquiry to generate the kinds of knowledge that will realize our specified purposes. We wish to get to grips with what happens when well-intentioned improvement efforts come unstuck, and why it happens. We wish to understand what educators do when coping with the implementation of improvement efforts. We wish to use this knowledge as a platform for reflecting on how improvement efforts might be rendered more effective. Answering our questions necessitates drawing on a wider range of theory and research than is usually considered in the leadership and management literature. We need ideas and evidence from investigators who have asked different questions from most who work in the educational leadership and management field, and which relate to our questions because of the intellectual project these theorists and researchers have pursued. Five intellectual projects may be identified (Wallace and Poulson, 2003). Each is driven by a different rationale and value stance towards the phenomenon under scrutiny, leading investigators to ask particular kinds of question (Table 1.2).

Table 1.2: *Five intellectual projects pursued in the field of educational leadership and management*

Intellectual project	Rationale	Value stance	Typical question
Knowledge-for-understanding	understand through theory and research	disinterested	what happens and why?
Knowledge-for-critical evaluation	evaluate through theory and research	critical	what is wrong with what happens?
Knowledge-for-action	inform policy makers through research and evaluation	positive towards policy and improving practice	how effective are actions to improve practice?
Instrumentalism	improve practice through training and consultancy	positive towards policy and improving practice	how may this programme improve practice?
Reflexive action	improve own practice through evaluation and action	critical of practice, positive about improving	how effective is my practice, how may I improve it?

The two mainstream intellectual projects in this field are closely associated. The first is *knowledge-for-action*, directed towards developing knowledge with practical application from a positive standpoint towards current policy and practice. The second, usually informed by the first, is *instrumentalism*, imparting practice knowledge and skills directly to improve practice inside the prevailing policy framework. These projects attract external funding and generate most practical prescriptions for educational leadership and management. But the combination of operating largely within current policy and attempting to improve practice tends to deflect the attention of investigators from the more searching questions to which we seek answers. Our intellectual project lies closer to *knowledge-for-understanding*, consistent with Popper's (1963: 125) dictum that 'it is the task of social theory to explain how the unintended consequences of our intentions and actions arise'. We believe that deepening comprehension leadership and management in the context of schools as organizations is essential to underpin the development of more realistic knowledge-for-action and instrumentalism. Indeed, ignoring the potential insights to be gained from knowledge-for-understanding is one reason why managerialism continues to be pursued despite the ironies it generates.

We take an explicitly negative normative stance towards what we judge to be a deleterious consequence of excessive leadership and management: unintentionally inhibiting the educational improvements that they are intended to foster. In this respect our intellectual project has some affinity with *knowledge-for-critical evaluation*, but we part company with those whose purpose is restricted to demonstrating what is wrong with what happens. The constructive goal of our intellectual project is to use the insights from knowledge-for-understanding to inform knowledge-for-action that, in turn, could support more realistic policy-making and leadership and management practice to improve education in conditions of endemic ambiguity.

The ironic perspective presents school leadership and management in a new light. It offers no prescriptive theory but seeks to generate understandings which *might* – not *will* – contribute to more effective leadership and management of schools. Texts on educational leadership and management born of knowledge-for-action and instrumentalism are vital in providing practitioners with guides to action. But because of their narrow focus on improving practice within the bounds of current policy they may inhibit understanding of the wider context in which leadership and management take place, and the often unforeseen and unnoticed consequences of actions taken by leaders and managers. We will draw on two bodies of literature which figure only marginally in conventional, practice-oriented leadership and management texts. We will call them *organizational studies* and *professional workplace studies*.

Organizational studies differ from most knowledge-for-action and instrumentalist project-driven leadership and management studies and the form of theory that they generate. While a broad distinction can be made between leadership and management theory and organization theory we recognize that they interpenetrate in many ways and are ultimately interdependent. Indeed, organization theory is not a tight, self-contained body of thought. It embraces a diversity of approaches (reviewed in Hoyle, 1994). But overall, the organizational approach does represent a different way of viewing organizations from that of leadership and management texts.

First, the intellectual project of organization theory is knowledge-for-understanding. While many organization theorists hope that their work will have positive consequences for practice, they are more likely than leadership and management theorists to orientate their findings towards broader social and political concerns surrounding the practice being examined. Second, organization theory is oriented primarily towards understanding what happens, whereas leadership and management theory are oriented more towards specifying what should happen and towards

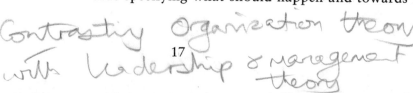

Contrasting Organization theory with leadership & management theory

improving what does happen. It should be noted that the stance underlying the attempt to understand, rather than improve, cannot be wholly disinterested. Organization theory is certainly not value-free, many contributors having a more or less explicit political or educational agenda – as we have. But leadership and management theory are more directly orientated towards changing practice according to implicit or explicit values. Third, organization theorists are more likely to engage in general social scientific theory-building, in contrast to the reliance of leadership and management theorists on practical experience, consultancy and applied research in developing normative applied theory.

Despite the different orientations of organization theory and leadership and management theory, it is possible to draw eclectically on both. We will do so, but our priority to deepen understanding by questioning what so many leadership and management studies take for granted draws more heavily on organization theory than most leadership and management texts.

Organization theory is included, if under represented, in the study of educational leadership and management. By contrast, professional workplace studies are conspicuous by their absence in the leadership and management literature primarily because, like organizational studies, they reflect the intellectual project of developing knowledge-for-understanding. They explore the experiences of professionals who work in educational organizations, including leaders and managers. We employ the umbrella term 'professional workplace studies' to connect investigations rooted in different social science traditions in order to enhance our understanding of the daily realities of schools and their leadership and management. Such work includes:

- *Studies of teaching as a profession*: these can be divided into studies of the teaching profession in society – its institutions, prestige and power, and studies of professional practice and the school context. Studies of practice are particularly relevant to our argument;
- *Studies of the school as a workplace*: these cover similar ground to studies of the professions and professional practice, but have different theoretical roots and lean more towards the intellectual project of knowledge-for-critical evaluation, with more emphasis on conflict and constraint. We do not, however, draw extensively on these studies since they have a stronger orientation towards policy than our own approach;
- *Studies of responses among teachers and headteachers to policies entailed in the reform movement*: they cover somewhat the same ground as the above but are focused on specific issues, such as responses to the introduction of the National Curriculum into English state schools. We will draw heavily on a number of these studies including those of Helsby (1999), Osborn et al. (2000) and Woods et al. (1997).

Collectively, professional workplace studies convey a sense of the reality of school life for teachers and headteachers, not least their responses to managerialism, which so many studies of school leadership and management fail to convey because their orientation is much more towards what organizations could and should be like. It is largely on the basis of professional workplace studies that we hypothesize the ironic response and the underlying ironic orientation. Among the insights offered by the professional workplace studies is the depiction of varied responses to managerialism in schools. We will adopt as our starting point the following categories of orientation that underlie responses:

1 *True believers*, who have internalized managerialism in language and in practice.
2 *Ironists*, who have not internalized managerialism and are often critical of it, but who have fashioned their own commitment by being 'flexible, adaptive, creative, opportunistic, collaborative with a drive towards self-improvement and self-development' – the description of a primary school headteacher labelled as a 'composite' head by Woods et al. (1997).
3 *Uncommitted*, who are less positive than either of the other types and have responded to managerialist reforms in a variety of ways including surface adaptation, minimal compliance, retreatism, resistance, and exit (as we have seen, approximately one-third of teachers are seeking to leave the profession).

Our heroines and heroes are, of course, the *ironists* who adopt creative means to meet the contingent needs of students where their needs are perceived as not being appropriately met through official policies. These are the headteachers and teachers who fulfil the professional function of the flywheel of education by their steadfast focus on pupil interests, throughout the vicissitudes of repeated changes in policy and associated modes of accountability.

We have said more by way of introduction about organizational studies and professional workplace studies than about educational leadership and management studies. The latter literature also reflects different perspectives, which we will not seek to map. Instead, we set out in a condensed, breathless and intentionally provocative form what we see as constituting the current orthodoxy in educational leadership and management studies, particularly as expressed in texts on school improvement:

> School improvement is the outcome of the capacity of a transformational leader driven by moral purpose to harness distributed leadership in creating a learning organization, underpinned by a strong organizational culture which reflects shared values and is expressed through a clear vision, encapsulated in a distinctive

mission, and internalized through a school-focused staff development programme by a collegial staff who contribute to a corporate development plan which gives unified direction to their synergistic and continuous improvement efforts.

This summary constitutes the touchstone of our analysis, yielding key concepts such as transformational leadership, culture, the learning organization and vision that we discuss separately. There is a strong body of work within this tradition and we in no way deny its value. Most contributors are well aware of the complexities of improvement. However, some readers, and not a few teachers of educational leadership and management, bring an oversimplification to their reading. We are concerned with the ironies of unintended consequences which flow from writers pressing these concepts too hard and from readers over-interpreting the prescriptive element of such texts. Here and in the rest of the book we generally avoid referring critically to specific texts from this genre in order to keep the length of our own text within bounds. But we can assure readers that we are not attacking a 'straw person'. The current orthodoxy is widely prevalent, as anyone who has read the school improvement literature will appreciate.

From intemperate to temperate leadership and management

We appreciate that this book is unlikely to influence any 'true believer' who ventures to open it. But we hope to reassure those headteachers and teachers that we have identified as ironists, who continue to sustain a focus on the well-being of pupils but who feel pressured, and perhaps stressed, by managerialist expectations. We also hope that it will provoke our colleagues involved with the professional development of educational leaders and managers to join us in giving this reassurance, and to consider the possibility that effective leadership and management may entail reducing their compass. We aspire to inform any policy-makers who recognize the problems induced by managerialism, and are willing to consider, in principle, moving towards a more temperate approach to educational improvement.

We will attempt to show how an understanding of contemporary educational organizations can support the stance which many headteachers and teachers are currently taking towards managerialism. But we offer no general prescriptions. It would be contrary to our position to do so. Our view is that we must look to local, contingent and temporary solutions to educational problems and accept ambiguities and dilemmas as endemic problems which may be amenable to the achievement of temporary equilibrium, but never fully resolved. In saying this we are sensitive to March's (1999: 5) dictum: 'Balance is a nice word but a cruel concept.'

2
Endemic ambiguities:
the preconditions of irony

Why is irony integral to leading and managing organizations? Why does change increase the likelihood of irony? Why can't irony be eliminated? Answers to these questions imply understanding what generates irony in the first place. Here we examine sources of perennial ambiguities which, in turn, create preconditions for irony: the situational irony of unintended consequences, and the semantic irony of intended or unintended ambiguity in language. There is no escaping irony in social life: it is ubiquitous and endemic. As Robert Burns put it: 'The best laid plans of mice and men gang agley [go awry].' While the preconditions for irony can sometimes be ameliorated or reduced, general experience and abundant evidence imply that they cannot be entirely managed away. We focus now on the endemic ambiguities generating ironies in educational organizations and elsewhere, in preparation for examining how managerialism designed to reduce ambiguities produces the unintended consequence of increasing them.

Ambiguity entails uncertainty in meaning. Perhaps the best-known form is semantic: uncertainty in the meaning of words. One of the key literary critical texts is Empson's (1930) *Seven Types of Ambiguity* which explores both the deliberate and unconscious use of irony as a mark of great literature. The problem of ambiguity in the meanings of everyday speech and in the relationship between words and the world remains one of the central issues in philosophy. Years ago a colleague of one of us sent a complimentary copy of a book he had recently published to his head of department. The latter replied with a note which read: 'Thank you for sending me a copy of your new book. I shall waste no time in reading it.' This person, who took great care over correct language use, was probably being deliberately ambiguous. Not only is language capable of different meanings but so also are actions and organizational structures.

Ambiguity captures an aspect of organizations that we guess readers will intuitively recognize. It is typified by complaints from organization members

21

like 'why does everyone else know what's going on except me?', 'why can't they see things my way?' or 'who's *really* in charge here?'. While organizational life may be partly characterized by clarity, certainty and predictability, it includes another element which is less than clear, somewhat uncertain, rather unpredictable. What is happening, should happen or will happen may be open to different interpretations and judgements. A dictionary definition of 'ambiguous' gives a sense of this side of organizational experience: 'doubtful; undetermined; of intermediate or doubtful nature; indistinct; wavering; having more than one possible meaning; equivocal' (Chambers, 1998). It is the area of organizational life where people waver between alternative interpretations, or where they are equivocal about judging what to do, that we argue can sometimes be reduced but never eradicated.

There is a lengthy tradition of organizational studies oriented towards knowledge-for-understanding that support our claim. People have to work at making sense (Weick, 2000) of what they experience as disjointed, sometimes confusing, and frequently frustrating situations. Brunsson (1989) has explored the ambiguities arising from the discrepancy between speech and action in organizations. Such experience is characterized by varying organizational ambiguity – which March and Olsen (1976) define as experienced opaqueness over internal decision-making, by unpredictability concerning the short and longer-term outcomes of managerial actions, and by enduring organizational dilemmas (Ogawa et al., 1999) that are not amenable to definitive and permanent resolution.

Change inside any organization adds to chronic ambiguity, and can make it acute, as is acknowledged in organizational and leadership and management studies alike. Fewer acknowledge that an ineradicable degree of change is endemic to organizational life, even in the most stable and routinized settings. Endemic change contributes to endemic organizational ambiguity because it brings uncertainty surrounding the learning that individuals and groups must acquire to put the change into practice.

Students, parents and school staff come and go. Staff turnover means that new members periodically joining the organization must familiarize themselves with their new situation. Their longer-serving colleagues must learn to work with the newcomers. Whenever individuals are allocated a new task – however routine – they have to learn for themselves how to fulfil it competently (Wallace, 1996). Ask teachers, headteachers, administrators or policy-makers how they have developed their ability to perform their present tasks as well as they do now. They will probably say they learned primarily through trial and error in their current job. Some will acknowledge the value of previous job experience, training or other support in rendering their learning less of a trial, and with less error, than might otherwise have been the case. Few will claim that past experience or training were all they needed.

Adding innovation to the endemic level of change flowing from the passage of time, typically with improvement in mind, temporarily increases ambiguity because of the additional learning required for implementation. Even modest change challenges existing practices and assumptions of people in and around the organizations implicated. In his synthesis of research, Fullan (2001: 8) argues that educational change concerns the individual struggle to find meaning in an experience that, intrinsically, involves venturing into the unknown, and so into the realm of increased ambiguity:

> The problem of meaning is central to making sense of education change. In order to achieve greater meaning, we must come to understand both the small and the big pictures. The small picture concerns the subjective meaning or lack of meaning for individuals at all levels of the educational system. Neglect of the phenomenology of change – that is, how people actually experience change as distinct from how it might have been intended – is at the heart of the spectacular lack of success of most social reforms. It is also necessary to build and understand the big picture, because educational change after all is a sociopolitical process.

Fullan refers to the common failure among policy-makers or leaders and managers to take into account what the change experience will be like for those in educational organizations who are expected to modify their practice. How can they make sense of it? They cannot fully understand the new practice before they have experienced it for themselves. To begin with, its meaning will be doubtful, undetermined, indistinct, equivocal. Nor can they be sure how to make this shift before trying it out. No amount of preparation can get round what they can learn consciously or tacitly only through attempting to modify their practice in their work setting. Knowing how to do things differently emerges from doing things differently. People come fully to make sense of a significant change only once its ambiguity diminishes as it becomes their normal way of doing things.

Ambiguities generated by change also flow from attempts to change the practice of people in organizations across an entire system. Government reform efforts reach beyond the small picture of life inside any organization to the big inter-organizational picture of policy drivers stimulating new policies. They herald system-wide changes in practice. Innovations connected with central reform policies are implemented through the coordinated activity of individuals and groups based in organizations at intermediate and peripheral administrative levels. Most of those involved in large-scale change never meet face-to-face – and often do not even know of each other's existence.

Augmenting endemic ambiguities: a school-based innovation

To anchor our account of sources of ambiguity forming the preconditions of irony, we recount the story of a planned change in one school with

23

which one of us was associated. It happened before the advent of central government educational reforms, when the English state school system was a 'national service, locally administered'. Headteachers and teachers had considerable scope to innovate. There was minimal legislation governing the curriculum and teaching methods, and the only national assessment comprised examinations for secondary school students. Inspections were rare. In a political context favouring risk-taking this school setting offered exceptionally favourable conditions for the headteacher (who we will call John) to be innovative, adding to the everyday level of ambiguity. He was appointed as the headteacher of a new middle school in an English town, designed for students aged 9–13.

John was the first staff member to be appointed, while the school was still a building site. He had previously held a senior post in a private school whose hallmark was child-centred, progressive education for the children of affluent middle-class parents. His often-articulated goal was to implement this progressive approach in the contrasting context of a state school serving a predominantly working-class area. Compared with most headteachers, who inherit a going concern on appointment, John had unusual scope for creativity. He was centrally involved in appointing other staff, so could attract like-minded colleagues who would implement his progressive educational vision. His talent for writing lively job advertisements yielded hundreds of applications. Those who were successful could anticipate contributing to a dynamic and progressive school.

Yet John did not entirely get his own way. Even a large field of applicants had limits. In the event, most teachers came from local secondary schools. The deputy headteacher's post was the sole appointment where John's preferred candidate was not selected. A teacher from a nearby secondary school was invited by officials from the local education authority (LEA) where the school was situated to apply for this post. At the time, LEA officials had sufficient authority to over-rule the headteacher during the selection process. The new deputy headteacher subscribed to a more traditional view of education: she had gained her high local reputation by preparing students for public examinations in separate curriculum subjects taught through didactic methods.

John's jurisdiction over the curriculum and pedagogy lay within wide parameters. As the school was being constructed and opened in stages, he was able to influence its internal design and how it would be furnished and equipped. Facilities for older students were built first, the school opening with 350 students aged 11–13. There were specialist areas, and most teachers recruited from secondary schools expected to continue teaching their subject. Students were initially grouped in single-ability sets for the more academic subjects, circulating between specialist teachers working in specialist curriculum areas. Several staff who had been recruited from primary schools, together with a teacher who had worked in the headteacher's previous school, were more ready to consider the progressive approach which John wished to implement.

He called staff meetings to nurture what is now called a 'culture for change', building the enthusiasm of teachers for a more progressive approach that gave students greater scope to develop a love of learning by following their individual interests. On one occasion he brought his tape-recording of students in his previous school expressing appreciation of the progressive education they had experienced. He stated his hope that the recording would convince his more sceptical colleagues of the value of this approach. But he did not know how to operate the school tape-recorder. Several minutes of struggle and the assistance of a colleague were required before he succeeded. An unintended consequence was his loss of credibility with most teachers. He had transgressed their professional beliefs: lesson preparation included learning how to work equipment, and headteachers should be exemplary teachers.

All staff experienced a heavy workload as they endeavoured to establish arrangements for teaching and pastoral care of students. Teachers appreciated their allocation of 'non-contact time', freeing them from teaching for a few hours each week to do preparation and marking. When John walked into the staffroom one day and asked a teacher there what she was doing, her facetious reply was: 'Killing time!' He immediately cancelled non-contact time for all staff, proclaiming the new rule that every teacher should be in the classroom throughout the school day. Staff stress levels rose.

Embracing an uncertain future: from vision into practice

John pressed ahead with implementing a school-wide 'individualized curriculum', supported by the few staff sharing his vision. He allocated to each teacher responsibility for pastoral support and monitoring the academic progress of about 20 students (but excepted himself). Teachers of mathematics, science and modern languages argued vehemently for continuing with single-ability sets. John acquiesced, aware that he needed their cooperation. So the timetable for students was then constructed around their requirements. Most other teachers were to teach individual students who could choose when to attend their lessons. Humanities subjects were integrated, students having choice of activities inside broad topics like 'our neighbourhood'.

Students were required to register in their pastoral group at the beginning of the morning and afternoon sessions. They must carry a record sheet on which teachers confirmed their attendance for particular lessons, and report to their pastoral tutor regularly during lesson times so that their progress could be monitored. In that pre-computer age, it proved difficult to design a timetable according to these parameters that was flexible enough to cope with changing requirements (say, a group of students going on a field-study trip). Several teachers spent many evenings constructing a timetable. They embossed labels – letter by letter – onto strips of magnetic tape, placing the labels on a metal timetable matrix fixed to the staffroom wall.

Students and staff were issued with timetable and record sheets, and the new regime was launched one Monday morning. The immediate outcome of this progressive educational venture did not conform to John's vision, but was consistent with what his opponents predicted. Many students headed towards popular areas like art, rapidly filling them to capacity, while seeking to avoid less favoured activities. Some disappeared after registration. Most intruded repeatedly on their pastoral tutor's lessons to report on their progress. Others mislaid their record sheet. Even the teachers taking single-ability sets of students – who at least knew whom they would be teaching and when – had to cope simultaneously with being a pastoral tutor. Tutees might enter the classroom at any moment for their record sheet to be signed.

John rejected pleas from teachers to abandon the initiative. Staff meetings became increasingly conflictual, polarized between the traditionalists led by the deputy headteacher and the progressives led by John. The deputy headteacher began holding unauthorized meetings with her supporters to campaign for a return to the earlier, formal approach. Staff absenteeism soared. Colleagues in school were frequently required at short notice to cater for extra students. The abolition of staff non-contact time, coupled with an LEA policy to provide supply cover only after an absence of three days, meant that no-one except John was available to take the classes of absent colleagues. But he refused all requests: his job was to run the school, not teach. At one crisis point he entered the school hall during a physical education lesson, wearing the caretaker's overall and carrying a can of brown paint and a paintbrush. He began painting noticeboards that lined the walls, remarking to the teacher taking the lesson that he was feeling stressed and this activity was his therapy.

Student indiscipline increased, as indicated by competitions to climb classroom curtains during the lessons of certain teachers. At lunchtimes, parents whose houses backed onto the school playing field were treated to a display of the amorous adventures of older students – in contravention of school rules. A few teachers resorted to direct action when confronted with unintended consequences of the new order. John instructed a recognized mathematics teacher to take an absent colleague's geography class instead of his mathematics set. The teacher informed the students that he was not a geography teacher and would not teach them. He sat reading a book while the students amused themselves. John did not discover what had happened until the absent teacher returned to work.

Calls to abandon the individualized curriculum increased as hitherto progressively oriented teachers defected to side with the traditionalists. They and parents put pressure on John to invite LEA officials to inspect the school, hoping that the individualized curriculum would be judged a failure. John refused. He countered by appearing on local television, extolling the virtues of the progressive education that he claimed was being provided. Afterwards he stayed mostly in his office. An electric 'traffic-light' message system installed outside his door usually informed those who knocked that John was 'engaged'.

Ambiguity subsides: outcomes of the innovation

One teacher secured a job elsewhere, capitalizing on his new-found immunity from John's authority. He visited the LEA officials to reiterate the request to inspect the school. The officials refused because the headteacher had not invited them. However, a few weeks later the individualized curriculum was discontinued and a more traditional approach reinstated. Within a few years John had taken early retirement, replaced by a headteacher with traditional educational beliefs and values.

The well-intentioned attempts of an innovative school leader, whose moral purpose was to realize progressive educational goals for students, proved to have unintended consequences that undermined their achievement. None of those involved foresaw what would happen. None had realized how their educational beliefs would be so deeply challenged. None had expected such a chasm to appear between the rhetoric of contributing to a dynamic new school – attracting them to the job – and the reality they experienced.

This salutary tale illustrates sources of ambiguity precipitating situational and unintended semantic ironies. It culminated in the re-establishment of the traditional approach to teaching, drastically reducing ambiguity generated by the individualized curriculum. This account may be used to exemplify sources of endemic ambiguity characterizing all social interaction, and their augmentation by change.

Complexity and the sources of endemic ambiguity

The foundations of ambiguity in educational leadership and management rest with its *complexity*. One definition of complexity is 'composed of more than one, or of many parts; not simple or straightforward; intricate; difficult' (Chambers, 1998). The core idea is of multiple relationships between the parts constituting a whole. The 'whole' constituted by any leadership and management activity (such as John's presentation at the staff meeting) is made up of constituent parts (including beliefs and values of the people present, their interaction during the meeting, and the shift in perceptions when John could not work the tape-recorder).

Decades of experience, theorizing (e.g. Dimmock and Walker, 2003) and research suggest that leadership and management practice in different settings may be affected by multiple factors that inter-relate in multiple ways. Effects may impact recursively to become causes. (John's focus on his presentation may have caused him to forget that he would need to operate an unfamiliar tape-recorder. The unintended effect was to cause the loss of John's credibility with colleagues.) Effects may be indirect, mediated by intervening factors (John's change initiative eventually brought his early retirement). It takes only a moment's pause to appreciate how many factors and their inter-relationships were salient for John's ill-fated effort: from the political context allowing him freedom to innovate plus immunity from inspection; through the school setting precipitating responses of the students to progressive educational opportunities; through the mix of personalities among the staff, with their evolving professional beliefs and values; to the flow of interaction among them.

It is beyond the capacity of leaders or managers to grasp all the factors conditioning their perceptions and actions at any point, and how they inter-relate in the contingent circumstances at hand – never mind what all the intended and unintended consequences will be. (Referring back to Chapter 1, could Haber have guessed when inventing Zyklon B gas that it might be used to exterminate his relatives?) Even if leaders or managers did have such capacity, they could not do so during the fast-pace interactions of practice. Hence the epithet of 'analysis paralysis'. Too much thinking about doing inhibits getting things done, because judgements have to be made rapidly and intuitively, drawing on conscious and tacit knowledge.

In our earlier example, a frenetic period of iterative decision-making was precipitated on the fateful Monday when the individualized curriculum was launched. This story also illustrates how the complexity of leadership and management follows from its nature as a people-intensive activity, unequally distributed within and between organizations. Such activity is expressed among individuals and groups inhabiting an intricate network of relationships. For leadership tends to connote followership, just as management connotes there being people to be managed. Leaders and managers achieve their goals with and through the contribution of others based in or beyond their organization, and just as libraries would be easier to run if people did not borrow the books, so organizations would be easier to lead and manage if leaders and managers did not depend on the *agency* of those whom they lead and manage. John failed in implementing his progressive vision because he could not go it alone. He depended on support from the colleagues he had appointed, they depended on his decision to abandon the experiment, and ultimately all staff depended on responses of the students.

Human agency implies that people can choose between alternative courses of action (Giddens, 1984) according to their interpretation of a situation. Leaders and managers commonly possess agency related to authority accompanying their formal position. But the led and managed may also possess sufficient agency to give them recourse to alternative actions according to their interpretation. Choices may range from enthusiastic support for managerial projects to open resistance. Individuals may attempt to *channel others' agency* in the direction they favour through encouragement (as John did in making his presentation), the stuff of mutual trust and collaboration. Or they may seek to *delimit others' agency* by trying to pre-empt or correct any action transgressing the limits of this favoured direction (as John also did in curtailing the non-contact time allocated to teachers), the stuff of monitoring and corrective action. The potential of all involved to act in alternative ways according to beliefs which cannot be directly controlled generates unpredictability alongside the more predictable. The led and managed always have some capacity to mediate the goals of leaders and managers.

When the added ingredient of change is incorporated in the leadership and management mix, the complexity imposed by multiple factors and their inter-relationship increases. The outcome of many actions cannot be predicted before they have happened (as John discovered after launching the individualized curriculum), and when the added ingredient of reforming an entire education system is incorporated, complexity increases manyfold. Here is an indicative list of 'characteristics of complexity' identified in one study of change (Wallace and Pocklington, 2002: 38–43). Leaders and managers based in organizations at central, local and school levels had to take all five characteristics into account, each consisting of more detailed components.

1 *Large-scale*: a multitude of stakeholders with an extensive range of specialist knowledge and priorities; the allegiance of stakeholders to partially incompatible beliefs and values, within limits.
2 *Componential*: a diversity of sequential and overlapping components affecting different stakeholders at particular times; a multiplicity of differentiated but interrelated management tasks.
3 *Systemic*: a multidirectional flow of direct and mediated interaction within and between system levels; an unequal distribution of power

between stakeholders within and between system levels who are never-theless interdependent; the centrality of cross-level management tasks.

4 *Differentially impacting*: a variable shift in practice and learning required; variable congruence with perceived interests and its associated emotive force, altering with time; a variable reciprocal effect on other ongoing activities; variable awareness of the totality beyond those parts of immediate concern.

5 *Contextually dependent*: interaction with an evolving profile of other planned and unplanned changes; impact of the accretion of past changes affecting resource parameters.

Source: Wallace and Pocklington, 2002: 38

First, complex educational change is *large-scale*, implicating many people. One has only to consider any change designed to affect the staff of over 20,000 organizations making up the English state school system. An example is the National Curriculum. School staff will probably have some stake in the content of the change and perceive it differently according to their varying circumstances. Instigators of the change will probably wish to involve a multitude of stakeholders possessing a range of specialist knowledge, but who are also likely to have different priorities. These stakeholders may hold diverse and partially incompatible beliefs and values, inside limits imposed by assumptions about their entitlement and constraints on alternative courses of action.

Second, complex educational change is *componential*, constituting interrelated and differentiated parts which vary as time unfolds. The National Curriculum comprised multiple curriculum subject sub-innovations. It was introduced subject by subject and school phase by school phase over several years. The content of the change is likely to consist of sequential and overlapping components affecting different stakeholders at particular times during the introduction, implementation and consolidation of the change. The variety of components, perhaps coupled with their cumulative impact over time, will dictate that a multiplicity of different but interrelated change management tasks have to be addressed at different times. In primary schools, staff had to cope with introducing changes in up to nine National Curriculum subjects (plus religious education) at different implementation stages.

Third, complex educational change is *systemic*, spanning two or more administrative levels of an education system which both shapes and constrains interaction among stakeholders. A cross-level change process embodies a multidirectional flow of direct and mediated interaction within and between system levels. A change must involve interaction between groups based at different system levels where it is initiated either centrally or at an intermediate system level for implementation at the sites where education is provided. Many interactions will take place through interme- diaries. They interpret communications of stakeholders at one administrative level seeking to influence those at another, as where central government ministers employed trainers as their change agents to prepare school staff for implementing National Curriculum subjects.

Power will be distributed unequally between stakeholders within and between system levels who are nevertheless interdependent (extending the point made in relation to the individualized curriculum). The authority of stakeholders may differ widely, especially between administrative levels of the education system. Yet none are powerless. Ultimately even the formally most powerful initiators are constrained by their dependence on the for- mally less powerful. Cooperation of the latter may be required where they implement the change. Whenever policy-makers at one administrative level aspire to modify practice at another, many leadership and management tasks will span system levels. Typically, a leader or manager at a more cen- tral level is responsible for achieving a change implementation task with and through others at a more peripheral level. In respect of the National Curriculum, LEA officials were made responsible by central government ministers for much preparatory in-service training of staff in the schools under their jurisdiction. Interaction across such an extensive network of stakeholders, based at different system levels, will almost certainly generate unintended consequences of actions. Such consequences may remain hidden from their perpetrators. Policy-makers at the centre may not be party to further interactions among stakeholders at other system levels which they have stimulated.

Fourth, complex educational change is *differentially impacting* on people affected, contributing to the array of associated tasks. Individuals and groups must make a variable shift in practice and learning according to the novelty of whatever they have to do. Primary school teachers intro- ducing National Curriculum subjects experienced a steeper learning curve than their secondary school counterparts, who were mostly concerned with one subject. Shifts in practice will have variable congruence with perceived interests and associated emotive force for different individuals and groups, whose perceptions and feelings may alter over time. Many teachers who resented the imposition of the National Curriculum became more accept- ing as they gained familiarity with the new practices. Any change is bound to have some reciprocal effect on other ongoing activities – change is never launched in a vacuum. Teachers were busy before the National Curriculum was introduced. They had to make time for preparation, procuring resources, and trying out new practices alongside their other work.

31

There will be contrasting levels of awareness of the totality of the change beyond parts of immediate concern to particular individuals and groups. Grasp of the change and its parts may be hierarchically distributed. Breadth of knowledge of the National Curriculum centrally and at the intermediate LEA level was marked by superficial awareness of circumstances in most schools. Conversely, depth of knowledge of the scene at school level was marked by superficial awareness of the totality. Central government ministers had an overview of the entire National Curriculum programme, though they were shorter on appreciating the impact of their efforts on schools and communities than the people based there. Most school staff possessed only an impression of the National Curriculum as a whole, little knowledge of its impact on schools elsewhere, but detailed awareness of what lay inside their first hand experience.

Fifth, complex educational change is *contextually dependent*, facilitated and constrained by the wider political and historical milieu with which it interacts. We noted earlier how John's capacity to innovate rested partly on his autonomy as a headteacher when there was little external pressure for change. But in the present reform era, any change is likely to interact with an evolving profile of other planned and unplanned changes. Policy initiatives are likely to impinge on each other. The National Curriculum had to be implemented alongside other innovations flowing from central government reform polices, LEA initiatives and other crises or events.

Even in a reasonably 'steady state', the complexity of leadership and management generates endemic ambiguities that are the preconditions of irony. They are exacerbated by change, whether affecting a single organization or a large system. We now examine more closely factors creating the ineradicable baseline of endemic ambiguities in educational organizations.

Organizational pathos and the problem of goals

A major form of endemic ambiguity arises from the unintended but inevitable shortfall, or *organizational pathos* (Hoyle, 1986), between the lofty, diffuse and diverse goals that central government ministers, parents and other stakeholders generally ascribe to education and the possibility of their achievement in educational organizations. Recall from Chapter 1 the legal requirement that the curriculum 'promotes the spiritual, moral, cultural, mental and physical development of pupils at the school and of society'. How can teaching the curriculum to a group of students in any school promote the spiritual, moral, cultural, mental and physical development of society as a whole, except insofar as these students comprise a very small part of their very large society? And how could we determine whether the aspiration to make a difference to society had been achieved? While there is universal agreement that the prime goal of schools is education, problems arise over the detail. The following observations on school goals suggest reasons for these difficulties:

- goals are diverse, ranging from the search for beauty, truth and goodness to the acquisition of personal hygiene and road safety skills. The former may be more grand but the latter are hardly unimportant;
- they are diffuse, concerned with the development of 'the whole child' or 'the whole person'. Education is expected to have long-term impacts (as in promoting 'a lifelong love of learning') or those that are indirect (as in developing society through teaching a specific group of students);
- some goals attributed to educational organizations are incompatible. Students are expected to be creative and conformist (even in the liberal setting of the individualized curriculum, student competitions to climb classroom curtains were deemed not to conform to norms of acceptable creativity held by teachers);
- as school goals are so diverse they cannot all be pursued with the same vigour, so there is a tendency to prioritize goals espoused for the most recent policies (a problem emerged with implementing the National Curriculum because whichever subject was being introduced at any time tended to concentrate the minds of teachers, at the expense of other subjects not currently in the spotlight);
- school goals are often 'displaced' during implementation, so education may give way to selection and differentiation of students. Sometimes narrow managerial efficiency can become a virtually autonomous goal. But running a 'tight ship' financially is not equivalent to providing a valued education.

The problem of operationalizing lofty goals cannot be resolved by changing the terminology and referring to mission, vision, philosophy, goal, objective, need, policy, programme, priority, rule or plan. For whatever the language, an inherent pathos will remain between official organizational aspiration and its achievement. We doubt that the overarching goal of schools could ever be restricted to measurable outcomes. Education is expected not only to generate the social, moral, physical and aesthetic outcomes we have discussed, many of which cannot be meaningfully quantified. It is also expected to provide a 'repair' function for society in relation to family breakdown, antisocial behaviour or public order. And how could this be meaningfully measured? Therefore, as Caldwell and Spinks (1992: 38) assert, an educational goal can amount to simply 'a statement of broad direction, general purpose or intent, it is general and timeless and is not concerned with any particular outcome at a point in time'.

Paradoxically, *goal* is a problematic concept, but we cannot do without it. In practice, a distinction may be made between the stated or official goals of an organization and the operational goals held by individuals and groups. They may, in principle, include covert goals that would not withstand scrutiny when set against official goals. An example might be a teacher's unarticulated goal of minimizing time spent on lesson preparation and marking. Current orthodoxies of educational leadership and management directed towards knowledge-for-action portray organizational goals as unproblematic. They typically start with official goals and seek to identify the most efficient and effective means of achieving them. By contrast, approaches informed by organization theory (directed towards knowledge-for-understanding) focus less on goals than on actions resulting in what might, with the benefit of hindsight, be termed 'goals'. In short, goals can be a guide to successful practice but successful, intuitive practice often becomes identified as a goal only retrospectively. Of course, it is a task of leadership and management to operationalize official goals where possible. But the impossibility of achieving them fully leaves school staff to cope with perennial goal ambiguity.

To support this generalization, we will take an instance that, though not contemporary, is instructive. In *The Open-Door College*, Clark (1960) investigated a new junior college in California that had been established to achieve two official goals. The junior college was structurally situated between high school and the four-year college or university. The prime goal was to provide a vocational education for the majority of students. The minor goal was to provide an academic education for students retaining the aspiration to enrol in a four-year college, having failed to do so at the end of their school careers. The junior college was staffed and organized on the assumption that most entrants would be *terminal students* taking vocational courses, and that a few would be *transfer students* following university-oriented academic courses.

However, the college also had an 'open-door' policy. Students could choose their courses. Goal ambiguity was embodied in this policy, because it was unpredictable whether most students would opt for vocational courses in line with the prime goal. When the college opened, a situational irony was indeed precipitated. The open-door policy produced the unintended consequence that most students chose to enrol for the *transfer* courses, only a few opting for *terminal* courses. Adjustments were made in staffing and structure to meet these unanticipated demands and formally both goals were maintained.

Staff teaching the transfer students soon judged that many lacked the academic ability needed to meet entry requirements for a degree course at a college or university. They adopted an implicit operational goal, becoming 'agents of consolation' persuading these students to switch to vocational courses. Clark describes the strategies used as part of the 'cooling-out function'. They included counselling, issuing 'need for improvement' notices, and a compulsory course for all transfer students called 'Psychology 5: Orientation to College'. It was ostensibly to prepare students for college education. But intelligence tests, interest inventories and grade point scores were used to convince many students that a degree course was beyond their reach. Thus three sets of students emerged: terminal students, transfer students, and *latent terminal students* (who thought they were transfer students but were in the process of being cooled-out).

Organizational pathos here entailed a gap between the aspiration of most students to qualify for a four-year college education and judgements of staff that many were incapable of doing so. The situational irony arising because such students could not be cooled-out before admission was compounded by the irony of staff pursuing a covert anti-educational goal to lower the educational aspiration of these students. Yet they did so for the best of educational intentions: to steer the students towards vocational courses whose educational demands they were deemed capable of meeting.

Pursuing the goal of efficiency versus the goal of effectiveness

'Efficiency and effectiveness' are frequently linked in the leadership and management literature as if they were synonymous. If this were so, one term would be redundant. Efficiency implies 'achieving intended outcomes with minimal wastage of resources'. Effectiveness implies 'achieving valued outcomes' whatever the resource implications. Ambiguity arises where pursuing efficiency comes at the expense of effectiveness or vice versa.

The difference between efficiency and effectiveness may be illustrated as follows. Hypothesize a class of 20 students studying physics for an examination. Aptitudes for physics within the class differ and school staff must decide on their policy for presenting students for the exam. Staff might enter only the best 10 students, all of whom pass – representing 100 per cent efficiency. Or they might enter all 20 students, of whom 15 pass. This option represents only 75 per cent *efficiency* compared with the first option. But it is 50 per cent more *effective* since five pupils passed who would not have been entered under the more rigorous presentation policy. Here the more efficient strategy is the less effective; the more effective strategy is the less efficient.

Ironic consequences of pursuing effectiveness and efficiency ensued when the headteacher of a prestigious school known to one of us was dismissed by school governors because examination results were 'inferior' to those of a less-prestigious school nearby. Newspaper reports indicated that the dismissed headteacher had adopted a more liberal attitude towards entering students for examinations than the headteacher of the more 'successful' school. Governors judged the headteacher who was potentially more effective (in maximizing the proportion of students offered the chance to pass) as less successful than the one who was more efficient (in minimizing the proportion of students offered the chance to fail).

Limits to rationality

Classical management theory was predicated on a 'scientific' means–ends rationality. A key contributor was Frederick 'Speedy' Taylor, the time-and-motion specialist whose influence on early managerialism in education is discussed in Chapter 4. (Taylor had a nervous breakdown and died in the night while feverishly trying to wind his watch. Ironic?) In their critique of the assumptions underlying what became known as the scientific management movement, March and Simon provided a detailed argument for the *bounded* nature of rationality in organizations. They noted how the classical model assumed that when making decisions, leaders and managers were aware of the range of alternative choices, could estimate the likely outcomes of each alternative, and could rank each alternative in order of preference. As March and Simon (1958: 198) pointed out: 'One can hardly take exception to these requirements in a normative model – a model which tells people how they ought to choose ... But the notion of objective rationality assumes that there is some objective reality in which the 'real' alternatives, the 'real' consequences and the 'real' utilities exist.'

What leaders and managers actually do is to *satisfice* (p.140–1):

> Most human decision-making, whether individual or organizational, is concerned with the discovery and selection of satisfactory alternatives; only in exceptional cases is it concerned with the discovery and selection of optimal alternatives. To optimize requires processes several orders of magnitude more complex than those required to satisfice. An example is the difference between searching a haystack to find the sharpest needle in it and searching the haystack to find a needle sharp enough to sew with.

What March and Simon conceptualized is what every teacher and headteacher experientially knows: that they work in circumstances where they daily make a multitude of decisions 'on the run' in contingent and evolving circumstances. Despite the increased scope for rational planning made possible by management systems, electronic means of communication, and sophisticated data storage and retrieval technology, there remain limits to scientific rationality for several reasons.

First, there are *cognitive* limits to rationality: decision-makers cannot know in advance what all the possible immediate and longer-term outcomes of a particular decision will be. They will have variable, but always limited, awareness of what is happening inside and outside the organization. They will have even less idea about what will happen in future which might impinge on the decision outcomes. In the case of our school-based innovation, could John have reliably predicted that the immediate consequence of his decision to cancel non-contact time would be to lower staff morale across the school? Or that an indirect consequence would be an increase in staff absenteeism because of stress to which lack of non-contact time contributed? Or that the longer-term consequence would be staff antipathy towards his leadership?

Cognitive limits to internal organizational decision-making are exacerbated in such a change context. But this was a single school-based innovation. Consider how these limits become further tightened under conditions of complex change, as in the introduction of the National Curriculum. We discussed earlier how central decision-making affected people based in intermediate organizations (such as LEAs) responsible for supporting implementation of the National Curriculum, and the staff in schools countrywide responsible for teaching it.

Second, rationality is subject to *logical* limits, brought out by game theory (see Elster, 1978). Individual rational pursuit of a particular goal can prevent it being achieved when everyone else happens to pursue it as well. This source of ambiguity arose over John's individualized curriculum. The logic behind the principle of giving students individual choice over when to study particular subjects assumes that genuine alternative choices exist. But most students made a similar individual choice: to study the same few subjects. Their *collective* choices prevented the majority from studying the subject they had chosen. The logic of the individualized curriculum offered the students as a group little choice over making different individual choices from the menu of subjects. They must do so if they were to distribute themselves among the finite number of spaces available. The logical ambiguity here was that individuals had a real choice between studying alternative subjects at any time only if their collective choices matched the prespecified pattern of alternatives dictated by the capacity of the specialist facilities.

Third, there are *phenomenological* limits to rationality arising from competing interpretations of events. March and Simon (1958: 138) write: 'From a phenomenological viewpoint, we can only speak of rationality relative to a frame of reference, and that frame of reference will be

determined by the limitations on the rational man's (sic) knowledge.'
Social phenomenology has been applied to educational organizations by
Greenfield (1975). From this perspective schools are social constructs.
Although a school has a materiality in terms of buildings, a clear membership and a reasonably stable organizational structure, as a social institution
it remains amenable to different interpretations (as emphasized in our
account of reification in Chapter 1). Individuals and groups construe the
school differently. The potential range of constructions is limited by the
parameters for official school goals, the unequal distribution of power
among those associated with them, and the fact that constructions can
constrain perception and action (Giddens, 1979). But incompatible perspectives will be regarded as 'rational' by their protagonists.

The frames of reference governing social constructs are not linked solely
to limited knowledge. They may also relate to contradictory beliefs, norms
(rules about how people should behave) and values held by any individual
or distributed between different groups. The ambiguity of incompatible
perceptions and values about the same situation will be familiar to any
teacher or headteacher who has arbitrated when students or colleagues
come into conflict. The account offered by each protagonist seldom
squares with that of his or her adversaries. Yet all protagonists were party
to the same conflict.

It is common experience that actions expressing contradictory beliefs
and values can coexist without conflict, as long as actions according to one
belief are kept separate from actions according to the other. With our
school-based innovation, it was not until John began trying to win the traditionalist teachers over to his progressive vision that staffroom arguments
began. When the school opened, the traditionalist teachers made their preferred teaching approach work in their classrooms, while the progressive
teachers made a radically different approach work in classrooms next
door. Students moved frequently between the two groups. They adjusted
seamlessly to the contrasting norms held by different teachers. In one
lesson the teacher was called 'sir' or 'miss' and students should sit still and
do the work allotted them. In the next the teacher and students were on
first name terms and students should be proactive, taking responsibility for
achieving what they wished to learn.

Conflict between the traditionalist and progressive teachers was generated when actions according to their different beliefs, norms and values
were brought together in the same interaction. Launching the individualized curriculum compromised their incompatible approaches.
Traditionalists resented their lessons being interrupted by students for
whom they had pastoral responsibility coming to have their record card

checked. Progressives resented the restrictions on student choice imposed by colleagues who insisted on teaching single-ability sets. The conflict was resolved only when the individualized curriculum was abandoned, allowing the traditionalists to teach single-ability sets uninterrupted, the few remaining progressives to teach sets in their own way, and the headteacher to retreat to his office. Peace returned once the traditionalists and progressives were again able to express their contradictory educational beliefs and values in different classrooms. The phenomenological ambiguity of contradictory constructs remained, but incompatible actions were safely compartmented-off behind different doors.

Fourth, there are *control* limits to rationality, because no single person in normal organizational life can achieve absolute control. Ambiguity relates to the potential of other organization members to act in ways that may not be wholly predictable from the perspective of the would-be controller. Power is distributed – however unequally – within and between organizations. Whatever position of authority formal leaders may hold, and whatever the sanctions available to them, they still depend on cooperation from other organizational members. We have already implied that leaders need followers, managers need someone to manage. So all organization members have recourse to informal influence (Bacharach and Lawler, 1980), not least the negative capacity to resist or undermine work towards achieving official goals. Staff may wield considerable influence who become 'whistleblowers' and reveal wrongdoing by their leaders and managers. In these unusual circumstances, informal influence can prove more powerful than formal authority.

In the aftermath of the individualized curriculum, John was the target of whistleblowers over whom he had no authority: parents, and a teacher who had left the school and so no longer depended on John for a job reference. LEA advisers had authority to inspect the school. But they were unwilling to stand on this authority by carrying out an inspection without the headteacher's invitation, because of his potential to resist. Control by any protagonist was not a foregone conclusion. Even where John could directly control a colleague's behaviour, as when he ordered the maths teacher to take a geography class, the teacher still had recourse to covert influence by refusing to teach the students without informing John. Nor could John control the beliefs and values held by others. When he appeared in the hall with his therapeutic pot of brown paint, he could not have anticipated the negative interpretation that the teacher working in the hall would place on his well-intentioned action. Control ambiguity is even greater across large multi-organizational systems, where policymakers depend on a series of cooperative relationships between themselves and all the intermediaries and implementers involved in putting policies into practice.

Chance and emergence

Further limits to control exerted by leaders and managers are imposed by ambiguity flowing from the occurrence of *chance* events. The one-time British Prime Minister Harold Macmillan was once asked what had been his main problem in the post. He replied: 'Events, dear boy. Events.' Although events have causes these may be so complex that they can rarely be apprehended in their entirety. Notoriously, events which are seemingly minor can lead through a chain reaction to events of far greater significance. The element of chance in systems forces us to reverse our usual top-down perspective where we attribute events to the conscious agency of those who run organizations. Instead the focus shifts towards *emergence*, the process by which individual actions and decisions taken at the periphery of a system become linked in unplanned ways and eventually bring about radical change 'from below'.

March and Olsen were early investigators of emergence in educational organizations. Ambiguity in decision-making relates to the loose relationship in the 'organized anarchy' that they label educational organizations to be among goals, management structures, decision-making processes, technology (including curriculum and pedagogy) and outcomes. Goals, we noted earlier, can emerge from activities rather than prestructuring them. A policy or practice which might be assumed to flow from a strategic decision and a systematic implementation strategy turns out on investigation to have been the result of chance, personal interests, opportunities and choices. In their famous metaphor March and Olsen conceive this opaque decision-making process as a 'garbage can'. An outcome may not be the result of a logical or rational sequence of events, but rather of four streams of metaphorical rubbish that pour into the garbage can, get mixed together, and spill out when the garbage can is emptied to become the decision. These streams comprise (1976: 26–7):

- problems – whatever people are concerned enough to voice, whether connected with official goals, personal interests, life outside the organization, or status differentials;
- solutions – a product or idea of what works proffered by advocates, often their preferred answer to most organizational problems, and sometimes their ready-made solution for which they actively seek almost any problem to solve;

- participants – those entitled to become involved or who otherwise wish to do so, depending on their other priorities, and whose attendance or non-attendance at meetings may be crucial for the outcome;
- choice opportunities – occasions when it is expected that organizational behaviour which can be called a decision will be produced, and where an old problem may sometimes be resolved by becoming attached to the solution of a new problem.

The process is one where what happens depends on 'a relatively complex intermeshing of the mix of choices available at any one time, the mix of problems that have access to the organization, the mix of solutions looking for problems, and the outside demands on the decision-makers' (p.82). Organizations can even be said to 'run backwards' where what becomes regarded as a decision may be nothing more than a retrospective rationalization of what emerged obscurely as a regularized practice.

Chance and emergence are the focus of complexity and chaos theory, at root mathematical and concerned with fundamental and abstract relationships between system components. Their status as predictive theory is debateable since what they predict is unpredictability. A distinction may be made between complexity as a normative theory and complexity as a device for developing knowledge-for-understanding by examining patterns in leadership and management and of change, as we have done here. Attempts to build knowledge-for-action through applying abstract complexity theory to create normative prescriptions are more equivocal, as in the treatment by Morrison. Complexity theory is more attuned to chance and emergence than prescriptions for increasing predictive control. Elements of complexity theory that Morrison (2002: 9) lists include: 'effects are not straightforward functions of causes'; 'uncertainty and openness prevail'; 'the universe is irregular, diverse, uncontrollable and unpredictable'; 'systems are indeterministic, non-linear and unstable'. Given this list and such statements as 'long range planning is futile ... control is a chimera, and ... the power of bosses is limited' (p.189), one wonders what complexity theory can offer to leaders and managers. But Morrison's practical prescriptions actually reflect the contrary assumption, with which we broadly concur, that leaders and managers can at least give a steer to emergent events. In other words, there is a place for the conventional leadership and management activity of structuring, planning and evaluating but it cannot eliminate endemic ambiguities. Excessive activity may merely increase them.

The dilemmas of educational organizations

The essence of a *dilemma* is the double ambiguity, first, of being faced with choosing between alternative courses of action, and second, of realizing that no alternative is fully desirable, feasible, and guaranteed to bring success. Whichever course is taken, something that is valued will be lost. Coping with dilemmas incurs unavoidable *costs*.

We saw how John experienced ambiguity over winning his colleagues' acceptance of the individualized curriculum. He was lobbied by traditionalist teachers wishing to continue teaching their subject to single-ability sets of students. We imagine John to have faced a leadership dilemma, ambiguity arising because he could not resolve the issue to everyone's satisfaction. One alternative was to use his authority to over-rule the traditionalists, insisting that they teach whichever students came to their classroom as long as there was space. This alternative would be undesirable for John because it could cost him the cooperation of traditionalists, which he valued because he depended on it. The traditionalists could potentially use negative influence, from his perspective, to undermine the innovation by, say, providing tuition which was not individualized or by complaining to parents.

Another alternative was to surrender to the traditionalists by letting them continue teaching single-ability sets. This alternative would be undesirable for John because it would dilute the individualized curriculum. It would constrain the study choices for students and would be resented by the progressive teachers, potentially costing him support on which he depended to make the innovation work. Which way to go? He opted for the latter alternative; it cost him dearly. An unintended consequence was the situational irony that the school-wide design of the individualized curriculum envisioned by John was compromised. What was launched was merely half individualized and half set by ability.

Dilemmas have long been a focus of organization theory. They are particularly salient in educational organizations because of their diffuse and diverse goals, and research is oriented towards understanding how participants cope with these dilemmas. Related leadership and management theories vary in their prescriptiveness. Some offer definitive solutions to, say, the conflict between organizational goals and individual needs. Others focus more pragmatically on achieving a temporary balance in contingent circumstances. But the current orthodoxies of educational leadership and management and school improvement depict organizational dilemmas as less procedurally 'solvable' than 'dissolvable' through leadership, collaboration and organizational learning. We are sceptical of such approaches, since dilemmas are endemic. We will argue (Chapters 6 and 7) that education reforms have more often exacerbated than dissolved them.

Woods and colleagues (1997) offer a perceptive approach to understanding educational dilemmas from a professional workplace perspective, investigating the responses of English primary school teachers to educational reforms. They focus on dilemmas in learning and teaching, but they point out that these can be manifestations of dilemmas across administrative levels of the education system. In contrast to our usage, they reserve the term 'dilemma' for alternatives presenting teachers with a single ambiguity because they are amenable to a contingent solution by applying professional judgement and expertise. They use the term 'tensions' to cover what we have called dilemmas because they incorporate a double ambiguity in presenting teachers with incompatible choices. For those externally structured dilemmas preventing teachers from exercising choice over potential alternatives they use the term 'constraints'. They see teachers as facing extended unresolvable tensions because of education reforms: the OFSTED inspection regime has tightened constraints on the use of professional judgement and expertise by teachers, since inspectors judge only a restricted range of practices to be effective.

Schools as organizations face collective dilemmas. Ogawa et al. (1999) conceive organizational dilemmas in terms of contradictory values that, we have argued, contribute to phenomenological ambiguity. Organizational dilemmas represent dichotomies: incompatible alternative ways of operating, both of which are valued. Decision optimization (finding the sharpest needle in the haystack) is impossible. Satisficing (finding a needle which is sharp enough to sew with) is the best that can be done. An ironic consequence flows from actions favouring either of the dichotomous alternatives.

The more actions favour one pole of the dilemma, the more emergent circumstances may bring pressure for ameliorative action favouring the opposite pole. Actions to cope with organizational dilemmas vacillate between the alternatives, like a swinging pendulum. It cannot be stopped, for there is no stable balance between actions in accordance with the opposing values (consistent with March's observation quoted in Chapter 1 that balance is a cruel concept). Four internal dilemmas (Table 2.1) and three concerning external relations (Table 2.2) are identified by Ogawa and colleagues. We have offered illustrations from the North American research they discuss. We have also indicated how a likely consequence of action favouring one pole of the dilemma is to stimulate a pendulum swing towards action favouring the opposite pole.

Table 2.1: *Endemic internal organizational dilemmas*

Dilemma and its two poles	Example from US school reforms	Why it is unresolvable
Organizational goals Organizational purposes *versus* individual needs and self-interests	Performance-related pay for teachers was introduced to harness their individual interest in maximizing their remuneration towards more effective achievement of official goals. But teachers resisted because individual reward is gained intrinsically from teaching rather than pay, competition between teachers is inequitable, and teachers' performance cannot be reliably measured.	Individual action to realize diverse individual interests may support or hinder the pursuit of official goals. But individual interests cannot be tightly controlled through managerial action. Attempts to harness particular interests towards the pursuit of organizational goals are likely to trigger activity to protect other individual interests.
Task structure Formal management structures *versus* emergent informal structures	Innovations were introduced that employed the formal management structures directly to target individual teaching of the curriculum. But impact was low because teachers continued to be guided mainly by inherited practices that were valued among particular colleagues and by their individual decisions.	Informal structures may facilitate or hinder activity conducted through formal management structures. But the emergence and operation of informal structures cannot be tightly controlled by managerial action according to formal structures. Attempts to formalize informal structures are likely to trigger new informal structures of resistance.
Professionalism Bureaucratic control *versus* professional autonomy and judgement	Involving parents as educational partners is challenging teachers' assumption that they know what is best for students and parents. It is not yet clear whether	Pressure for coordination by powerful stakeholders other than teachers enables them to contribute to how students are taught. But coordination of teachers' work limits their discretion to make judgements in contingent situations,

teachers' capacity to make judgements in contingent classroom circumstances will be compromised.

applying an incomplete body of knowledge about what works. Attempts to reduce teachers' discretion inhibit their capacity to adjust effectively to contingent circumstances. Attempts to expand it compromise other powerful stakeholders who expect to make an input to teaching activity.

Hierarchy

Centralization *versus* decentralization of organizational decision-making

The innovation was introduced by school district administrators of creating a parent and community-dominated council for each school to decentralize educational decision-making. But it led to demands from some powerful stakeholders to re-establish district office direction because they perceived that delegation had gone too far.

Centralization of decision-making denies a voice to some stakeholders who wish to contribute. But decentralization may result in contradictory decisions. Universal acceptance of any balance is difficult to achieve because some stakeholders' interests are always compromised. Attempts centrally to decide practice are likely to generate differential adaptation by teachers making decisions in their diverse classroom circumstances. Attempts to decentralize are likely to generate what some powerful stakeholders will regard as unacceptable practices, which they will attempt to curb.

Source: Ogawa et al., 1999

Table 2.2: *Endemic external organizational dilemmas*

Dilemma and its two poles	Example from US school reforms	Why the dilemma is unresolvable
Persistence Organizational certainty *versus* adaptation to the external environment	School principals (headteachers) were expected to oversee the implementation efforts of teachers in enacting policies adopted by district administrators to increase the certainty and	Teachers and leaders and managers have to establish and sustain enough internal organizational certainty to operate routinely in contingent circumstances, but they also have to adapt to the changing demands of an uncertain external environment. Externally initiated

45

Table 2.2: *Continued.*

Dilemma and its two poles	Example from US school reforms	Why the dilemma is unresolvable
Persistence *Cont.*	effectiveness of teaching. But teachers expected their principal to buffer them from ambiguities introduced by the innovations that flowed from these policies.	attempts to increase internal organizational certainty are likely to trigger an unintentional increase in internal ambiguity. The increased ambiguity reduces the capacity of teachers, leaders and managers to operate routinely and therefore it is likely to be resisted.
Organizational boundaries Maintaining the integrity of the organization *versus* bridging the boundary with its external environment	School principals acted as buffers, protecting staff from some external stakeholders, including assertive and demanding parents. But they made bridges with other stakeholders who were supportive of educational activity in the school.	The boundaries between the internal and external environment of schools are permeable and ambiguous. Teachers and leaders and managers work to develop and sustain internal coherence, while other stakeholders from outside the organization bring uncertainty that threatens coherence. Bridging attempts to forge strong community links are likely to trigger increased ambiguity about the boundary of school membership and non-membership. The increased ambiguity reduces the capacity of teachers and leaders and managers to sustain internal coherence, so they are likely to respond by buffering to strengthen the organizational boundary.
Compliance Adaptation to enhance internal organizational operation *versus* adaptation to enhance external legitimation of the organization	School-based [local] management was introduced as a result of a campaign by policy-makers, teacher union representatives and academics who claimed it would improve educational effectiveness. There is little evidence to	There is a technical need for teachers and leaders and managers to import ideas and resources from outside in order to improve internal school operation directed towards attaining official goals. But there is also a symbolic need to be seen to adopt practices which meet the approval of powerful stakeholders from outside the organization who control

| Compliance Cont. | support this claim. But school district administrators adopted the innovation to legitimate themselves, being seen to support what powerful stakeholders believed in. | resources that could contribute to enhancing internal operation. Compliance with externally initiated attempts to improve school operation for symbolic reasons is likely to draw the attention of organization members away from the technical need to import other ideas that might enhance internal operation. If these symbolic attempts do not turn out to improve educational effectiveness, it is likely that new demands will be triggered for compliance with the unmet need to enhance internal organizational operation. |

Source: Ogawa et al., 1999

This work on the unresolvability of dilemmas supports our stance outlined in Chapter 1: knowledge-for-understanding gained through organization theory and related research is vital to inform the development of realistic knowledge-for-action to improve practice. Policy-makers may have to work with these dilemmas, rather than expect to resolve or dissolve them. With considerable prescience about English reforms, Ogawa and his associates argue that:

school reform is still a matter of active choosing, even if among equally valued alternatives and equally true but contradictory consequences. To be sure, such solutions as site-based management [local management] and decentralization may unknowingly contain the seeds of re-centralization. Similarly, market solutions and charter schooling [independently operating public-funded schools] could prove to be but the beginnings of a new regulatory spirit in public education. Or, more deeply into dilemma-effects, efforts to balance opposing values (the power of standards while simultaneously preserving local initiative and autonomy) could only serve to mask temporarily some fundamental contraries in state–local relations.

Not to choose and not to act in school reform, however, is just to swing with the pendulum. The key importance in an understanding and awareness of organizational values in conflict, and in the tendency of one of two poles to define/produce the other, is that choice implies consequence – with side effects, trade-offs, and compromises, plus problems that are reintroduced again and again. To act meaningfully in educational reform is to act with an informed sense of these phenomena. (1999: 291)

The ironic double bind

We have explored how endemic ambiguities of organizational life constitute preconditions of irony. A degree of change is also endemic because of learning to perform tasks which are novel for particular individuals and groups. Innovation brings more substantial change, exacerbating endemic ambiguities. Ambiguity-reducing reforms across a large system temporarily increase ambiguity through the change process. We turn next to the endemic ambiguities of policy implementation and their impact on the endemic ambiguities of organizational life.

We make this connection to underline how ambiguities are ever-present in educational organizations and externally initiated improvement efforts. It will set the stage for examining how UK reforms since the 1980s have been designed to reduce such ambiguities. The movement for reform arose from a perceived lack of clarity about goals and desired outcomes of the education system, and so problems over judging its effectiveness. We will argue that there was a case for ambiguity reduction, within the limits of feasibility. But reform efforts, uninformed by knowledge-for-understanding, created an ironic 'double bind'. In seeking radically to reduce ambiguity, and hence the preconditions of irony in education, reformers have generated the irony of excessive leadership and management.

3

The ambiguities of policy implementation

We have so far considered schools as organizations with some allusion to their policy context. Now we consider schools as organizations from the perspective of central and local government policy-makers and their officials. For them, schools are sites where the education service is 'delivered' to students and parents, and the target of innovations flowing from their policies to change how teachers and headteachers work and relate to their community. Ambiguities paralleling those endemic to individual schools are generated by policy implementation across organizations and administrative levels. Why is irony integral to implementing policies? Why can't ironies of implementation be eliminated? Most sources of endemic organizational ambiguities identified in Chapter 2 can be applied to policy implementation. It implies change which increases ambiguity, not only inside any organization but between organizations and administrative levels of the service system.

We will anchor our account through illustrative cases. But we will also examine the variety of means of implementation that policy-makers have at their disposal, considering how every instrument brings its own ambiguities and potential for situational irony. There is no such thing as a cost-free means of policy implementation.

Ambiguities of policy implementation: an LEA-based innovation

We begin with an English LEA policy initiative during the 1980s, just prior to the major reform legislation of 1988. It represented a concerted attempt to improve education in some 230 primary schools in the city of Leeds, and cost almost £14 million (over $20 million). We draw on Alexander's (1997) report of the LEA-commissioned independent evaluation of this initiative. State education in England was still a 'national service, locally administered'. In Leeds, elected councillors in local government and their LEA advisers enjoyed considerable autonomy to create policies for schools under their jurisdiction. Such autonomy was, of course, delimited by central government legislation and the amount of funding that could be raised through local taxation and central grants. Local councillors decided to reverse years of low expenditure on primary education through the inception of a 'Primary Needs Programme' (PNP) in their primary schools. The stated aim of the PNP 'to meet the needs of all children, and in particular those children experiencing learning difficulties' was to be achieved through three goals:

1 developing a curriculum which is broadly based, with a stimulating and challenging learning environment;
2 developing flexible teaching strategies to meet the identified needs of individual pupils, including specified practical help for individuals and small groups, within the context of general classroom provision;
3 developing productive links with parents and the local community.

The language of these official statements brought enduring implementation difficulties in schools:

> First, the problem of ambiguity ... many school staff were uncertain whether PNP was about the special educational needs of certain children or the provision of 'good primary practice' for all. Second, the problem of amorphousness ... few of the phrases in the three enabling or subsidiary goals conveyed any clearly defined meaning. Finally, the problem of application: it was difficult to see what practical function, if any, aims expressed in this way could usefully fulfil. (Alexander, 1997: 5)

One headteacher commented: 'When PNP began I received two messages about its purpose: that it was for children with special needs but there again it wasn't for special needs, but for the general enhancement of the school.' (PRINDEP, 1987: 7) Rivalry between staff in the separate LEA departments responsible for special educational needs and for primary education, each vying for priority over PNP funding, helped perpetuate uncertainty over the focus of the programme.

Nevertheless, the new money was spent. Most was invested in schools judged to have the greatest social and educational needs based on the proportion of students qualifying for free school meals, and on student scores in the LEA annual reading test. The bulk of expenditure went on appointing additional staff, including over 100 'PNP coordinators' responsible for managing the programme in their school. The remainder was used to support school staff bids for extra material resources, to refurbish dilapidated buildings (which included repainting, new furniture and carpets), and to provide in-service training courses for teachers.

The evaluation raised doubts over the return on this investment in terms of effectiveness. Not only were the goals diffuse enough to allow conflicting interpretations of the focus, but their linkage with the means employed was indirect. Achievement of the official aim and goals entailed implementing the PNP initiative through a complicated causal chain. LEA-based staff with school support responsibilities would work with and through school leaders and managers (primarily headteachers and PNP coordinators) and other staff to enhance the teaching environment, curriculum and pedagogy, so as to improve student learning. Envisaged links were that:

- *LEA advisers, advisory teachers and other support service professionals* would be involved in allocating resources, liaising with school leaders and managers and other staff, and providing some in-service training;
- *headteachers* would be responsible for procuring some resources and ensuring that students whose educational needs were greatest were identified and new resources deployed to meet their needs;
- headteachers would work through *PNP coordinators*, once appointed;
- PNP coordinators, in turn, would work with other *teachers* and *support staff* to realize the proximate goals of enhancing the curriculum, teaching it flexibly to match the diversity of learning needs, and improving links with *parents* and the local community;
- their combined endeavours in these areas would be directed, implicitly, towards the ultimate aim of meeting the educational needs of *students* through enabling them to improve their academic and social learning.

The evaluators explored each link. They found that interpretation of *students' priority needs* led to most resources being directed towards students with special educational needs, through enhanced staffing and training. They judged resources to be inadequate or lacking altogether for other categories of need, including those of students from minority ethnic groups and very able students. Specification was minimal of what should constitute a *broadly based curriculum*. LEA curriculum policies were drawn up without consulting most headteachers, whose responses ranged from acquiescent to critical. Further, 'the curriculum in action in many schools and classrooms was not, by any of the possible definitions of the phrase, broadly based' (Alexander, 1997: 156). PNP coordinators were differentially empowered and made very variable impact, dependent on what headteachers and other staff allowed them to do. Some were centrally involved in managing curriculum development, others were marginalized. One noted: 'Class teachers do not want to be responsible for slow learners or to have advice. They all want slow learners out of the classroom' (PRINDEP, 1987: 8). LEA advisers had offered a clearer prescription about classroom arrangements to provide curriculum breadth and flexibility, which was:

> consistently purveyed to teachers through in-service courses, documents and the work of individual advisers and advisory teachers ... The layout commended by advisory staff, and perceived by many of our interview and questionnaire respondents as being less a suggestion than a requirement, had work bays for each major area of the curriculum. These were intended to facilitate the patterns of curriculum provision generally denoted by terms like the 'flexible day' or 'integrated day', in which at any one time a classroom will contain children working on quite disparate tasks in different areas of the curriculum. Since some such tasks might involve children standing or working on the floor, advisory staff also encouraged teachers to make flexible use of furniture, some commending what was termed 'the concept of fewer chairs than children': the argument being that since the nature of the activity did not require one chair per child, more space for those activities could be created by dispensing with superfluous chairs. (Alexander, 1997: 40–1)

The advisers set up a model classroom at an in-service training centre to convey the 'quality learning environment' which teachers were encouraged to emulate, but:

> Some teachers adopted the recommended practices; some found difficulty in doing so, others rejected them. However, while the advisory team's views had the undoubted consequence of making many Leeds primary classrooms seem busier and more attractive, the beneficial consequences for children's learning were less clear; and for some teachers, the claim of 'flexibility' had exactly the opposite effect, strait-jacketing them into practices to which they had no real commitment and which they had difficulty in managing. (Alexander, 1997: 157)

Monitoring of curriculum provision revealed wide variation in coverage. Student reading scores in the annual LEA screening tests indicated that standards had dropped slightly during the PNP period, suggesting that the extra resources had made no positive impact on this curriculum area. The initiative had proved ineffective, insofar as these tests represent a valid indicator of the extent to which its ambiguous aim had been achieved.

In-service training placed strong emphasis on *flexible teaching strategies*. But it highlighted improving the quality of the learning environment, such as displaying work done by students and classroom organization, rather than directly stimulating student learning. While groupwork was advocated, classroom monitoring showed that students in groups actually worked mainly on individual tasks. Least activity was evident on *developing links with parents and the local community*, as the LEA policy here remained underdeveloped.

Implementation of the PNP initiative was therefore patchy, evidence suggesting that the official goals, their ambiguity notwithstanding, were far from fully realized. Yet the discourse of the LEA advisers and their advocated practices were adopted among many school staff, even though some did not believe in them. They perceived that the patronage of advisers was needed to support their career advancement:

> many teachers and heads felt that getting on in the primary sector required verbal and practical allegiance to certain quite specific canons of 'good primary practice', and that anything less, let alone any open challenging of the orthodoxies in question, could damage their professional prospects. Moreover, this normative process was felt to operate at several levels, from appointments, promotions and other career aspirations to the much more subtle everyday processes whereby individuals come to acquire a sense of their professional worth from the comments and valuations of 'significant others' – advisers, advisory teachers and heads in particular. (Alexander, 1997: 134)

When local councillors and LEA advisers decided to launch the initiative, and later to commission the evaluation, they could not have predicted the situational ironies that would ensue. Their benign effort would be roundly criticized in the published summative evaluation report alongside acknowledging its benefits. The report would be interpreted by newspaper journalists, whose eye for a sensational story led to their 'discourse of derision' generating headlines like '"Progressive" teaching in schools was £14 million failure … advisers said that children should sit on the floor' (Daily Telegraph, 1991) – a reference to the account in the evaluation report of the 'fewer chairs than children' advice. LEA advisers would become the butt of commentators critical of 'progressive' methods, including the teacher (McGovern, 1991) who published a national newspaper article entitled 'Very peculiar practice for state schools', claiming: 'The Leeds Report shows that these child-centred methods are a major cause of under-achievement in our schools. The education authority advisers who peddle this nonsense as "best practice" have been found out at last. They must go.'

Still less could they have expected that the evaluation report, published three years after the initiative ended, would offer a timely gift to central government ministers. The latter were by then committed to educational reforms curtailing LEA authority over education. Ministers compounded the negative spin of media reporting by seizing on the evaluation report as evidence justifying their policy thrust, one junior minister describing it as 'a parable for our time'. Through the PNP initiative, hapless local councillors and LEA advisers unwittingly triggered the unintended consequence of a series of uncontrollable events, reinforcing the determination of ministers to reduce the power of LEAs through national reforms. How did this deepest of situational ironies ensue?

The complexity of the change process

The LEA advisers who orchestrated the PNP initiative created a change expressing to some extent all five characteristics of complexity identified in Chapter 2. Implementation of PNP was bound to increase endemic ambiguity. The initiative was *large-scale*: more than 500 new teaching staff including PNP coordinators were appointed to over 200 schools. The teachers, support staff, headteachers, LEA advisers and advisory teachers (employed by the LEA to provide training and advice in schools) all had different kinds of expertise and priorities. Contrast the PNP coordinators who had a vested interest in implementation with class teachers who did not. There was variation among all these groups of stakeholders over what constituted 'good primary practice', and not all teachers were comfortable with the 'integrated day' approach promoted by LEA advisers.

PNP was *componential*. Funded activities spanned three annual phases, beginning with the schools deemed most in need of support. LEA advisers concentrated on supporting staff in different schools each year. We mentioned above how expenditure ranged from appointing additional staff, through increased capitation (the annual allocation of money to purchase consumable materials and books), through in-service training courses, to refurbishing buildings. So in the most 'needy' schools staff, advisory teachers and advisers might be involved in activities connected with all these categories.

As an LEA initiative to improve practice in its schools, PNP was moderately *systemic*, spanning two administrative system levels. Here most interaction between stakeholders based at LEA and school levels could be face-to-face. But LEA advisers driving the initiative were intermediaries for the local councillors who provided additional funding. Those stakeholders based at LEA level depended on headteachers and PNP coordinators to promote implementation in schools, on responses of teachers, and ultimately on the measured learning of students and parental support.

PNP was *differentially impacting*, the anticipated shift in the practice of teachers depending on the degree to which it already matched the definition of 'good primary practice' adopted by LEA advisers. Variable congruence between the initiative and individual self-interests is indicated by contrasting responses among teachers to the efforts of LEA advisers, advisory teachers and PNP coordinators promoting the 'quality learning environment' of the model classroom. Some reported complying solely for career reasons. Impact on the other work of individuals similarly varied. The initiative was central to some LEA advisers and all PNP coordinators. But it was more peripheral for most teachers and headteachers, especially those becoming fully aware of PNP only when their school became incorporated in the initiative. Interviews conducted by the evaluators revealed wide gaps in awareness. What was perceived by LEA advisers as a clear set of aims was confusing to many school staff: to what extent was PNP about meeting special needs or improving education for all primary school students?

Like any other change, the PNP initiative was *contextually dependent.* The impetus came from elected councillors acknowledging the need to compensate for years of low expenditure on primary schools. LEA advisers were in an authoritative position to harness the new resources to promote their view of 'good primary practice'. The initiative interacted with other changes, not least pressure from national legislation, passed a few years earlier, for students with special educational needs to be educated in mainstream classrooms rather than in withdrawal groups or 'remedial' classes.

Given the complexity of the PNP initiative, it is hardly surprising that ambiguities noted by the evaluators arose and produced ironic unintended consequences. Faithful implementation across all schools was unlikely where there was such varied awareness of the initiative among stakeholders at different administrative levels. The situation was exacerbated by ambiguity about what PNP was for, how individuals were supposed to contribute, and whether doing so would be in their best interests.

Policy pathos and the implementation gap

If operations within any organization generate endemic ambiguities that are preconditions of irony, the PNP initiative illustrates how conditions obtaining across organizations within and between administrative levels intrinsically multiply this ironic potential. The organizational pathos of individual institutions finds its complementary expression in *policy pathos.* This term describes the inherent gap between proclaimed goals embodied in policy initiatives, typically formulated at a central or local administrative level, and their achievement through implementation in organizations at the system periphery. International research confirms our contention that some disjunction between the aspirations of policy-makers and their achievement in target organizations is endemic to the policy process (Fullan, 2001; Odden, 1991). The ironic perspective allows for the possibility that goals will be only partially achieved. It provides conceptual tools for analysing the extent of the gap between policy aspirations and their realization, and for explaining why such a gap occurred. A gap seems certain to open up when new policy initiatives are introduced with the goal of increasing control over those who work in other organizations within a complex system. The only uncertainty is just how big that gap might be.

We noted earlier how policy-makers at one administrative level are constrained by their relative unfamiliarity with other organizations into which their policy initiatives are introduced. When new policies are launched their impact cannot be exhaustively predicted or predetermined. The greater the range and scope of new policies, the greater the novelty and effort for leaders and managers and others in target organizations, and the greater the potential for divergence between the espoused goals of policy-makers and their realization in the sites of implementation.

Policies originating outside the sites of implementation are of particular importance for the ambiguities endemic to the internal operation of educational organizations and the external dilemmas that organization members face. The mediation of externally initiated policies at the sites of implementation has long been acknowledged, though not in terms of irony. It is captured in such concepts as the 'implementation gap', the 'implementation problem' or the 'mutual adaptation' occurring between the content of an innovation connected with policy change and the practice of its users (McLaughlin, 1991). Mediation implies that policy-makers have limited control over those responsible for implementing their policies, even though they frequently have authority sanctioning their formal control. Those with the responsibility for implementation possess sufficient agency to behave in ways that do not necessarily support the espoused goals of policy-makers.

The pathos of the PNP policy initiative embodies ambiguities paralleling those of organizational life to which they contribute. The goals of local councillors and LEA advisers were diverse and diffuse enough to confuse school staff, and they were not fully realized. There was ambiguity about the relationship between these goals and their outcomes in the inception and implementation of the policy initiative. The aim and goals were expressed in positive but loose terms that failed to specify relative priorities or suggest any link between teaching the curriculum and student learning. Ideas like the 'broadly based' curriculum remained under-specified, with the unintended consequence that the curriculum remained narrow in many classrooms.

Ambiguous goals were compounded by indeterminacy following from the long causal chain embodied in implementation. Decision-making appears to have been partly emergent. The view of LEA advisers about 'good primary practice' represents what, by extrapolation from March and Olsen's 'garbage can' model of organizational decision-making, amounted to an LEA solution looking for a primary school problem. PNP provided LEA advisers with a 'choice opportunity' for proffering their blanket solution to the problem confronting primary school teachers over promoting effective student learning. Given the likelihood that whichever strategy works is contingent on the learning situation, advocating a universal approach may have had the unintended consequence of perpetuating this problem.

Certainly, the evaluators judged that the policy initiators could have acted more effectively. In our terminology, they could have reduced the magnitude of the ambiguities that underlay the ironic unintended consequences of their actions to their inherent core. But they could not have had complete knowledge of – let alone complete control over – all the factors contributing to the outcome. One uncontrollable irony-inducing factor was the increasingly turbulent national political environment. Powerful actors operating at this level pursued their interests at the expense of those of the architects of the policy. The very implementation gap exposed by the evaluation report was paraded by journalists and central government ministers to symbolize what was wrong with the historic position of LEAs being entrusted with local administration of the national education service.

Limits to the rationality of policy implementation

The pathos of the unrealized goals pursued by policy-makers, and other unintended effects of their policies, were epitomized by *situational* irony. Just how seriously the intent of LEA councillors and advisers had come unstuck was suggested by the dip in student reading scores despite the massive injection of resources into schools. The bounded rationality of the implementation process was fourfold, creating extensive ambiguity.

First, severe *cognitive* ambiguity surrounding the decision-making of policy-makers flowed from the multitude of factors whose individual or combined impact could not be precisely computed, even in the short term. The number of school and LEA support staff involved in implementation ran into thousands. All were differentially empowered to respond in ways that were relatively indeterminate. The level of indeterminacy along the causal chain increased exponentially. Implementation entailed linked actions where one set of individuals and groups must impact on the next, from LEA advisers to students in classrooms, and the actions of each individual along the chain was to some extent indeterminate. Small wonder that LEA policy-makers did not predict how all the others would respond. If we add the ever-present capacity to affect the initiative among others at the local level, such as parents, or at the national level, including central government ministers or journalists, the impossibility of taking all conceivable factors into account becomes even starker. For policy-makers to think of all possible consequences of all possible alternative courses of action was clearly unthinkable. However the evaluation report does imply that, in *satisficing*, more could have been done to think through the initiative's content and implementation requirements. We agree, insofar as ambiguity can feasibly be reduced. But no amount of thinking through could eliminate ambiguity over responses to the initiative.

A key contributor to sometimes incompatible rationalities of the various actors was their different levels of knowledge about PNP, depending on their location, as already discussed. The beliefs and values of advisers and school staff about 'good primary practice' and about the state of play with implementing the initiative reflected their contrasting experiences. The evaluators were commissioned to put themselves in the privileged position of obtaining an overview across administrative levels and to feed information back to those involved in the initiative. The latter were precluded from seeing the situation as a whole precisely because of their administrative level or organizational location.

Second, *logical* ambiguity followed from gaps in the logic of policy-makers over specifying their aim and goals. The aim to 'meet the needs of all children' does not sit easily with the simultaneous attempt to concentrate on a subgroup: 'those children experiencing learning difficulties'. How can the needs of all students be met while prioritizing one group? The unintended consequence is understandable. Staff from the LEA department supporting students with special educational needs found themselves competing with colleagues from the department supporting primary education.

The logic of meeting the needs of students was only partially unpacked in the official aims and goal statements. What were these educational 'needs', how they identified and how were they to be met? Reference was made to:

- the classroom context (a stimulating and challenging learning environment);
- the home environment (productive links with parents and the local community);
- the content of teaching (a curriculum which is broadly based);
- how it was to be taught (through flexible teaching strategies).

But no indication was offered of how these elements linked with student learning – surely a necessary condition for achieving the goals of policy-makers. The false assumption was that a favourable context, curriculum and pedagogy were sufficient to meet all student needs. Consequently implementation activity focused more on the context of learning than on learning itself, probably contributing to the irony that no positive impact on student learning could be discerned.

Third, *phenomenological* ambiguity delimiting the rationality of efforts made by LEA policy-makers was generated by different interpretations of those with and through whom the initiative must be implemented. They must interpret the policy goals, evaluate them according to their professional beliefs and values, decide their response, and take action – which could possibly lead to unintended consequences for the actions of other intermediaries, and ultimately for student learning. LEA-based staff in rival special educational needs and primary education departments came to alternative interpretations of the relative priority to be accorded to all children or those experiencing learning difficulties. Yet both groups were included in the aim expressed by policy-makers.

Some headteachers and teachers interpreted the initiative favourably and orchestrated its implementation in line with the vision articulated by policy-makers, empowering the PNP coordinator in their school. Others rejected it, resulting in their PNP coordinator's marginalization. Many teachers interpreted the overt encouragement by LEA advisers to implement their vision of 'good primary practice' in classrooms as an unspoken strategy for securing compliance in return for the future patronage of advisers (who contributed to appointing school staff at that time). Unintended consequences of the advocacy by advisers were, first, that many teachers responded by suppressing their criticisms and complying to safeguard their career prospects. Second, despite the intention of advisers to promote flexibility in teaching strategies through the 'flexible day' or 'integrated day', some teachers perceived what was advocated as being inflexible, forcing them into tightly specified teaching strategies in the classroom.

Contradictory beliefs and values featured strongly, both for individuals and between groups. The professional beliefs of some headteachers and teachers ran counter to those underpinning the view of LEA advisers concerning 'good primary practice'. Yet these same school staff also believed in the authority of the advisers to impose their view. Consequently, such staff adopted practices that were contrary to their beliefs because they felt this to be necessary, but it was adoption without a commitment to maximizing whatever the advisers were seeking to achieve. Where individuals and groups subscribed to incompatible beliefs and values they used what power they had to resist adoption. Advisers wrote LEA curriculum policy statements without consulting headteachers. Hence, where the latter did not agree with these statements, not only were they vociferous in their criticism, but they expressed their resistance through going slow over adoption.

Fourth, *control* ambiguity was generated by conflict between the view of LEA advisers concerning 'good primary practice' and the challenge it posed for the preferred approach of many teachers and headteachers. Authority over the school curriculum and pedagogy was then diffused largely across local and school administrative levels. Headteachers and teachers retained considerable autonomy over what and how they taught. Consequently LEA advisers were just that: advisers on good practice in schools, not directors or enforcers. They sought to channel the agency of staff in schools in their favoured direction primarily through the appointment of PNP coordinators, backed by in-service training. But there were few sanctions for non-compliance. Perhaps most powerful was the perceived threat that the patronage of LEA advisers might be withdrawn. Whether this patronage was real or not, belief in it was enough to shape the behaviour of those who sought it. Those not seeking patronage had sufficient latitude to reject the innovation, as where teachers marginalized their PNP coordinator because they wanted 'slow learners out of the classroom'.

Overall, the policy implementation process generated enough ambiguity to precipitate extensive situational ironies following from the disparity between official stated goals at one administrative level and practice in the sites of implementation at another level. The policy pathos connected with limits to the rationality of the implementation process because of cognitive, logical, phenomenological and control ambiguities. Ironies stimulated by the endemic ambiguities of the implementation process were not only situational. There was also evidence of *semantic* irony affecting implementation. The official LEA rhetoric of policy statements, together with descriptors of 'good primary practice' proffered by advisers, did not wholly match practice in the schools. This hyperbole was almost certainly unintentional. But competition among staff from different LEA departments between prioritizing all students or those with special needs resulted from what Alexander viewed as the 'ambiguity' and 'amorphousness' of the key goal statement. A consequence of the under-specification of notions articulated by advisers, such as the 'integrated day', coupled with the loose use of such terms among teachers – what Alexander (1984) earlier had dubbed 'primaryspeak' – was confusion among teachers and variation in their practice.

Intentional *semantic* irony was the province of commentators and headline writers at the local and national levels, where, for example, evaluation findings like the 'more children than chairs' advice were taken out of context. What had been stated was distorted (advisers did *not* say that children should sit on the floor) to suit the interest of journalists in implying that whatever LEA advisers had regarded as good practice was in fact the opposite.

The evaluation report does not record whether headteachers and teachers expressed ironic humour in coping with the change. Evaluation reports are intended to be taken seriously, so it is unlikely that humour directed against policy-makers would surface here. We leave readers to decide whether headteachers and their colleagues, many born and bred in this Yorkshire city, did indeed engage in ironic humour.

Ambiguities of implementing policies in organizational practice

The PNP story illustrates our claim that endemic ambiguities in policy implementation breed situational and semantic ironies, producing the pathos of failure by policy-makers fully to achieve their goals. Policy implementation adds to endemic organizational ambiguities. The encounter between the attempts of leaders and managers to cope with the implementation requirements of externally initiated policies, together with their other responsibilities, gives rise to policy pathos. The outcome of implementation is unlikely to match up to the claims of policy-makers for their policy. This encounter simultaneously contributes to internal organizational pathos: leaders and managers struggle to cope with what, for them, is a new external demand which may constrain their ability to realize their goals for the organization.

The disjunction between goals pursued by policy-makers and organizational practice in the sites of implementation is created because organization leaders and managers and those for whose work they are responsible are empowered in some degree to act in accordance with their existing professional culture. They do not necessarily do what policy-makers envisage. A corresponding gap is created between the goals pursued by leaders and managers and the practice of their organizational colleagues. Policy-makers are equally empowered to operate according to their political culture. They do not necessarily do what leaders and managers require to avoid exacerbating endemic ambiguities that are preconditions for the ironies of organizational life. Hence the implementation gap.

We have so far concentrated on the direct impact of policies like the PNP initiative on the leadership and management of organizations where they are to be implemented. But ironies surface elsewhere in the policy process and can also impact indirectly on organizational ambiguities. PNP was a local policy, initiated one administrative level away from the sites of its implementation. The scope for unintended consequences of policy changes expands as the number of administrative levels increases, especially between policy in conception and policy in practice. Multi-level corporations and national welfare systems are structurally vulnerable to policy pathos linked with policy-makers' attempts at 'remote control' of organizations more than one administrative level removed from the centre.

Let us illustrate this point by building on the story in Chapter 2 of the school-based innovation, examining how a national policy impacted indirectly on the establishment of the middle school. In those pre-reform days, national policies for schools were typically implemented through intermediate LEA policies, giving rise to considerable potential for the good intentions of central policy-makers, LEA policy-makers and school leaders and managers to become unhinged. Each group inevitably enjoyed limited appreciation of others' context.

The innovation of middle schools

Why did establishing a novel form of school generate organizational ambiguities and consequent ironies, particularly those resulting from staff subscribing to either a primary school or a secondary school professional culture born of their previous teaching experience? Answering this question entails going beyond the actions of the headteacher and teachers. The school-based innovation was contextually dependent on the national and local policy framework that had brought the LEA decision to create middle schools. An explanation suggested by the ironic perspective focuses on causes of policy pathos which led, in this instance through a somewhat tortuous route, to the organizational pathos previously described. Our account is informed by the work of Hargreaves and Tickle (1980) and Hargreaves (1983) on the origin of middle schools. We concentrate on the factors most salient to the middle school at hand.

From the 1950s policy-makers in a few LEAs had been implementing the goal of creating non-selective comprehensive secondary schools. Their purpose was to replace the existing selective system comprising grammar schools for the most able students and secondary modern schools for the rest. Policy-makers assumed that larger organizations than the typical grammar or secondary modern school were required to cater for the full range of student ability, and to provide a viable sixth form of the academically most able who stayed on beyond the minimum school leaving age. However, they were frustrated by the policies of government ministers. Driven by the pursuit of economies in public expenditure, ministers stipulated that existing school buildings must be used except where population expansion or urban renewal warranted new construction.

An unintended consequence of the interaction between these LEA and national policies was for LEA policy-makers to seek alternative means of creating a comprehensive education system where they were precluded from undertaking new building. In 1964 central government ministers legislated to allow students to transfer between phases of schooling at ages other than 11. They thus created conditions for LEA policy-makers to find new means of achieving their goal of creating comprehensive schools. Present school buildings of modest size could be used if primary and secondary schools were replaced by a three-tier system. One such plan was to establish a junior high school or middle school in a secondary modern school building. A nearby grammar school building would become a senior high school for older students. Middle schools emerged as much out of *administrative convenience* as out of any desire to create a distinctive form of education for students making the transition between primary and secondary schooling. They represented a neat LEA compromise to circumvent central government restrictions: an economical way to realize the comprehensivization goal of LEA policy-makers.

In 1968, West Riding LEA established the first middle schools for students aged 9–13. Other LEA policy-makers soon adopted this policy, leading to the creation of the middle school described in Chapter 2. Its location in an area of rapid population expansion allowed new construction rather than using existing buildings. An unintended consequence of the middle schools policy was to create establishments which, in the early days, could be staffed only by teachers from primary or secondary schools. But members of each group subscribed to their own professional culture. John, the headteacher of our middle school, had an exceptionally free hand in selecting staff. But we have seen how his freedom was limited. Apart from one colleague from his previous private school, applicants for teaching posts came from state primary or secondary schools. Their respective professional cultures proved more enduring than John's ability to blend them through the individualized curriculum into a distinctive middle school tradition. The situational irony of a divided staff followed. Unintended knock-on effects of policy goals across administrative levels can be as diverse and diffuse for organizational leadership and management practice as the diversity and diffuseness of the goals themselves.

This and our earlier illustration of policy pathos and its impact on organizational pathos differ radically in many respects. What the ironic perspective reveals they have in common are features of a generic process of policy implementation. This process entails attempting to bring about change in organizations across two or more administrative levels. It generates endemic ambiguities resulting in some split – whether crack or chasm – between the espoused goals of policy-makers and their realization through practice among stakeholders at other administrative levels.

Endemic ambiguities of policy instruments

We conclude with a consideration of the restricted choice of *policy instruments* or mechanisms that policy-makers may employ to promote implementation at other administrative levels. Each instrument generates a degree of ambiguity that may trigger situational ironies in the form of policy *costs* alongside what count as benefits, from the perspective of policy-makers. They parallel the organizational costs, discussed in Chapter 2, of coping with enduring dilemmas. Just as no action to cope with a dilemma avoids the possibility of losing something that is valued, so no instrument (or combination of instruments) comes cost-free or guarantees implementation success. McDonnell and Elmore (1991: 158) distinguish four instruments, determined by the access of policy-makers to three types of resource: the ability to make rules, to spend money and to shift the balance of authority between organizations at different administrative levels. They define the instruments as follows:

1 *Mandates* are rules governing the action of individuals and agencies, and are intended to produce compliance.
2 *Inducements* transfer money to individuals and agencies in return for certain actions.
3 *Capacity-building* is the transfer of money for the purpose of investment in material, intellectual or human resources.
4 *System-changing* transfers official authority among individuals and agencies in order to alter the system by which public goods and services are delivered.

Inducements and capacity-building may operate not only through providing additional funding but also by withholding it unless potential recipients comply with the requirements of policy-makers, or by distributing funds following a process of competitive bidding. (These instruments may be construed as an 'offer you dare not refuse' where those at the sites of implementation depend on resources which inducement or capacity-building money provides.)

The four instruments operate differently in channelling and delimiting the agency of stakeholders at more peripheral administrative levels. Each tends to generate ambiguities related to the potential for costs which militate against achieving the stated goals of policy-makers. *Mandates* are based on securing compliance. Endemic ambiguity will thus be a function of the degree to which compliance is be attained and the degree to which policy-makers can know to what extent it has been attained. Surveillance is required to detect any avoidance, evasion or rule-bending by stakeholders at the sites of implementation, coupled with the authority to impose sanctions. Minimal compliance can be guaranteed only if sufficient enforcement can be applied. But the capacity for monitoring and corrective action is costly, draining resources that might otherwise have been deployed to promote substantive changes. A further ambiguity arises over how much variation in implementation should be permitted, especially where positive unanticipated outcomes might emerge that accord with the spirit of the policy change as envisaged by its instigators. Mandates are likely to inhibit desired variation, and do little to build mutual trust between policy-makers and other stakeholders or to promote enthusiasm for the policy.

Inducements rely on surfacing the latent capability of stakeholders at the sites of implementation to do what is required in exchange for extra money. As with mandates, ambiguity ensues over the extent to which the inducement will stimulate the required response. Further ambiguity arises over the extent of variation that might be considered to comply with the conditions of an award, given the range of possible consequences. These range from resources being accepted without any corresponding changes in practice through to positive unanticipated outcomes. Where there is sufficient response to the offer of an inducement, costly surveillance is incurred if policy-makers wish to ensure that the money is spent on what they intend.

The scope of *capacity-building* is broader. This instrument is designed to enhance whatever general capability exists at the sites of implementation. Ambiguity is an integral feature because the impact of capacity-building is diffuse, long term and therefore unpredictable at the point the policy is launched. The diffuseness of capacity-building leaves more room for agency on the part of other stakeholders than in the case either of mandates or of inducements. It allows outcomes to be achieved that policy-makers never envisaged – whether good and bad from their perspective. The ambiguity of capacity-building presents policy-makers with unavoidable costs in the short term: there are unlikely to be immediate and measurable returns for the investment, so it may be difficult to gain support for such expenditure.

Finally, *system-changing* operates by altering the balance of authority, frequently between administrative levels. Ambiguity emerges over the possible responses of stakeholders who stand to lose or gain authority. Conditions are created which may prove costly if losers are provoked into a defensive response, undermining the exercise of the new authority accruing to the gainers. Conversely gainers experience the ambiguity of change in learning how to use this authority, generating the possibility of variation in outcomes and the medium-term cost of providing learning support.

Whichever instrument is selected, it is guaranteed to generate ambiguities as implementation proceeds, the preconditions for the irony of negative unintended consequences. For what cannot be guaranteed is the desired outcome of policy-makers. We will say more in Chapter 4 about the ironies that these four instruments have produced during the implementation of policies to introduce managerialism in schools.

In summary, the endemic ambiguities of policy implementation parallel those of organizational life because they also rest on achieving goals with and through other people. Yet the greater complexity of change across large systems, involving more people, enhances the potential for ambiguities and consequent ironies. However, it is important not to overstate the extent of endemic ambiguity. The depiction by March and Olsen (1976) of organizations as 'organized anarchies' implies limits to internal ambiguity: life may feel anarchic, but some organizing is also going on. Similarly system-wide policy implementation, even during a reform period of policy frenzy, operates inside structural parameters. They govern what can be done, in terms of resourcing in a capitalist economy where expenditure on social reproduction cannot be allowed to undermine economic competitiveness. They govern what can even be imagined, in terms of assumptions about what is feasible and desirable.

PART TWO: IRONY AND MANAGERIALISM

4

From management to managerialism

Part Two amplifies what we mean by managerialism in school education, tracks its manifestations, and shows how endemic ambiguity is exacerbated, resulting in unintended ironies that threaten to undermine the aims of policy-makers, administrators, leaders and managers alike. In this chapter we elaborate our normative definition of managerialism, distinguishing it from leadership and management in general. We then take a selective historical look at the emergence and re-emergence of managerialism in schools. We explore how the amount of leadership and management activity in schools associated with managerialism has radically increased, and point to indicative ironies resulting from the change process to introduce contemporary managerialist practices.

In Chapter 5 we will examine how excessive leadership and management promoted by government policies threaten not only to become a self-sustaining distraction from the core purpose of education in schools, but also to swamp the educator role – which is far more crucial to educational improvement. History suggests that schools can be run successfully where few teachers are involved in their leadership and management. However, research on learning and teaching suggests that schools cannot be run successfully without giving all teachers scope to teach in creative ways that are responsive to the contingencies of each school, each class and each student.

Managerialism as an ideology

We see a fuzzy but important distinction between, on the one hand, leadership and management, and on the other hand, what we term managerialism. We reiterate our commitment to the improvement of school leadership and management as a means of enhancing the quality of education. Together with positive and forward-looking leadership, management functions to support learning and teaching, the core of the educational enterprise. Effective leadership and management 'take the strain' by creating structures and processes which allow teachers to engage as fully as possible in their key task. Managerialism, on the other hand, is leadership and management to excess. It transcends the support role of leadership and management and in its extreme manifestation becomes an end in itself. Underpinning the hyperactivity of managerialism, the constant creation of new tools for organizing work, is an ideology which holds that not only *can* all aspects of organizational life be controlled but that they *should* be controlled. When a fresh problem is encountered the first resort is to a leadership and management solution, notwithstanding the probability that the 'problem' is the result of the unintended consequences of an earlier managerial decision. The folk wisdom suggesting that when one is in a hole the best plan is to stop digging, has no place in the ideology of managerialism.

At a policy level, as well as at an organizational level, the ideology of managerialism demands that a specific problem is dealt with by means of some piece of legislation that has universal application. Or else by a revised set of procedures which might deal with the specific problem but has the consequence of generating further, unanticipated, problems thus instigating a continuous flow of policies. Whilst the majority of headteachers seek to cope as best they can with this wave of policies, a minority would appear to have so internalized the ideology of managerialism that each specific 'problem' encountered at the school level provokes a managerial response. So rather than taking the strain, leadership and management end up creating stress.

That the agency of other stakeholders can and should be channelled within limits tightly specified by central policy-makers, or leaders and managers acting on their behalf, is a key tenet of managerialism. Organizational leaders and managers, and the led and the managed, are allegedly empowered to express agency, but only within the bounds of the predetermined policy. They may become so acculturated to the vision articulated by policy-makers that they are totally committed to achieving it. In a recent UK government policy document on restructuring the teaching profession, the phrase 'freedom to manage, without losing accountability' (DFEE, 1998: 21) was coined to justify the surveillance of headteachers. The aim was apparently to ensure that this freedom was used in compliance with central government requirements. Both leadership and management and managerialism are about one group achieving a degree of control alongside or over another. But managerialism departs from the wealth of leadership and management experience in its unrealistic act of faith that channelling the agency of others, and delimiting its boundaries, can and should be both comprehensive and enduring.

Managerialism in contemporary schools originated from their external environment characterized by an unrelenting series of innovations flowing from successive central government educational reform policies. These policies, in turn, were influenced by the view of policy-makers that private sector practices are applicable to the public services, including education. Distinguishing between versions of managerialism helps us to portray how they operate at school level. One difference is over the means suggested for channelling and delimiting agency to achieve their common goal of increasing control. Another turns on whether the control mechanism is direct or indirect. The three versions of managerialism identified here represent 'ideal types', but in practice there will be many hybrid variants (Table 4.1).

Table 4.1: *Characteristics of three ideal types of managerialism*

Characteristic of managerialism	Ideal type of managerialism		
	Neo-Taylorism	*Entrepreneurship*	*Culture management*
Form of control	direct	indirect	indirect
Centre–periphery power shift	centralizing	decentralizing	centralizing
Control mechanisms	overt	covert	overt and covert
Minimal aim behind the control strategy	behavioural compliance	behavioural compliance	beliefs and values governing behaviour
Trust relationship between policy-makers, organizational leaders and managers, and teachers	low trust, with strong top-down surveillance and sanctions	low trust, with reliance on consumers to monitor provision and apply financial sanctions to those who fail to be competitive	high trust, with occasional verification and sanctions

▶

Table 4.1: *Characteristics of three ideal types of managerialism*

Characteristic of managerialism	Ideal type of managerialism		
	Neo-Taylorism	Entrepreneurship	Culture management
Examples of generic mechanisms for channelling agency	target setting, specifying tasks, identifying performance indicators, task-focused training	financial inducements to compete, creating a diversity of market niches, devolving decision-making powers, training for competitive operation	contributing to the formulation of official goals, symbolic climate setting behaviour fostering commitment, rewards for high commitment, teambuilding training
Examples of mechanisms for channelling agency within UK school reforms	setting 'tough targets' for the performance of teachers, training for headship	basing the school operating budget on student numbers, financial inducements for secondary schools to specialize in different subjects so increasing the diversity of school types	a requirement that the school brochure must contain a statement of school aims, the expectation that headteachers will create a shared educational vision
Examples of generic mechanisms for delimiting boundaries of agency	surveillance through monitoring outcomes, appraisal, inspection	financial penalties for non-competitiveness, empowering consumer choice	self-discipline, sanctions for lack of commitment
Examples of mechanisms for delimiting boundaries of agency within UK school reforms	league tables of national test results, teacher and headteacher appraisal, inspection of teaching and of leadership and management	reduction in a school budget where student numbers fall, empowerment of parents to express their preference for a local school	identification of a lack of commitment through monitoring teaching

Neo-Taylorism opts for channelling agency and delimiting its boundaries through overt, directive control. It is unsubtle, with a strong 'top-down' orientation (though more sophisticated than the original version of Taylorism, to be discussed below). Power is concentrated in the hands of policy-makers and organizational leaders and managers. It operates through detailed specification of who is to do what to achieve specified outcomes, backed by narrowly focused training, strong surveillance, and accountability measures designed to ensure tight discipline. The aim is minimally to secure behavioural compliance. Teachers or headteachers do not have to agree with policy directives, but they do have to carry out specified tasks. Otherwise they risk sanctions.

Entrepreneurship is more subtle, opting for covert, indirect control by devolving power (although within predefined limits) over selected areas of organizational decision-making. It is a strategy of 'steering at a distance' (Whitty et al., 1998) with the 'hidden hand' of the market at the wheel. Agency is channelled and delimited through creating conditions which promote competition for student places, and so for the jobs of teachers. The discipline of the market maximizes efficiency through the aggregate of self-interested activity among stakeholders, ensuring that consumers receive value for money. The aim is minimally to generate competitive activity, pitching staff from each school against their counterparts in neighbouring institutions. They do not have to believe in competing, but they cannot afford to risk losing students. Entrepreneurship operates through consumer demand which channels and disciplines the response of teachers and headteachers as producers of education offered in the marketplace.

Culture management is most subtle, opting for indirect control through a mix of overt and covert mechanisms. These are designed to align the beliefs and values of teachers with those of their leaders and managers and to bring them, in turn, into line with those of policy-makers. Both the former groups may be invited to contribute their view on the choice of official goals. They may equally be subject to subliminal efforts to shape their beliefs and values through symbolic behaviour, as where 'Management By Walking Around' (MBWA) is designed to persuade teachers that their headteacher values them enough to show interest in their work. The minimal aim here is the most ambitious. It reaches beyond behavioural compliance to 'winning hearts and minds', so that teachers and headteachers come to trust those who set goals on their behalf and embrace the desired culture. They will be motivated voluntarily to channel their agency along the required lines with full commitment to the spirit of the enterprise. If it works as intended, culture management does not require the continuing threat of sanctions underlying neo-Taylorism, or the debilitating attrition of resources that entrepreneurship failure implies. Teachers and headteachers will delimit the boundaries of their agency for themselves through exercising self-discipline because they believe in achieving official goals.

Each ideal type of managerialism reflects a different combination of form and mechanisms of control but, in combination, they provide comprehensive control mechanisms: direct and indirect, centralizing and decentralizing, explicit and subliminal. The raft of innovations entailed in an educational reform programme may reflect aspects of all three ideal types where the intent of policy-makers is to secure maximum control over teachers and headteachers.

The popular, mainly US, business management literature has been a key source of managerialist ideas for policy-makers concerned with reforming education and other public services. Indicative is the advice offered by the management gurus Peters and Waterman, describing one of their 'attributes' of excellent business management: 'simultaneous loose-tight properties ... the coexistence of firm central direction and maximum individual autonomy ... organizations that live by the loose-tight principle are on the one hand rigidly controlled, yet at the same time allow (indeed, insist on) autonomy, entrepreneurship, and innovation from the rank and file' (1982: 318). In our language, Peters and Waterman are advocating a conditional looseness: entrepreneurship alongside culture management (insisting on individual autonomy to promote a culture of innovation, as long as it is directed towards more profitable products). Looseness through empowerment to innovate is conditioned by a central tightness. Neo-Taylorist 'firm central direction' both channels and, if necessary, delimits the agency of the 'rank and file'. Innovation must be pursued in compliance with company requirements.

The rise and fall of old managerialism

Managerialism in English schools reaches back to the early days of state involvement in elementary education. In the 1860s a central government policy of 'payment by results' was introduced to ensure that the government grant, by then part-funding elementary schools, secured good value-for-money (Maclure, 1970). Up to two-thirds of this grant was conditional on the annual examination by Her Majesty's Inspectors (HMI) of each student in reading, writing and arithmetic (incongruously known as the three Rs: reading, 'riting and 'rithmetic). Girls were also examined in 'plain needlework'.

The policy was an attempt to increase financial efficiency and educational effectiveness through direct control, using a crude version of inducement as its policy instrument. The jobs of teachers depended on securing the annual grant. The intentions of policy-makers were both to reduce ambiguity over what was taught and, through annual student performance assessment by HMI, to provide evidence that the required standards of learning had been achieved before approving future funds. So the inducement was allied with a heavy sanction for staff if their students failed to perform satisfactorily. An unintended consequence of reducing ambiguity was the situational irony of reducing elementary education to what was assessed. Yet official goals for elementary education were viewed even then as amounting to more than passing the annual inspection in the three Rs (plus needlework for girls). Teachers prioritized 'teaching to the test', coaching their students to increase their chances of passing – an irony echoed in today's OFSTED inspection regime.

External control of elementary school teachers was loosened as national and local government became involved with secondary education, and payment by results was discontinued. A national code of practice for secondary schools prescribed a strict academic curriculum, soon to be backed by a national examination system. But the corresponding code for elementary schools gave staff much greater autonomy. From 1905, the national Board of Education published a *Handbook of Suggestions for Teachers*, whose title implies that teachers could choose whether or not to adopt these suggestions. A case was made for teaching the three Rs, 'health and physical training' and 'practical instruction'. It was left to headteachers to decide on curriculum content and methods. But presciently, the authors implied that effective teaching requires sufficient freedom for teachers to adapt to contingent circumstances in each classroom, a fundamental tenet of professionalism:

> The only uniformity of practice that the Board of Education desire to see in the teaching of Public Elementary Schools is that each teacher shall think for himself (sic), and work out for himself, such methods of teaching as may use his powers to the best advantage and be best suited to the particular needs of the conditions of the school. Uniformity (except in the mere routine of school management) is not desirable even if it were obtainable. But freedom implies a corresponding responsibility in its use. (Board of Education, 1937: 3)

Management was viewed as the servant of education. The detailed specification of teaching was left to individual teachers within parameters set by headteachers, taking the national code into account. At a time of widespread consensus over what official school goals should be, and with national examinations in effect governing the curriculum in secondary schools, it is unsurprising that external controls on teaching were relaxed. Policy-makers did not expect that teachers might step outside the boundaries of conventional wisdom. Not until the 1960s did political disquiet surface over the exercise by teachers of what had become a high degree of individual professional autonomy in the classroom, resulting in the emergence of diverse practices. By then, central government controls had been removed – explaining the appeal of managerialism to government ministers as a means of reimposing their will.

Taylorism and education: a parable for our time?

Intriguingly, the first manifestation of managerialism in US school education had little influence on the pre-1960s temperate leadership and management context of the UK. It has since been revived in the elaborated form of neo-Taylorism described above. Frederick 'Speedy' Taylor's notion of 'scientific management' was applied to schooling in the USA during the 1920s and 1930s. Our account draws on Callahan's (1962) critical history, concentrating on policies affecting leadership and management introduced by school superintendents. Each was responsible for a school district (equivalent to a small LEA) in a devolved system of state funded schooling.

Taylor (1911: 5–7) claimed that 'the best management is a true science, resting upon clearly defined laws, rules and principles', and that these 'fundamental principles of scientific management are applicable to all kinds of human activities, from our simplest individual acts to the work of our great corporations, which call for the most elaborate cooperation'. A legacy of his work for classical management theory was the optimistic assumption that there could be one best way of leading and managing. Universally applicable best practice could be determined through a rigorous investigation paralleling the natural sciences. Leadership and management practices embodied in scientific management were originally conceived as distinct from politics because they are concerned with efficiency of means. Educational ends were the province of employers or politicians.

Taylor blamed management for industrial inefficiency, allowing workers to rely on 'rule of thumb' rather than 'scientific' methods for doing their job. They could therefore engage in 'soldiering' – underperforming. Soldiering arose from the 'natural' laziness of humankind (presumably Taylor excepted himself) plus a more 'systematic' version, where workers deliberately slowed down production while looking as if going flat out for fear of increasing production levels expected of them. Taylor subscribed to a different rationality, believing that eliminating inefficiency would allow goods to be produced at lower cost and sold for a lower price, so expanding consumer demand (embodied in the logic of mass production for which his ideas proved seminal).

The answer was scientific management: a four-step systematic approach to maximizing individual productivity:

1 Develop a 'science' for each element of work, through a time-and-motion study and analysis of the tools required, leading to a comprehensive specification of the job, broken down into standardized units.
2 Select and train workers to carry out each unit, removing their capacity to do it by rule of thumb.
3 Set workers detailed tasks and pay them through a bonus scheme, calculated according to the earlier analysis, to motivate them. A supervisor responsible for particular units of work conducts the training and monitors the performance of workers.
4 Ensure that managers plan and control the work process in detail. Workers do as they are told or else face lower wages or dismissal.

Scientific management suited the interests of many powerful players in the American laissez-faire capitalist economy of the period. Profits could be maximized not only through elimination of inefficiency in production. The costs of publicly funded education necessary to supply the workforce for that economy could also be minimized by eliminating inefficiency here. Business people and consumers were resistant to year-on-year increases in public taxation to resource an expanding education system. Applying scientific management to this sector promised to reduce taxes: more efficient schooling could enable less input to produce the present standard of educational output. The new discourse, which Callahan labels the 'cult of efficiency', proved hard to resist. Who could argue that the drain on the public purse brought by inefficiency should be cherished?

Some superintendents were converted to believing in the new science of management. Others were merely keen to keep their job. The insecurity of their employment rendered them vulnerable to changes in public opinion, their priority of professional survival disposing them towards appeasement. A common response among superintendents to being held accountable for public money invested in their schools was to cover their backs by demonstrating that they ran an efficient operation. University academics were soon involved, several becoming pioneer management gurus offering 'efficiency expert' consultancy.

From pathos to bathos

Many ideas to eliminate waste of human effort in schools were implemented in the spirit of scientific management, as state funded school education became increasingly conceived as a business. They included:

- cost accounting – concern with analysing the financial cost of providing education for students reaching a particular standard;
- analysing measured student learning outcomes across schools in the district to determine their relative efficiency;
- calculating expenditure on teaching different subjects which was required for students to reach a specific grade, as a basis for decisions on which subjects to offer or cut;
- reducing costs by increasing class sizes;
- adopting quantifiable standards for student achievement, in consultation with local businesspeople;
- introducing comprehensive record keeping, from the consumption of basic materials to measured student learning outcomes;
- rating teachers (for example, on time spent in class passing round and collecting in papers, on their 'influence on students – in study, in life goals, in nobler ideals', on their 'energy – snap, go, force in classwork', and on their 'results'), together with students, principals and even school janitors (site managers);
- employing university consultants to conduct efficiency surveys of school districts;
- designing schools on the basis of the 'factory system' where students circulated between specialist areas so that all spaces were in constant use. The school day was lengthened, increasing the workload for teachers, and a shift system was trialled to increase use of the buildings;
- maximizing savings on school premises and operating costs.

As university training programmes came under the influence of scientific management, superintendents receiving this training came to perceive themselves more as business executives than as educators. They sought business links through such means as membership of local chambers of commerce. Superintendents even developed public relations techniques to 'sell' their schools to the public on whose goodwill and taxes they depended. One strategy took the metaphor of schools as a service enterprise to the point of absurdity. Placards were placed where visitors would see them, carrying messages like 'America's service station, a public school', 'the school desires to serve the public', 'business transacted in the office' and 'pleasing the public is our pleasant duty. The principal desires your comments.'

Policy pathos ensued because the official goals for schools, even as 'service stations', retained the aspiration to educate first, and do it cheaply second. Pathos became bathos in what Callahan calls 'the descent into trivia'. Obsession with efficiency became pervasive, expressed in everything from the subject of doctoral theses written by future superintendents (such as an analysis of the tasks of the school janitor), through advice from federal government (reducing expenditure by increasing class sizes, coopera-tive purchasing of consumables like paper clips, or repairing dripping taps), to textbooks. One entitled '*Practical School Economies*' was largely devoted to 'plant' operation and maintenance, including sections on 'toilet bowl cleaners', 'toilet paper', '[cock]roach powders', 'reducing laundry costs' and 'purposes of painting'.

The time of scientific management passed when the economic recession of the 1930s jolted administrators into attending to what had been missing all along. In Callahan's judgement:

> the introduction into education of concepts and practices from fields such as business and industry can be a serious error. Efficiency and economy – impor-tant as they are – must be considered in the light of the quality of education that is being provided. Equally important is the inefficiency and false economy of forcing educators to devote their time and energy to cost accounting. We must learn that saving money through imposing an impossible teaching load on teachers is, in terms of our free society, a very costly practice. (1962: 263)

This application of scientific management might seem a 'very peculiar practice' for state schools. We saw in Chapter 3 how in the Leeds PNP ini-tiative policy pathos flowed from the sights of policy-makers being set too high through their visionary but ambiguous goals. Here the opposite obtained. Policy pathos flowed from the sights of policy-makers being set too low, their sharply focused goal being too prosaic to impact positively on students' learning.

Ironies abound, not least unintended semantic irony which is the very opposite of hype: the trivialization of education in writings imbued with 'efficiencyspeak' by exponents of scientific management. Their espoused policy goal of eliminating waste of human effort through maximizing effi-ciency was deceptively clear, their quantifiable methods of calculating it unambiguous. But their rationality was tightly bounded. The logic of the enterprise was flawed, concentrating on efficiency while ignoring its impact on effectiveness. Taylor's system was concerned solely with means, the intermediate goal of efficiency with which a commodity of given qual-ity is produced at minimum unit cost. This system left ends – the quality and worth of the product – for others to decide. So in education the possi-bility remained unaddressed that the efficiency drive might have negative consequences for effectiveness along the causal chain from quality of edu-cational provision, through quality of student learning outcomes, to their resultant capability to join the labour force.

The false clarity of the scientific approach masked inherent ambiguity in the endeavour of superintendents. Their ideology predisposed them to fail to notice the gap between their goal of improving efficiency and implicit educational goals. Scientific management ruled out questions of alternative values while actually embodying highly contentious values: about the desirability of restricting educational goals to the intermediate efficiency goal, the possibility of one best way to achieve efficiency, and the validity of adopting a particular method for achieving it. Lowering unit costs brought the situational irony of unintentionally inhibiting educational effectiveness by:

- narrowly constraining the capacity of teachers to take initiatives;
- overloading them with large classes;
- tiring them out with long teaching days;
- diverting their attention from teaching through extensive record keeping;
- subjecting them to detailed surveillance;
- focusing the attention of superintendents on resource management and accounting for this expenditure to the exclusion of educational leadership.

The logical ambiguity of a single-minded belief in efficiency is obvious. Teachers could be pushed into doing more with less, but not into doing everything with nothing. Efficiency savings must have limits, where the costs to education and so the preparation of tomorrow's workforce would outweigh the financial benefits to today's taxpayers. There was a compounding phenomenological ambiguity. Business people and consumers seemingly lost sight of their implicit, contradictory belief that educational quality was, and would remain, a constant.

Some unintended consequences of the original form of managerialism in education, such as overloading teachers, have contemporary resonance in the UK (Chapter 1). But now they represent unintended consequences of reforms to increase effectiveness as well as efficiency. New managerialism is more sophisticated, and creates conditions for more complex ironies.

The rise of new managerialism

When Taylorist managerialism was popular in US education, school leadership and management in the UK were little discussed in academic or policy circles. It was a period of 'proto-management' during which the terms 'leadership and management' were rarely used. When used, they generally connoted day-to-day administration necessary to support learning and teaching, consistent with the description of school management as 'mere routine' in the Board of Education handbook quoted earlier.

In educational discourse before the mid-1960s schools were not 'managed', they were 'run' by their headteachers, who were primarily just that:

head *teachers*. In larger schools, they would be supported by a secretary and by a deputy head with a near-full teaching load. Headteachers undertook routine desk-work or 'admin' and spent much of the day on a wide variety of tasks, devoting relatively little time to each. They also oversaw the curriculum, pedagogy and social aspects of education. Running a school was largely about keeping things on track – the 'mere routine' of school management. The spheres of activity occupied by headteachers and teachers did not greatly overlap. There was widespread tacit agreement that headteachers should run the school while teachers would be left to exercise their professional judgement in the classroom. The role of headteachers had historically acquired a legitimacy whereby the power of the incumbent was accepted as 'natural' and deference prevailed outside the classroom. A flavour of traditional headship was given by Eric James, later Lord James, in the 1960s when High Master of Manchester Grammar School. He described his management style as drinking his morning coffee in the staffroom and being approached by teachers with requests and proposals, to which he would generally reply 'Why not?' thereby inviting them to go ahead.

The era of proto-management was succeeded by a movement to improve the quality of school management. This growing interest stemmed from practitioners including headteachers, LEA advisers, representatives from professional associations for headteachers and teachers, and academics, including contributors to the symposium edited by Baron and Taylor (1969), and Glatter (1972). One impetus for the development of the 'educational management movement' was the government policy of creating comprehensive secondary schools.

A source of logical ambiguity was generated by the necessity for specialist teaching of the menu of academic and vocational curriculum subjects deemed appropriate for students of all abilities. Under the preceding selective system, grammar schools provided an academic education for students judged to be most able while secondary modern schools provided a vocational education for the remainder. Catering for all abilities and aptitudes required a large enough organization to offer the full range of academic and vocational subjects. It also had to be structured to provide adequate pastoral care for maybe 2,000 students. Comprehensive secondary schools tended to be twice the size of the neighbouring grammar school and secondary modern school they typically replaced. Twice the staff and twice the subjects brought change: creating complex administrative structures and new staff roles, and learning how to make them work.

Central government had been little involved with developing school management. The HMI committee on the Staff, Management and Organization of Schools (COSMOS) in the late 1960s was responsible for some of the first so-labelled 'management training' courses in the UK. Management training for headteachers and senior teachers remained patchy and unsystematic, attracting little government sponsorship despite recommendations from government advisory committees, as with proposals for training primary school headteachers in the Plowden Report (CACE, 1967), and for career-long professional development in the James Report (DES, 1972). Political support for headteacher training emerged only with the drive for accountability in the 1980s, a result of the perceived necessity to rein-in teachers following a period, in the eyes of politicians, of misguided innovation.

Despite these trends the term 'management' was still seldom used in the UK, perhaps in part because primary school governors were called 'managers'. The term had a distinctive legal meaning which excluded headteachers, except in their capacity as members of the Management Committee of their schools. Ambiguity surrounded what to call the activity of achieving tasks with and through other adults in educational organizations. 'Management' had long referred to business practice. At this time it was widely thought to be an inappropriate concept for education, since schools were not factories and the term connoted an undesirable image. Academics tended to employ the term 'administration' in line with US usage (Hoyle, 1965). Yet 'administration' was also misleading since it had two connotations in the English education system: administration as routine desk-work, and administration as the activity of LEA officials and civil servants. With increased willingness to learn from business during the 1960s, management became a more acceptable term, as signalled in the book title: *Secondary School Administration: A Management Approach* (Hughes, 1974).

Weakening the boundaries: the decade of school-based innovation

The ensuing period of radical innovation up to the early 1970s posed considerable challenges for those managing schools. Traditional boundaries that had framed what was taught, by whom, how, and to whom were being eroded. This shift, first noted by Bernstein (1967), was characterized by Hoyle (1975) in terms of boundaries becoming more open, flexible and permeable (Table 4.2).

The school-based individualized curriculum innovation discussed in Chapter 2 and the PNP initiative discussed in Chapter 3 reflected a movement to transcend traditional boundaries. The individualized curriculum was designed to break down boundaries created by timetabling single ability sets of students, labelling students by ability and dictating when and what they studied. The PNP initiative was designed to soften the boundary

Table 4.2: *Opening up educational boundaries through school-based innovation*

Boundary	Direction of innovations initiated at school and LEA levels
Between subjects	a move from the traditional 'disciplines' such as physics, chemistry and biology to 'combined science' and from history and geography to 'humanities'
Between teacher and taught	a move from largely front-of-class didactic pedagogy to pedagogy based on discovery and resource-based learning
Created by school staff	a move from the class as the key unit of organization and the fixed time period for a lesson to increased flexibility in group size – a year group, a class, a working group, individual learning – and in the allocation of blocks of time to departments, faculties or years according to negotiation and agreement among teachers
Between categories of student	a move from the grouping of students by ability in terms of school (comprehensivization) and school class (mixed ability grouping) and, in some infant and primary schools, from age grouping to vertical grouping
Between teachers	a move from the isolation and privacy of class teaching to greater collaboration between teachers at the levels of pedagogy (team teaching), planning (of the curriculum) and policy-making (across the school)
In student assessment	a move from assessment by tests or examinations, taken by individual pupils at the same time and with the outcome being norm-referenced, to modes of assessment entailing course-work, group work and criterion-referenced tests
In student choice	a move from limited student choice over courses and their content to a more extensive degree of choice over courses taken, projects pursued and modes of working
In the physical characteristics of schools	a move in school architecture from an egg-box or 'cellular' structure towards open-plan schools allowing for flexibility in pupil grouping
Between school and community	a move from a strong boundary to a more permeable boundary arising from dual school and community use of buildings and facilities, greater involvement of parents and participation of students in community activities

between teacher and taught by promoting flexible teaching strategies, groupwork, discovery learning, and a 'broadly based curriculum' instead of subjects.

Such innovations reflect a fundamental shift in assumptions about schooling characterized by:

- emergence (structures emerge from activities);
- agency (teachers have a greater role in determining the nature of the school);
- flexibility (roles and structures become open to creation and re-creation);
- collaboration (teachers gain freedom to negotiate policies, structures and pedagogies).

Implementing this shift potentially entailed a transformation in school management towards supporting teachers in implementing these innovations. The interest of practitioners and academics in day-to-day management was replaced by concern with managing innovation for school improvement.

A strategy evolved which entailed integrating curriculum development, organizational development (staff collaboration) and professional development (to facilitate their continual learning). This was intended to strengthen the combined capacity of a school staff to manage innovation supported by external agencies, including 'change agents' (exemplified by the creation of PNP coordinators, discussed in Chapter 3) and teachers' centres. The strategy was 'school-focused' (Bolam, 1982), school staff taking principal responsibility for improvement, rather than LEA advisers, inspectors or curriculum development bodies. The role of HMI swung from inspection to consultancy. The intention was to strengthen generic school-wide capacity for improvement, rather than to promote specific innovations.

For headteachers and teachers, learning to cope with the management of innovation at the same time as they were innovating in curriculum, pedagogy and assessment was a considerable challenge – 'changing the wheel on a moving car' as the metaphor has it. Headteachers experienced difficulty in reconciling their authority and accountability with the expectation that they would encourage school-focused and increasingly teacher-led innovation. Teachers experienced a tension between their treasured individual autonomy and the expectation of greater collaboration. Many were suffering from innovation fatigue. Parents were often bemused by innovations in curriculum and pedagogy.

Enthusiasm for school-based innovation subsided as uncontrollable international events threatened to destabilize the UK economy. The 1973 oil crisis precipitated economic uncertainty. Political concern shifted to the importance of school education in creating an economically competitive workforce that would meet the growing global competition. The attention of government ministers turned towards the effectiveness of the state school system in achieving this instrumental goal in the interests of economic prosperity. Government concern with efficiency surfaced as pressure on the economy forced the realization that the rate of increase in expenditure on providing public services, including education, was far greater than the rate of economic growth needed to sustain it. Economically efficient, instrumental educational effectiveness became the leitmotif of reform, paralleled in many western countries facing similar economic problems.

By the mid-1970s, UK Labour government ministers became concerned about school-focused developments lacking accountability, just when attention to the instrumental goal of education required assurances that schooling would be capable of delivering the skilled workforce that would be needed. The philosopher Richard Peters described the dangers of curriculum innovation as moving from a 'mesh' to a 'mush'. This metaphor can be extended to include the entire profile of innovations as multiple boundaries were eroded. Most specific criticisms of education in the 1960s leading to the era of reform were underpinned by a perceived need to restore the tight boundaries of more traditional schooling for instrumental ends. An example of the potential for idiosyncratic school-level boundary-shifting was the decision by the headteacher in a middle school known to one of us. This classics enthusiast unilaterally introduced Latin for the oldest students – and horse-riding, for girls only.

Improving the capacity of school staff to innovate and to pick from the menu developed by external agencies was overtaken by a very different approach to management. It was stimulated by the growing complaint among politicians that many school-based innovations were failures, allied with their growing faith in accountability. They construed academic support for curriculum innovation as part of the problem. Emergent ideas such as school-focused professional development and school self-review were seen as improving the capacity of school staff to manage the 'wrong' innovations. Ironically, the subsequent marginalization of academics and their 'trendy theories' did not stop many of these ideas being later adopted by government-sponsored developments in leadership and management. But they were adapted to the more prescriptive and instrumental purpose of ensuring the implementation of government reforms.

Administrative convenience: reinforcing management hierarchy

Radical redirection of education policy in the UK from the early 1980s flowed from the determination of the incoming Conservative government to tighten control over state-funded education. An ironic consequence of the years of consensus over education, from the perspective of ministers, had been the erosion of central legal controls over the curriculum that we have described. Now, when legislative levers were urgently required, they no longer existed, and would have to be laboriously recreated.

HMI, whose role now swung back from consultancy to inspection, contributed significantly to paving the way for expanding school leadership and management to assist the 'tightening grip' (Lawton, 1984) of central government on the curriculum. National HMI school surveys conducted between 1978 and 1985 reflected a common prescriptive assumption that all teachers holding 'posts of special responsibility', attracting a higher than basic salary, should provide some leadership of colleagues and so influence their work (Wallace, 1986).

Seeds of situational irony were sown here. Many headteachers and governors had long enjoyed their autonomy, with LEA acceptance, to award such posts to some teachers in acknowledgement of their loyalty to the school or the quality of their classroom performance rather than for clear responsibilities. The duties attached to these posts were often token and no more than a means of legitimating the bestowal of financial rewards on valued teachers. We know of one primary school post of special responsibility being awarded for supervising the staff noticeboard, another for 'looking after the head's things'. It was not uncommon to award a post of special responsibility to teachers who would shortly retire, thereby enhancing their pension. An unintended consequence of the new HMI expectation that all postholders should be leaders (rather than custodians of noticeboards or 'the head's things') was to generate ambiguity over expectations and relative authority (Wallace, 1989). Many postholders had been awarded their additional allowance – legitimately at the time – on quite other grounds. In primary schools, the curriculum adviser role, with school-wide responsibility for a subject, sat uneasily alongside that of the leader of a group of classes with leadership responsibility for their teachers, covering all subjects: an obvious source of ambiguity.

The system of posts of special responsibility had evolved into a career structure which would attract and reward good class teachers. HMI chose to interpret these posts as forming a hierarchy. Postholders could be expected to influence the work of their colleagues in order to curtail their individual professional autonomy. Administrative convenience probably played a part. A means was sought to implement an externally initiated curriculum. The system of promoted posts already in place could provide it. Headteachers and deputy headteachers were seen to have a major leadership role, responsible for overseeing colleagues with posts of special responsibility, whose leadership role was more modest. They included heads of department and teachers with a pastoral role in secondary schools, and curriculum advisers in primary schools.

An implicit official model of the 'well-managed school' is detectable from positive comments in the survey reports applauding good practice and, by inference, criticizing alternative practices (Table 4.3). The model implied hierarchical distribution of responsibility for managing the curriculum that would delimit the agency of teachers, curbing their individual professional autonomy to ensure consistency and progression of the educational experience for students. The well-managed school would feature a management hierarchy as the vehicle through which external specification

Table 4.3: An implicit HMI model of curriculum control in the 'well-managed school'

Role	Responsibility for curriculum management
Headteacher	maintaining oversight of the management process by: ● coordinating the work of colleagues ● delegating responsibility for planning and supervising the curriculum through acting as consultants ● inducting new staff ● making provision of time during the school day for those with management responsibility to carry out their tasks ● making available opportunities for school-based in-service training and external training courses
Deputy	offering support to colleagues with management responsibility by: ● assisting the headteacher with maintaining oversight of the management process ● assisting other colleagues with carrying out their delegated responsibility for planning and supervising the curriculum
Secondary school heads of department, primary school curriculum advisers	planning and supervising the curriculum, and so influencing the work of colleagues through acting as a consultant in respect of one or more curriculum areas by: ● consulting teachers ● producing guidelines or a scheme of work ● procuring necessary resources ● assessing the effectiveness of guidance through means which include observation of colleagues at work in their classrooms ● adopting a tactful approach towards colleagues ● demonstrating exemplary teaching of their subject ● arranging school-based in-service training

of the curriculum could be implemented. In smaller primary schools, head-teachers should embody both headteacher and curriculum adviser roles, especially where they had responsibility for a class.

Policies for implementing managerialism in schools

In succeeding years the model of a well-managed school has been made explicit. Its implementation has been promoted by past and present governments primarily through neo-Taylorism, retaining a legacy of Taylor's 'science'. Reminiscent of the first step of scientific management – studying the 'science of the job' – is the case for expanding leadership and management developed in HMI survey reports and, more recently, OFSTED inspections and reports on school leadership and management (see OFSTED, 2003b). If 'soldiering' was a cause of poor productivity for Taylor, insufficient or poor leadership among headteachers, deputy headteachers and teachers with posts of special responsibility was a cause of ineffective education for government ministers. A parallel with breaking the job down into 'standardized units' is the specification of national standards (e.g. DFES, 2004), refined to strengthen the directive (not merely advisory) capacity of curriculum leaders.

The second step of scientific management – selecting and training – resonates with the provision of in-service training (e.g. the National College for School Leadership's 'leading from the middle' programme for 'middle managers'). The third step – setting tasks, instigating a bonus scheme and supervising the work process – connects with mandating a performance management and pay system in schools, an example of applying private sector practice to a public service. A scheme of performance-related pay for teachers and headteachers is linked to individual appraisal and associated targets (the equivalent of setting tasks) that may run to test or examination results. Annual salary increments for teachers (the equivalent of a bonus) are conditional on satisfactory performance, and are subject to a 'performance threshold'. Those judged through appraisal as having achieved outcomes and developed expertise that merit passing the threshold are entitled to a salary within an 'upper pay range'. Appraisal itself includes monitoring performance (the equivalent of supervising the work process) against previously established targets. The implementation of the performance management scheme has been evaluated and enforced through inspections.

Since neo-Taylorism relies on securing behavioural compliance, we should not be surprised if the mandate is the core instrument for bringing about policy implementation. It is sometimes backed by the inducement of additional resources. In the case of performance management, additional money was made available for pay increases dependent on a satisfactory outcome of individual performance assessment. But as mentioned in Chapter 3, mandates carry the enduring cost of continual surveillance because people cannot be trusted to comply voluntarily.

It now appears that government policy, intentionally or otherwise, is sponsoring a combination of neo-Taylorism and culture-management. If the short-term policy goal is rapid compliance, the longer-term goal seems to be acceptance and endorsement through the absorption of new practices into the school culture. Performance management is intended to 'engender a strong culture of professional development' (DFEE, 1998: 5) among teachers. Headteachers are urged to accept that performance-related pay for themselves would have a symbolic function in the task of achieving this cultural shift: 'Rewarding heads well for good performance is appropriate in its own right. It is also central to the development of a school culture which encourages and rewards excellence' (p.23). Vital to policy implementation, therefore, was the acculturation of headteachers so that they would respond positively to the central steer and, as central government change agents, implement the policy for the teachers in their schools.

The obverse of generating a management hierarchy at school level was to deploy system-changing as the main policy instrument to remove the intermediate layer of authority over the curriculum between central government and schools, which might otherwise impede central prescription. The state was gradually 'hollowed out' (Rhodes, 1997) in respect of schooling by stripping away much LEA authority and capacity to resource innovations in curriculum and pedagogy. It is thus small wonder that ministers seized on the evaluation of the PNP initiative (Chapter 3) as ammunition for this policy. In their perception, a high-spending Labour-controlled LEA had been empowered to produce an educational 'mush' at local taxpayers' expense. LEA power must be redistributed between central government and schools.

The rhetoric was of decentralization and school self-management. Greater school-level financial autonomy from LEA control was designed to foster entrepreneurship in what Conservative government ministers conceived as an educational marketplace. The 'marketization' of schools had been advocated by some North American academics (Chubb and Moe, 1990; Osborne and Gaebler, 1992). Their ideas were ideologically attractive to New Right members of the Conservative Party who pressed ministers to implement them. Parents were to be empowered to choose among an increasing diversity of schools on the basis of their preference, informed by league tables of test and examination results, inspection reports, and the marketing activity of senior school staff. Under LMS and associated reforms, headteachers were conceived as chief executives with the budgetary mechanisms to exercise greater autonomy, subject to the oversight of school governors. The report of Coopers and Lybrand (1988: 7) illustrates the confidence of private sector-based consultants that the public services could benefit from private sector practices. In advising on the introduction of the local management of schools (LMS) initiative the authors concluded:

> Good management requires the identification of management units for which objectives can be set and resources allocated: the unit is then required to manage itself within those resources in a way which seeks to achieve the objectives; the performance of the unit is held to account for its performance and its funds. These concepts are just as applicable to the public sector as they are to the private sector.

Note the reification – each unit is required to 'manage itself' – and the claim of universal applicability. At the time of publication there was little evidence from schools to justify this claim. A few LEA officials had experimented with increased delegation of the operating budget to schools, but fully-fledged delegation required changes in legislation yet unmade. The consultants proposed a generic 'self-management' solution to the problem of low standards, identified by the government-as-client to have resulted from strong LEA control over schools.

Accompanying the opening-up of competition for students between schools was a strongly neo-Taylorist thrust to centralize the direction of curriculum content through the complex innovation of the National Curriculum (Chapter 2). It was backed by the introduction of national assessment and league tables of test and examination results, and policed through the beefed-up OFSTED national inspection regime and publication of inspection reports. Decentralizing central government control over the inessentials (including greater autonomy to increase efficiency through creative budgeting), while centralizing control over the essentials (here, less autonomy over the curriculum to increase effectiveness according to the values of central government ministers) was part of a public service-wide strategy (Taylor-Gooby and Lawson, 1993). It served to replace the 'national service, locally administered' with a 'community enterprise, nationally directed, steered and disciplined'.

At the time of writing the successor New Labour government has retained most of these arrangements, supplemented with policies more directly focused on the learning and teaching process and the teaching profession itself (including performance management). We will take-up the push to refashion the teaching profession in Chapter 5. Central government intervention in state schooling is now to be 'inversely proportional' to standards of education achieved in relation to its targets. The degree of autonomy necessary for culture management and entrepreneurship to operate is therefore directly proportional to self-discipline in fulfilling central government requirements.

Ironies of managerialist policy implementation: the National Curriculum saga

In Chapter 3 we highlighted how policy implementation inevitably increases ambiguity, enhancing potential for the situational ironies of unintended consequences. Introducing managerialist policies has proved no less vulnerable. Indicatively, the incremental central government strategy for introducing the National Curriculum, after formal consultation subject by subject, soon produced the *policy pathos* of a widening gap between the stated aspirations of policy-makers and practice. (Our analysis of its characteristics of complexity in Chapter 2 suggested how complicated it was to manage.)

The change process created massive ambiguity across the entire school education system. *Organizational pathos* ensued in schools as it became increasingly difficult to plan for coherent curriculum provision (Weston et al., 1992). Academics and practitioner representatives in the consultative bodies were concerned solely with their own subjects. Each understandably argued for giving their subject sufficient teaching time. Thus the central government goal of creating a 'broad and balanced' curriculum became overlaid by pursuit of individual subject goals to the exclusion of others in all the consultative bodies, with resultant goal ambiguity.

Limits to the rationality of the implementation process abounded. According to Maclure:

> The creation of a broad and balanced National Curriculum was undertaken at breakneck pace without adequate time for preparation and planning. It is easy to see why the rapidly changing succession of ministers ... forced the pace. Given the pressures of confrontational politics, they did not feel they had time for pilot projects and careful evaluation. They were reluctant to discuss their plans in advance with experienced educational administrators. To do this would have given the old guard educational establishment the opportunity to regroup and counter attack. The momentum had to be maintained if there were to be any quick political dividends.
>
> So the whole thing was rushed. Wholly predictable pressures fell on the schools where time consuming curriculum development had to be undertaken alongside existing work. (1998: 13–14)

The policy implementation strategy appears to have incorporated *cognitive* ambiguity that was deliberate, if not conceived in such terms. The range of factors that might be taken into account was deliberately restricted to hold-off stakeholders with an interest in preserving the status quo. Ministers also wanted to maximize the opportunity within the 'political business cycle' (Mueller, 1989) to introduce possibly unpopular policy changes well before the next general election.

Logical ambiguity became apparent with the publication of the recommendations from each consultative body for a subject and the amount of time required for teaching it. The subject parts threatened to add up to more than the sum of the 'broad and balanced' whole. By the point when the final tranche of subjects was to be introduced, the National Curriculum had already expanded to fill more than the potential space available. Teachers struggled to squeeze in all the compulsory components.

Ideological controversy between different stakeholder groups over particular subjects was symptomatic of the *phenomenological* ambiguity generated by implementation. One notorious example was the LINC (Language in the National Curriculum) Project (Wallace and Wray, 2002). LINC was a major government investment during the early 1990s to support the implementation of a prescriptive model of language in schools. This model regards 'standard English' as superior to other dialects, and so the exclusive form that should be taught. Ministers commissioned academic linguists to develop teaching materials and provide in-service training for teachers. But project team members operated according to a more descriptive model of language variation, reflecting both mainstream linguistics and the views of many English teachers. This model emphasizes the appropriateness of language for its purpose, rather than the correctness of 'standard English'. The two models are mutually incompatible: one language dialect cannot best fit all purposes if different dialects best fit different purposes.

This instance also exemplifies how implementation produced *control* ambiguity. The agency enjoyed by linguists enabled them to interpret their brief according to their preferred model of language. Among different stakeholder groups with a legitimate interest in English teaching, whose preferred model of language should hold sway? Government ministers hold political authority to impose their preferred model but do not know much about the nature of language and how to teach it. Academic linguists know about language but do not have the political authority to impose their view. Teachers know most about the contingent characteristics of the students in their classrooms and pedagogy, but do not have political authority. And what about parents, employers, students?

In the case of the LINC teaching materials, ambiguity over which model of language should underpin English within the National Curriculum spanned two administrative education system levels: central government and university academic intermediaries through whom implementation was to be moved forward. Control ambiguity was reduced when the Secretary of State for Education blocked publication of the draft LINC teaching materials, on the grounds that they were overly concerned with the social context of language and insufficiently concerned with grammar (Carter, 1992). But phenomenological and control ambiguity did not stop there. A short-term irony stemmed from the unintended consequence that the central government investment in LINC (and so the money of taxpayers) had been squandered. More long term was the perpetuation of ambiguity over the English curriculum in schools, to which the government decision to marginalize academic linguists, thereby forfeiting their expertise, contributed.

The combination of these sources of ambiguity led to more substantial situational ironies. They included, first, the ordering of a major revision of the National Curriculum – meaning yet more work for teachers and headteachers to undo what they had just implemented – before this reform had even been fully formulated (Barber, 1996; Maclure, 1998). Second, some £750 million (over $1 billion) of taxpayers' money was estimated to have been wasted by government ministers – who were also publicly pursuing the economic goal of reducing public expenditure.

Excesses of the New Normality

Conceiving school leaders and managers as a conduit for educational reforms and teachers as the 'deliverers' of reformed practices has meant extra work beyond the implementation period. The National Curriculum and its assessment regime indirectly affected pedagogy, because teachers could not afford to ignore the tests. Other reforms amounted to mechanisms for facilitating the implementation of the ones focused directly on learning and teaching. They included development planning (to be examined in Chapter 7), staff appraisal, staff development and in-service training, and school governance attuned to the conditions of a quasi-market. These reforms added to what might be termed 'normal' leadership and management and implicated classroom teachers, ostensibly under the liberal banner of their *participation* but in effect coopting them into the managerial enterprise. A new array of leadership and management tasks must now be undertaken. There is no realistic choice in schools over whether to engage in them because accountability measures are so tight. But there is room to manoeuvre over how far to enter into the spirit of these tasks, as opposed to doing the minimum required. The increased workload is summarized in Table 4.4.

Table 4.4: *The new 'normal' leadership and management in state-funded schools in England*

Change connected with national reform	Indicative leadership and management tasks
The National Curriculum	managing the development, resourcing and teaching of the curriculum for each key stage
The literacy and numeracy strategy within the National Curriculum	managing the development, resourcing and teaching of the literacy hour and numeracy hour in primary schools, plus the equivalent in secondary schools at Key Stage 3
Religious education and collective worship	managing the development, resourcing and teaching of the curriculum, arranging the timetable to include daily collective worship
Assessment of the National Curriculum	organizing the assessment procedure for each subject to be assessed at each key stage and the marking and recording of results, informing students and parents, sending results to the Department for Education and Skills
Target setting for the National Curriculum	negotiating with LEA officials to set school targets taking into account national targets set by ministers
League tables of National Curriculum assessment results linked with national targets and truancy rates	orchestrating the work of teachers to ensure that students perform as well as possible in the assessment procedure and to keep the truancy rate down
Regular OFSTED inspection, whose results are published	managing preparation including the provision of documentation, the presentation of practice, facilitating inspectors' conduct of the inspection, reporting to parents, drawing up an action plan for improvement in the light of the inspection results
The code of practice for students with special educational needs	ensuring that the practice of teachers complies with the code
Revised arrangements for supporting students from minority ethnic groups	ensuring that specialist teachers and support staff provide student support within the new arrangements
An increased proportion of parents and local community representatives on school governing bodies	representing a professional view of school practice and priorities to lay people on the governing body through the full committee and subcommittees

Budgeting and staff appointments under LMS	setting, operating and monitoring the annual budget, preparing an account for governors' oversight, managing buildings, use of services and internal repairs, managing staff appointment procedures with governors
More open enrolment of students	providing information for prospective parents, competitive marketing of the school
The expectation that schools have a development plan	preparing the plan document, gaining the approval of governors, arranging for the implementation of initiatives, monitoring and evaluating the plan
Staff development budget and training days	managing a staff development policy and programme of activities to meet identified needs, planning and conducting training days
Performance management, including staff appraisal	managing the appraisal, threshold and performance related pay procedures within the oversight of governors
Operating with a remodelled workforce	reallocating tasks between teachers and support staff and monitoring who fulfils tasks deemed appropriate for teachers or support staff
Competitive tendering for services, including training support, grounds maintenance	inviting tenders, contracting (including negotiation with LEA service providers)
The system of school bids and securing of matched funds for central government-sponsored initiatives	developing, costing and submitting individual school and collaborative multi-organizational proposals to central government agencies, seeking matched funds from the local community, managing initiatives where bids are successful and reporting to the funding agency on the conduct and outcomes of these initiatives
Contribution to initial teacher training	managing the mentoring procedure for students on teaching practice

Notwithstanding the attempt to 'gentle' this additional burden for head-teachers and teachers by presenting it as 'professional development' or 'school improvement', there is clearly an intensification of work overall, marked by a striking expansion of leadership and management tasks. They all take time, and because no increase in staff working time could be allocated, one predictable cost was staff overload as headteachers and teachers coped with the extra tasks. Another was to curtail the time that headteachers and teachers – and especially those teachers now deemed to have leader-ship and management responsibility – could spend on educational tasks. Headteachers had long fulfilled the role of 'leading professional', even in large secondary schools (Hughes, 1973). They were educators first, engag-ing collegially with other staff in promoting effective teaching and pastoral care, and more directive administrators – or 'chief executives' – last. They now found the balance of their role reversed. It is because the expansion of leadership and management tasks has been so extensive, because before the reform movement schools were run and students were educated without them, and because they take time which could have been spent on direct educative tasks, that we claim them to be excessive.

Ironies of managerialist policy implementation

We have suggested that improving the quality of educational leadership and management as a route towards improving educational practice was neces-sary, but that the shift from management to managerialism may be going too far. The reform policies of the last two decades have not allowed sufficiently for endemic ambiguity or its inevitable enhancement by the change effort. Whichever versions of managerialism are adopted – the direct control of neo-Taylorism or the indirect control of entrepreneurship and culture man-agement – policy implementation generates ambiguities contributing to policy pathos. An ironic consequence is that the ever-tightening grip of cen-tral government unintentionally creates conditions for losing its grip. The policy implementation process causes the proliferation of further ambigui-ties. Many endure, contributing in time to endemic ambiguity, and so cannot be discounted as temporary side-effects. The more the attempt to assert con-trol, the greater the potential for ambiguities militating against it.

Early experience in the USA with scientific management showed the inadequacy of exclusive pursuit of efficiency. It underlined the importance of adopting a more sophisticated and less directive approach towards edu-cational improvement. The steady growth in educational provision during the 1960s was largely due to a combination of practitioner demand and academic response. Central government was little involved. Demands for accountability emerging in the 1970s challenged the self-interest of educa-tion and other public service professions. They challenged innovations in curriculum, pedagogy and assessment emerging in schools, seen as out of control because of the individual autonomy enjoyed by teachers, fuelled by ineffective LEA initiatives and bolstered by 'trendy' academic theories.

The response of successive central governments by increasing control over these matters and by strengthening school leadership and management as the means of implementing national reform policies has had some positive impacts, alongside the ironies of policy implementation. The extent of practitioner agency has been sufficiently delimited to obviate the excesses of educational practice that were seen in the era of school-based innovation, and the quality of education for all has thereby been to some degree enhanced. But we question whether these improvements have been of a magnitude that justifies their heavy costs, financially and in terms of sapping the energy and lowering the job satisfaction of teachers and head-teachers who have had to implement so many reforms, so often, and so fast. We move on to consider how the additional leadership and management tasks of the new normal practice in schools may be distracting teachers and headteachers from their core purpose. The new normality creates conditions for leadership and management to become an end in themselves, not just the means to an educational end.

5

A solution in search of a problem

Managerialism is a classic instance of 'a solution in search of a problem' (March and Olsen, 1976). Leadership and management deal with problems; managerialism generates problems. Given the level of pressure on contemporary headteachers, it may seem bizarre to suggest that they actively generate problems. We are not suggesting that all headteachers seek to identify or create them. Perhaps this is true only of the minority. But all headteachers are likely to experience pressures towards demonstrating problem-finding behaviour and either generating problems or overcomplicating existing problems to which there may be relatively simple solutions. There are several reasons for these pressures. First, they result from the pervasive spread of the ideology of managerialism in which problem-finding is regarded as a moral imperative. Second, problem-finding is representative of the proactive behaviour that is held to be a key indicator of leadership. Third, it is widely assumed that the skills acquired during the training of educational leaders and managers cannot be allowed to remain under-used. Finally, it is in the career interests of leaders and managers to display a problem-solving orientation. We begin by discussing and illustrating the phenomenon of a solution in search of a problem, then consider several developments associated with it.

A solution in search of a problem

The paradox of 'a solution in search of a problem' was discussed in Chapter 2. It is particularly apt in considering the ironic consequence of proactive managerialism whereby those in leadership and management roles must not only solve problems but must manufacture them. Problems legitimize roles, underpin promotion opportunities, and justify requests for additional resources. There is a parallel with the phenomenon that 'work expands to fill the time available', enshrined in Parkinson's Law

(Parkinson, 1985). Problems expand so as to legitimate leadership and management roles. It is uneconomic for the tools of leadership and management to stand idle. For 'true believers' the search for problems and the opportunity to exercise their skills may become something of a mission. We suspect that even the majority of teachers and headteachers, who are not 'true believers', nevertheless find it in their interests to sustain a high level of leadership and management activity – especially when shaping up to meet the criteria for an OFSTED inspection.

Associated with the phenomenon of solutions preceding problems is the increasing degree of professional specialization. There is a long tradition of sociological studies about the degree to which professional specialization has generated 'problems'. A classic case study undertaken by Cicourel and Kitsuse illustrated how student counselling in an American high school became a self-justifying semi-profession. Engagement with the normal trials and tribulations of adolescent development generated the 'need' for ever-more specialist counselling. As the authors put it:

> It is our thesis that the bureaucratization of counselling in large, comprehensive schools leads to an emphasis upon and concern for professional status among counsellors, and that this professionalization will produce a greater range and frequency of student problems (e.g. over- and under-achievers) than in schools in which counselling duties are assigned to and performed by less professionalized teacher counsellors. (1963: 77)

Professions are continuously 'in process', constantly generating new specialisms (Bucher and Strauss, 1961). Many professional specialisms emerge as a result of scientific and technological advances. This has perhaps been most obvious in medicine but developments in information technology have, for example, given rise to new specialisms in education. More frequently, new specialisms have been generated not as a result of fresh knowledge or technological advances but as a result of adding more functions to the educational enterprise, or by reconfiguring and relabelling existing functions.

The previously diffuse roles of teachers and headteachers have become more specialized, stimulated by the large schools created by comprehensivization and by the establishment of 'posts of special responsibility' in 1956 (Wallace, 1986). We saw in Chapter 4 how the increasing subject, pastoral and administrative role specialization which followed was less a response to a perceived need for greater specialization than a device for recruiting, retaining and rewarding valued staff. In secondary schools, most new posts were allocated to subject specialists. But new pastoral roles were created to reward well-regarded, often non-graduate, teachers without subject responsibilities. When equity required the creation of similar allowances in primary schools where there existed few subject specialisms, rewarding valued teachers necessitated the creation of new job titles. We do not deny the emergence of new needs as the educational enterprise became more complex, but the 'push' of needs has been complemented by the 'pull' of new roles. It is difficult to determine in some cases whether new tasks generated new job titles or whether new job titles preceded the identification of new tasks.

Understandably, few studies of contemporary school leadership and management have been designed to explore the contribution of increasing specialization to generating 'problems'. However, as an indicator of how the process occurs we can consider the proposal (Tan, 2000: 33, cited by Morrison, 2002) that each school should have a specialist 'human resource manager' whose functions would include the following:

- planning how the development of teachers (up to 100 hours per year) fits into the overall planning of the school;
- sitting on staff selection panels;
- establishing criteria for recruiting staff;
- assessing applicants' openness and willingness to learn;
- assessing interpersonal and social skills;
- assessing teamworking skills;
- arranging job previews (e.g. presentations by applicants to posts);
- assessing applicants' and teachers' abilities in multi-tasking;
- arranging pre-school oriented placements for students considering becoming teachers;
- developing transparent pay systems in the school, which includes payment for skills and skill development.

No doubt incumbents of such a role could find plenty to do and thereby legitimize the role – which would probably also entail the involvement of other staff whose workload would be thereby increased. But the question can be asked whether any school would benefit more from having an additional human resource on the staff in the form of an extra *teacher*, rather than a specialist human resource *manager*.

Meetings are particularly rich in opportunities for finding problems. Meetings have now become a major leadership and management tool. In many schools, attending meetings has become almost a way of life. They occupy time during the school day and also after school hours, contributing to the high number of hours worked each week by teachers. Meetings take many forms. Some are highly informal and initiated by groups of teachers collaborating on aspects of curriculum or pedagogy. But what we have in mind are particularly the formal meetings which are ostensibly concerned with leadership and management. The key example is what used to be called the SMT – the school or senior management team – now increasingly termed the SLT (school or senior leadership team) in line with managerialist discourse. Such meetings exist to enable staff to solve problems and make decisions. But they also fulfil many other functions, including reporting, mobilizing, motivating, reinforcing group identity, impressing colleagues, or parading grievances. They have the strong symbolic function of expressing the collegiality that has in recent years become a strong theme in educational leadership and management. Such has always been the case.

But meetings have increasingly become opportunities for *generating* problems. Constructing an agenda often entails a search for problems but, as March and Olsen (1976) have shown, problems flow into and out of meetings depending on who is present and who is not. Moreover, 'problems' can be of a different order of significance yet, unless the continued existence of the organization is threatened, their significance is not necessarily reflected in the amount of time and effort devoted to them. Some committees and working parties are dumping grounds for 'problems' that are not resolvable at a particular point. Managerialism thrives on meetings. To reduce the number of meetings may be to reduce the number of 'problems' that unproductively absorb staff time. But to do so would be heretical to the managerialist mind.

Partial professionalization

One consequence of the reform era has been the professionalization of educational leadership and management. This is highly ironic since one of the aims of educational reform can be interpreted as halting the professionalization of teaching. This irony results from the fact that the professionalization of leadership and management has been only partial.

Traditionally professions were regarded as occupations with distinctive characteristics including:

- a specialized knowledge base;
- a lengthy period of education and training;
- a clear boundary between members and non-members;
- a high degree of practitioner autonomy (though limited in some measure by legal and political control);
- self-regulation;
- a strong voice in determining policy within the area of members' expertise;
- a commitment to client-interest values expressed in a code of ethics.

Professionalization is the term generally used to connote the process by which occupations gradually acquire these characteristics and thereby come to be accepted as professions. However, professionalization may usefully be construed as having two components (Hoyle, 1974). The *institutional* component refers to the process by which an occupation increasingly meets such criteria as a strong boundary, self-regulation and accredited practitioners. By contrast the *service* component of professionalization refers to the process by which members of the occupation improve their core skills, give priority to the needs of clients, are unstinting of time and generally enhance the quality of provision. It can be too readily assumed that the two components of professionalization proceed together, but this need not necessarily be the case.

By the mid-1970s many social historians and social theorists had come to the view that 'the rise of professional society' (Perkin, 1989) which occurred broadly over the previous century could be viewed as the institutional dimension of professionalism having come to dominate and status interests to prevail over service interests. Thus professionalization in education, and in the public services generally, came to be regarded as a manifestation of a self-serving rather than a client-serving ideology, 'providerism' having prevailed over consumer interests. In the late 1970s the professions became a focus of reform as politicians increasingly adopted a market perspective. Autonomy, the core principle of professionalism, came under attack. Successive governments introduced measures to render the professions more accountable to government and to immediate clients. These measures ensured that the professional model of organizing work was squeezed by the increasing emphasis on the bureaucratic (accountability to government) and market (accountability to client) models within the 'new public management' (e.g. McLaughlin et al., 2002). The result can be viewed as 'de-professionalization' or as a 'new professionalism' (see Hoyle 1995).

Ironically, one of the means adopted to curb teacher professionalization in the institutional sense was that of increasing the professionalization of educational leadership and management. This was, however, a 'partial' professionalization since it was far from being a return to the traditional model of a profession, particularly in relation to practitioner autonomy. Although headteachers were given greater autonomy in certain areas such as budgeting and staffing (under the 'self-management' thrust discussed in Chapter 4), their autonomy was constrained by the iron cage of government policy. It is possible to construe the new professionalism as, in fact, incorporating the ideology of managerialism. But in Chapter 9 we will argue that notwithstanding this trend, many headteachers and teachers have sustained some of the characteristics of teacher professionalism. We in no way deny the improvements brought about by the professionalization of school leadership and management, a process in which we have ourselves been involved for many years. But we want to argue that the new quasi-professionalization of educational leadership and management has the potential for producing solutions in search of a problem.

A focal point of successive government strategies since 1983 has been to establish some form of national body to promote school leadership and management, beginning with the National Development Centre for School Management Training, a development project for the stimulation and evaluation of management training for headteachers and other senior staff. The latest manifestation of this trend is the National College for School Leadership, inaugurated in 2000, whose contribution to professionalization includes:

- documenting and extending the *specialist knowledge base* through commissioning reviews of research and small-scale empirical studies, and contributing to funding larger research projects;
- developing a suite of leadership *training* programmes, whose coverage includes leadership for 'middle managers', preparation and induction for aspiring and newly appointed headteachers respectively, and refreshment and mentoring skills for experienced headteachers;
- within this provision, offering the National Professional Qualification for Headship (NPQH). It has become compulsory for new headteacher appointments, so sharpening the *boundary* for membership of the national headship cadre and in effect extending the training that all aspiring headteachers will have to undertake in future;
- revising National Standards for headteachers originally introduced in 1997, prescribing *commitments* (DFES, 2004: 6–11) which are consistent with an ethical code (though not articulated in such terms), including 'the entitlement of all pupils to effective teaching and learning', 'involvement of parents and the community in supporting the learning of children and in defining and realizing the school vision', and 'the equitable management of staff and resources'.

The establishment of the NCSL is the most obvious way in which central government ministers are seeking to professionalize educational leadership and management. But other developments are contributing to the process.

Credentials and managerialism

Central to professionalization is *credentialism*, on which there are two major perspectives. Credentials, especially when linked to a licence to practice, define the boundary between members and non-members of a profession. Preserving this boundary can be seen as a form of exclusion and a means of sustaining or enhancing status and the perquisites which go with it. As such, credentialism contributes to the institutional component of professionalization. In terms of the service component, credentialism can be seen as assuring quality by excluding from the profession people who cannot demonstrate an appropriate level of competence, or, more positively, enabling would-be entrants to demonstrate their competence. We have noted how the NPQH is becoming a necessity for new headteachers. Hitherto, programmes offered by institutions of higher education have led to such credentials as master's degrees and doctorate qualifications but not professional qualifications.

The two traditions of preparation for understanding and preparation for practice coexist uneasily. As higher education academics, we observe that practitioners tend to experience some phenomenological ambiguity where they are exposed both to government-sponsored instrumental training orientated towards the implementation of central government policies and to advanced education programmes. The knowledge base for their training is founded on knowledge-for-action and instrumentalist intellectual projects. It is not wholly compatible with the knowledge base for their advanced education founded more on knowledge-for-understanding and, occasionally, knowledge-for-critical evaluation. Most management students seem to be ironists, knowingly compartmentalizing the two experiences. They act in accordance with the prescriptions of the training in their organizations, while developing critical purchase on what they are doing – some even choosing to write critical assignments deconstructing the training! But government-sponsored training and other development activities reach far more people than advanced education opportunities, which no longer attract much government funding. We therefore suggest that government-sponsored professionalization of educational leadership and management is promoting an instrumental managerialism rather than a reflective professionalism. A qualification for entry sharpens the boundary, and therefore the potential for self-protecting boundary maintenance, between the holders and non-holders of the NPQH qualification.

The knowledge base of the traditional professions entailed an interaction between practical skills (or know-how) and propositional knowledge based on scholarship and research. Hence the location of professional preparation for the older professions in universities. When the effectiveness and efficiency of public services was challenged in the 1970s, one strand of criticism was underpinned by the assumption that the professional knowledge base had expanded well beyond what practitioners needed to know. This expansion was increasingly seen as serving the aggrandizement of the professions, aided and abetted by academics. The backlash in school education was strong, with research and scholarship in university, polytechnic and college departments of education becoming a 'prime suspect' for causing the perceived decline in school standards. Central government education policies increasingly focused on tightening the grip of ministers on the content of teacher education courses and loosening their relationship with higher education through creating more apprenticeship-like patterns of entry (Hoyle and John, 1995).

As indicated above, educational reform has led to a clear *career structure* for aspirant headteachers. Previously there had been no single pattern, appointment to headship being based on diffuse, unsystematic and often quite idiosyncratic criteria (Morgan at al., 1983). The process is now much more 'professional' and selection has adopted some of the methods used in industry, the military and the civil service. It can be assumed that these developments have brought advantages to the system. However, one consequence has been to stimulate teachers who aspire towards promotion to think 'managerially' and to shape their careers to meet managerial rather than educational criteria. To do so they need to have occupied roles with managerial titles. We question, therefore, to what extent job titles may precede function. Advertisements for senior positions in schools do not always make clear just what the job really entails, and one suspects that the titles are sometimes more grandiloquent than the tasks involved.

Credentials and careers exert pressure on headteachers and teachers to internalize the culture of managerialism. *Culture* implies a configuration of beliefs, practices, relationships, language and symbols distinctive to a particular social unit. All occupations have their distinctive culture, and there is a recognizable culture of teaching. The relationship between the long-standing professional culture of teaching and the emergent culture of leadership and management is unclear. The reform effort has fostered the strengthening of a managerialist culture in education, the knowledge base has provided a distinctive conceptual base and language, and credentialism and career pressures have ensured its diffusion.

Talking the talk

A specialist language is central to an occupational culture and a new discourse has emerged in education over the past 20 years. Much has been absorbed from private sector management but an education-specific variant has been generated. This web of managerialist language has become so pervasive in education that even beginning teachers speak and write it. In Chapter 4 we noted how 'management' is itself a relatively new term in educational discourse. Revitalization of the concept of leadership is even more recent, adopted by central government policy-makers during the 1990s to emphasize how influencing people to change their practice is central to public service reform, rather than merely coordinating everyday activity.

The discourse now centres on words such as 'quality', 'performance', 'delivery' and 'personalization' which connote the client-orientation of a more professionalized leadership and management. It also incorporates semi-technical terms from the academic literature such as 'transformational leadership' or 'the learning organization', together with catchy phrases from leadership and management texts, many borrowed from the business world, including 're-engineering', 'zero defect' and 'high reliability'. In this respect the culture of educational leadership and management has been considerably influenced by the equivalent culture in the private sector, reflecting the affirmation of successive governments that leadership and management in this sector have something to teach the public services. It is probably also because the teaching of educational leadership and management in higher education has drawn heavily on concepts generated in the private sector, which have been absorbed by practitioners. It is the language of 'efficiency' and 'targets', and of such metaphors as 'right-sizing', 'sticking to the knitting' and 'the bottom line'. We speculate that this 'tough', 'masculine', 'can-do' discourse may have been more than willingly internalized by true-believer managerialists in education in an attempt to enhance their status – and salaries – by inviting a comparison between their role and that of private sector managers. If so, they are likely to be disappointed since the esteem which headteachers and teachers enjoy in the eyes of the general public is much more likely to stem from the 'educationist aspect' than the 'managerialist' aspects of their role (Hoyle, 2001). 'Everyone remembers a good teacher', in the language of the Teacher Training Agency, is likely to have more resonance for the general public than any slogan celebrating managerial efficiency.

A semantic irony, probably unintended, lurks here. Despite the extensive 're-badging' of educational leadership and management through hortatory leadership discourse (witness the NCSL's slogan 'every child in a well-led school, every leader a learner'), the 'can-do' imagery belies the 'must-do' of bounded professionalization in matters of curriculum and pedagogy. All headteachers and teachers have had to adjust to managerialism. The professional workplace literature suggests that the discrepancy between the 'right to manage' flavour of so much of the discourse and the expectation of 'ensuring the faithful delivery of education policy' is not lost on most. Perhaps the majority have accommodated to government-sponsored professionalization rather than fully internalizing a managerialist culture. It would also appear that teacher and headteacher associations have so far sustained an 'educationist' stance in the face of educational reforms and largely resisted the potential for serving their members' interests by embracing managerialism. Nevertheless, conditions have clearly been created for the ideology of managerialism at a political level to be converted into an ideology of managerialism at a practitioner level, whereby leadership and management become ends in themselves.

Provision of more comprehensive training support for those with and aspiring towards educational leadership and management posts is surely to be welcomed. Yet there is a danger that promoting this partial professionalization may, unintentionally, fuel a self-serving agenda concerned with enhancing status, remuneration and conditions of service. The service component of the professionalization of leadership and management is demonstrably the most important for educational improvement. If schools are to be led and managed effectively and efficiently it is vital that headteachers, aspirant headteachers and 'middle managers' maximize their leadership and management skills. Training and development activities to promote these skills connect the service component with the institutional component of professionalization. But an undue weighting on institutional aspects of professionalization may induce the idea that educational leadership and management constitutes a profession in itself, resonating with the notion of the career 'general manager' prevailing in the business world. The potential threat to education is that the professionalization of leadership and management fosters the emergence of an ideology which, first, bestows greater significance on leading and managing than on learning and teaching; and second, equates the professionalization of teaching with teachers internalizing the values of excessive leadership and management.

The private sector as model

Successive governments have increasingly turned to the private sector as their inspiration for strengthening public service leadership and management, on the twin assumptions that business practices are effective, and that they are directly applicable to educational organizations. The educational management movement in Britain in the 1960s (Chapter 4) tended to take a positive but guarded view of what could be learned from industry. However, policy-makers became less inclined to take an 'adjectival' view of management that entails perceiving educational management as having a set of problems and concerns which stemmed from purposes of education. They were much more inclined to make assumptions about the existence of a generic set of skills that could readily be transposed to educational settings.

It is something of an irony that private sector leadership and management practices were unequivocally accepted as offering solutions to the leadership and management of all schools – and perhaps 'failing' schools in particular – when there are daily accounts in the financial press of 'failing' companies. Perhaps there are only limited 'generic' solutions to problems in either private or public sector organizations. Yet management consultants generally operate on the basis of 'selling' generic procedural solutions to the problems presented by clients (Huczynski, 1993). What they had to offer ministers bent on implementing business practices in schools was a set of ready-made solutions, developed in non-educational contexts, in search of problems to which they could be applied. It is something of a puzzle why supposedly hard-headed managers of business organizations so unreflectively leap on to every passing management bandwagon in the face of experience – if, in fact, they do so in practice rather than just in terms of rhetoric. This has now extended to educational leadership and management as successive ministers become seized of the transformational possibilities of the latest theories. (As we make very clear, our ironic perspective is, we would like to think, a brake on the various bandwagons that hurtle down the educational highway.)

The contribution of academics, consultants and assorted gurus

We have to add to the forces generating solutions on search of problems: academics, consultants and management gurus. In the case of all three roles there are considerable pressures towards provision of solutions to problems and, in the extreme, solutions for problems which have not yet been identified or have been 'manufactured'. All three have been instrumental in spreading the idea of private sector solutions to public service problems.

In relation to academic work a number of trends can be noted. One is that academic careers are implicated in generating increased specialization in particular, and in contributing ideas consistent with a culture of managerialism in general. A second is that the expansion of knowledge in the area of leadership and management is a function of the theory and research which individual academics must produce to justify their position, their promotion, and their contribution to meeting criteria for external evaluation of their institution's performance. Success can be dependent on the identification of problems and recommended solutions disseminated through publication, teaching and consultancy. The funding of research – and, particularly, of development work – has to a greater degree than in the past favoured projects that carry the greatest potential for practical application. Also, as we noted above, there has been a growing tendency for the teaching of educational leadership and management to be orientated more towards practice than towards theory, particularly knowledge-for-understanding. That said, we believe that educational leadership and management have been less blighted than general management by the growth of 'sure fix' texts, and that the interplay between theory and practice is holding. Nevertheless the growth of prescriptive texts – specialized according to sector and to role – headteachers, deputy headteachers, heads of department, teachers, librarians, counsellors – is notable.

Tan's (2000) proposal for a human resource manager discussed earlier was cited in a text targeted at 'headteachers and middle managers, and those on higher level courses in educational leadership and management'. The idea of classifying teachers as 'human resources' is itself a translation from private sector discourse and practice. Academics may also play a part in the identification – and so generation – of leadership and management 'problems' and the nomination of new specialized roles whose incumbents would offer solutions. Teaching texts, driven by the intellectual projects of knowledge-for-action and instrumentalism, operate not only as aids to understanding but also as a source of prescriptions. Whether or not students internalize such ideas, they will be exposed to them.

A few academics and consultants who concentrate on offering their solutions to policy-makers and practitioners acquire something of 'management guru' status. We indicated in Chapter 4 how consultants have contributed to the legitimation of managerialism and so, indirectly, to ironic consequences. Whether through their writing, training programmes or private audiences with policy-makers, the discourse of management gurus typically offers the tempting vision of a simple 'model', or 'key attributes', 'lessons', or a 'sequence of procedures' which promise improvement in practice. Implicitly, the unproblematic implementation of whatever is advocated will reduce or even eliminate endemic ambiguities. Many gurus amount to what Ball calls 'policy entrepreneurs', whose practice consists of:

> the proselytizing, and in some cases the sale, of 'technically correct answers'. The policy entrepreneur is committed to the application of certain technical solutions to organizations and contexts which are taken *a priori* to be in need of structural and/or cultural change. The entrepreneur's interests, in terms of identity and career, are bound up directly and immediately ... with the success of their dissemination. (1998: 77)

Overblown belief in the potential for comprehensive control of practice in educational organizations owes something to the dissemination success of gurus who act as prophets, ambassadors and even trainers for managerialism. As Ball implies, the technical solution may precede the problem. Policy entrepreneurs have to problematize organizations and contexts in such a way that the nature of the problem identified appears amenable to their pre-specified technical solution.

Despite the widespread reservations about management consultants ('a management consultant is someone who steals your watch in order to tell you the time') there is a ready market among policy-makers and practition-ers for such prescriptions. Policy-makers are perennially on the lookout for ideas offering potential to realize their political interests. Endemic ambigu-ity, exacerbated by reforms, ensures that most practitioners rarely find themselves on top of the situations for which they are held accountable. But the buoyancy of this market for prescriptions also generates lively potential for an ironic unintended consequence. Prescriptions may con-tribute to creating more 'problems' rather than helping practitioners to cope with the endemic problem of ambiguity that they face. Among the diversity of relevant theoretical and research-based ideas produced by aca-demics, those pursuing knowledge-for-action and instrumentalist intellectual projects tend to be most ready to offer prescriptions, and these tend to be most consistent with the tenets of managerialism.

Which ideas become popular prescriptions for practice will depend on what practitioners who consume them are seeking, and who says what they need. Huczynski's analogy of a filter funnel illuminates why ambigu-ity and other potentially fruitful leadership and management ideas do not achieve the popularity of those ideas that promise the tightest leadership and management control. His analysis is adapted here (see also Wallace, 2003) to reflect the importance of external political intervention and aca-demic support in attempting to shape educational leadership and management practice. To reach teaching texts, handbooks or training guides, leadership and management ideas must survive a series of filters:

1 *The needs of leaders and managers* – ideas must be sympathetic towards perceptions among government politicians about the needs of practition-ers (e.g. to ensure smooth implementation of reforms).
2 *Idea benefits* – ideas must be consistent with the perception of practi-tioners about their immediate needs, typically to implement reforms (e.g. advice on generating staff 'ownership' of these reforms).
3 *Timeliness* – ideas must relate to commonly faced problems in this context (e.g. how to maximize organizational capacity to implement reforms).
4 *Promotion* – ideas must be actively disseminated (e.g. through govern-ment-commissioned research projects, sponsored training programmes, consultancies and web-sites, or advocated in higher education advanced courses).
5 *Presentation* – ideas must be engagingly presentable (e.g. simplified so as to be quickly grasped, and at a high enough level of abstraction for practitioners from diverse contexts to perceive that such ideas have rele-vance to their situation).

Since aspiring and serving educational leaders and managers and govern-ment politicians are the main operators of these filters, ideas that do not immediately appear to serve their interests are unlikely to get through. Unpopular ideas may run to those that are:

- out of line with the current approach to educational reform, so government politicians, who sponsor much training and dissemination, may judge them not to *meet the needs of leaders and managers* (e.g. ideas about organizational pathos);
- complex, as leaders and managers may not see them as giving immediate *idea benefits* (e.g. ideas on how to live with unresolvable dilemmas);
- inimical to the managerialist thrust of education reforms – very un*timely* (e.g. how to cope with the inflexibility of externally imposed planning requirements);
- restricted to academic texts, since without further *promotion* they will reach only a minority of practitioners (e.g. the long tradition of work on organizational ambiguity);
- tentative and ungeneralized, because they will not be *presentable* as guaranteeing success for any practitioner (e.g. ideas that are explicitly labelled as hypotheses or speculative reflections).

This book is indicative of the obvious scope for publishing ideas underpinned more by knowledge-for-understanding than knowledge-for-action or instrumentalism. Equally, academics are empowered to engage practitioners with a much wider range of ideas than those which become popular prescriptions. They have to persuade these practitioners that difficult ideas are worth exploring which might inform thinking about practice, rather than prescribing quick fixes. But central government is a key contributor to the filtration process where those academic ideas that appear most directly to support the current political agenda get to inform training programmes. As noted earlier, they reach far more practitioners than advanced education courses. It seems ironic that improvement in policy and practice may lie with ideas that get filtered out, including those about coping with ambiguity.

The solution is the problem

In this chapter we have continued our story of excess by exploring the phenomenon of a solution in search of a problem. A major part of the solution to perceived weaknesses in the educational system has entailed strengthening school management and promoting school leadership. On the face of it this is a reasonable strategy. However, the solution itself has become a potential problem. That it has not become as much of a problem as it might have been has been due to the fact that most headteachers appear to have held to their professional values as educators. The problem can be seen as the over-institutionalization of educational leadership and management. It has entailed promoting a managerialist ideology, sponsoring the new discourse of 'managementspeak', encouraging consultancy and professionalizing educational leadership and management by establishing a national college, authorizing credentials and creating a career structure. There is nothing inherently wrong with any of these developments. But the fervour with which they have been pursued has encouraged a search for problems. We offer as our own slogan 'If you want a problem, hire a consultant'.

Improvements in educational leadership and management are much to be welcomed. But education reformers have made the error of sponsoring managerialism as a policy lever for improving educational effectiveness. This error flows from the seductive but unrealistic belief that leadership and management can deliver high quality education. Only teachers in classrooms can do so. Partial professionalisation of leadership and management has accompanied the deprofessionalisation – though presented by central government as the re-professionalization – of teachers. But many functions now carried out by school leaders and managers are not new. They were components of the more diffuse, less specialized, roles of headteachers and teachers before the onset of the educational management movement, which the reforms overtook. There remains the question of how much professionalization of leadership and management has been necessary, and how much is proving to be counter-productive.

Managerialism is part of a political ideology that has been advanced by both the main political parties in the UK over the past two decades. Insofar as an ideology is a set of beliefs which legitimize a sectional interest, there is a danger that managerialism might itself become an ideology. The professional workplace literature suggests that this ideology has not yet become dominant in schools, though all teachers and headteachers are inevitably influenced by the culture of managerialism. But our analysis suggests that the ambiguity endemic in learning and teaching, in leadership and management, and in the change process entailed in reform, is being amplified by the ironic unintended consequences of managerialist policies. It follows that policy-makers may stand to gain more and lose less of what they aspire to achieve in improving education if they were to redirect their policy thrust to allow for the impossibility of eliminating ambiguity. Giving teachers somewhat more scope to teach in ways of their own choosing may offer greater educational improvement potential than fostering ever more pervasive leadership and management.

PART THREE: THE RHETORIC OF MANAGERIALISM AND LEADERSHIP

6

The myth of transformation

In Part Three we focus on the rhetoric of transformation that has come to dominate the discourse of educational leadership and management. Ministers of successive governments have set themselves the task of transforming the educational system. They have sought to do this through establishing structures of accountability. But they have also charged school leaders with transforming their own leadership approaches and, as a consequence, with changing the ways in which teachers work, their relationships with each other and ultimately their beliefs. The irony is that the potential for school improvement inherent in the transformational approach has been undermined by excess. In this chapter we examine how potentially valuable developments in three areas – organizational culture, organizational learning, and staff collaboration – have had unintended consequences as a result of some of their advocates having failed, wilfully or otherwise, to understand organizational constraints on transformation. In Chapter 7 we shift focus to the rhetoric that organizational leadership can be transformational and the reality that leadership is actually perceived as a conduit for implementing government-driven reform policies.

Transformation has become a dominant concept in contemporary leadership and management discourse. We take the term to connote a radical and ambitious change in educational goals and in the means of achieving them: doing better things. Transformation contrasts with *improvement*, which we use to connote enhancing existing procedures for achieving established goals – doing things better. We employ this distinction despite the fact that what is often claimed in the literature to be transformational turns out to be something more mundane, and despite the fact that many texts on school improvement equate improvement with transformation.

111

There was far greater opportunity for school-focused innovation in the 1960s and, ironically, it was school level attempts at transformation that provoked central government intervention. We have acknowledged, and reiterate here, that we regard the era of school-based innovation as generating a need for greater accountability, but we regard as somewhat dubious the continuing criticism of this period, some 30 years on, as a justification for current reforms. Those of the last two decades have certainly transformed the structures, procedures and legal framework in which schools operate. But these contextual factors delimit opportunities for transformation at the school level. The 'transformation' that is being urged upon schools amounts, in practice, to the required adoption of externally initiated policies. For people at school level, therefore, the scope for transformation is largely a myth. Its pursuit extends endemic ambiguities and enlarges the gap between increasingly lofty transformational goals and the decreasing possibility of realizing them. Such ambiguities create conditions for the ironic unintended consequence of setting expectations so high that they cannot be achieved. The endeavour risks demotivating teachers and reducing the scope of their autonomy to experiment with much more modest, everyday efforts to improve their teaching in the contingent circumstances of their classrooms.

We will explore the potential for situational irony in attempts to transform the teaching process in relation to our three themes of strong culture, learning organization, and staff collaboration. We regard these as developments well-worth promoting. However, problems arise – and ironies ensue – when these features are accorded a solely *instrumental* function. In each case a fundamental ambiguity exists because it is unclear whether culture, collective learning and collaboration are the *objects* of change or the *tools* of change. In the leadership and management literature they are implicitly, and often explicitly, deployed as tools to further the pursuit of goals determined by organization leaders and managers. The exclusively instrumental function accorded to culture, collective professional learning and collaboration differs from our view that their importance lies in their emergence from the daily activities of organizational members. Leaders and managers may shape them according to contingent considerations, but not determine them. The professional workplace literature suggests that most headteachers actually work with and steer the cultural, learning and collaborative resources of teachers with only a few adopting an aggressively instrumental stance. Our critique is thus aimed particularly at those policy-makers, academics and consultants who purvey the myth of transformation.

Culture

'Culture' is a contested concept. The anthropologist Adam Kuper (1999) goes as far as to question whether this 'hyper-referential' term has any continuing value as an analytic concept. Raymond Williams (1958: 77) claims that culture is 'one of the two or three most complicated words in the English language' and defies an agreed definition since, as he puts it, meanings stem from 'distinct and incompatible systems of thought'. Culture is a paradoxical word: there is no consensus about the meaning it has – no canonical definition, yet we cannot adequately discuss social life without it.

Indicatively, there is no agreement on the content of culture. It can include values, beliefs, attitudes, opinions, norms, behaviour, language, institutions, artefacts, symbols, codes and so forth: in short, 'the total way of life of a people'. Second, there is no agreement on the consciousness of culture. Some writers argue that culture refers to those values which are so taken for granted that they exist only at a pre-conscious level. Others attribute varying degrees of consciousness to culture, including what is purposively symbolic, such as artefacts, metaphors and rituals. Third, it is difficult to conceive of the boundaries of culture. A culture is the property of a group. Such groups may include humankind in general, major groupings of societies such as 'the east' and 'the west', nations, regions, organizations, occupations, religious and political institutions, and subgroups within any of these larger groupings. Boundaries will always be porous and there will be, inside any hypothetical boundary, individuals simultaneously identifying with several subcultures inside each overlapping culture. In education the term 'culture' has been applied to various configurations of values, behaviour, language, artefacts and so on, that are centred on a key idea. Thus there are cultures of 'excellence', 'learning', 'caring', 'achievement' and many more.

A prevailing assumption is that schools can be vastly improved if leaders and managers focus on changing their cultures. The 'cultural turn' in leadership and management theory occurred in the early 1980s. Culture became the new dominant frame joining, and to some degree replacing, 'structural' and 'human relations' approaches. It promised not so much to 'resolve' the organizational dilemmas listed in Chapter 2 as 'dissolve' them. Effective organizations became seen as those in which all members subscribe to common values and goals. The notion of organizational culture was not new. In education particularly, there had been several traditions of research directed towards developing knowledge-for-understanding about school and college climates and cultures. However, the 1980s witnessed a shift towards knowledge-for-action in which culture is conceptualized as an instrument of change. The task became not simply to understand culture but to 'use' it. A link was hypothesized between transformational leadership and the capacity to create strong, shared cultures.

Key works in the cultural turn include Peters and Waterman's *In Search of Excellence* (1982), introduced in Chapter 4. These writers attributed the success of a number of top companies to cultural leadership. (We note the irony that a significant proportion of these companies had become conspicuously less successful within five years of the book's publication.) There was an inherent attraction in adopting the cultural frame within educational leadership and management because of a potential isomorphism between cultural goals and cultural means. Some contributors were theoretically sophisticated (e.g. Sergiovanni and Corbally, 1984) but many adopted an unreflective instrumental approach whereby 'culture' was merely a slogan used to justify a range of directive practices. 'Culture' was not seen as a property that emerged from the daily practices of teachers and pupils but a creation of leadership. Smircich (1983) distinguished between culture as what an organization *is* and culture as what an organization *has*. It is the latter perspective which dominates the managerialist approach. If an organization *has* a culture, then it is readily conceivable that this culture can be instrumentally manipulated. But if an organization *is* a culture, then cultural change implies a much grander but less manageable undertaking: nothing less than altering the nature of the entire social construct that the organization constitutes. Few would regard change of this depth and breadth as lying comfortably within the span of leadership and management control.

Managerialist approaches to culture

We have asserted that managerialist approaches to culture are fundamentally instrumental. Cultural anthropologists and sociologists have long distinguished between the expressive and the instrumental. Expressive connotes ends (and values) and instrumental relates largely to means. The distinction between ends and means is difficult to sustain and thus the distinction between the expressive and the instrumental can be little more than heuristic. But, as we portrayed in Chapter 4, the educational enterprise has become much more instrumental from the point of view both of the individual and of the state. Less emphasis is placed on education as a good in itself, particularly in relation to those aspects of the curriculum such as the arts, which are essentially expressive. A recent Secretary of State for Education declared that he regarded the idea of 'learning for its own sake' as 'a bit dodgy'.

Managerialist approaches tend to charge organizational leaders with 'creating' a 'strong' culture by means of the manipulation of symbols. Some focus on the capacity of leaders to use language as a means of mobilization, particularly through the use of metaphor. In this context Deal (1998) is widely cited as correlating school effectiveness with a culture achieved through telling stories, maintaining myths, celebrating heroes and heroines and sustaining rituals (see also Bolman and Deal, 1984).

The leadership and management literature on culture almost invariably suggests that the cultural approach is values-focused. The problem is that 'value' as a concept is as complex as 'culture' and there are few scholarly attempts in this literature to engage with it (but see Hodgkinson, 1991). Values can range from the ultimate values of truth, justice and goodness to the proximal 'values' of an organization as expressed in Bower's (1966) definition of culture popularized by Deal: 'the way we do things round here'. The problem is that although values are generally claimed to be at the heart of culture, few writers spell out what these values are in relation to educational organizations. Caldwell and Spinks do list values of school leadership, noting that there is 'inconsistency' among them, that in matters of culture school leaders must lead and support, and that they must maintain a balance between stability and 'the harmful effects of continuous change' (1992: 89). Yet they still urge school leaders to identify value inconsistencies with a view to removing them and socializing staff into a shared set of mutually compatible values. Their view of culture implicitly accepts that dilemmas which we regard as endemic – such as that between efficiency and equity – can be ultimately dissolved through appropriate leadership.

Much of the literature appears to suggest that the role of leadership is to transform the deepest values of organizational members. Can this be a feasible, or indeed an appropriate, function of an organizational leader? An alternative, more realistic view sees culture as a set of codes that guide the daily work of teachers (Firestone and Louis, 1999; Swidler, 1986). Codes are undoubtedly underpinned by values but attention to these values arises only when matters of principle surface, as where one person's code is transgressed by another's and awareness is then raised of the subliminal values that each code reflects. Bower's definition of culture as 'the way we do things round here' is, as it happens, an apt summary of the operation of codes. Whereas writers like Caldwell and Spinks see culture as a settlement of values issues, the term can also connote 'getting by' on the basis of broadly acceptable norms, rather than value consensus.

The leadership and management literature on culture is highly integrationist. Notwithstanding the variety of subcultures within a school associated with leadership and management, teaching specialisms, educational beliefs, or simply the shared interests of friendship groups, the managerialist ambition is a unified culture. It is no accident that 'strong' and 'shared' are key words in this discourse. Dissent, anomaly, conflicts of interest or ambiguity are viewed from this perspective as aberrations instead of being endemic to organization (see Martin and Frost, 1996). Perhaps the most fundamental value which teachers might share can be expressed as 'doing my best for my students in the prevailing circumstances'. There are different pathways towards expressing this value that are worthy of cultural respect.

Ironies of culture

The managerialist approach to culture is a potent source of ambiguities and associated ironies. Let us offer some examples. First is the likelihood of unintended semantic irony through the *gap between symbol and substance*. There is a complexity about symbols that makes their manipulation hazardous (Hoyle, 1986). One instance of an attempt to make staff feel good about being a member of an organization and to identify with its collective endeavour is the use of the name of the school as a mobilizing symbol. The entrepreneurial headteacher of a school studied by Woods et al. (1997) would refer to 'the Meadowfields way'. Likewise the headteacher of a school studied by Nias et al. (1989) would speak of 'the Sedgemoor way'. (Another school in this study was called Lavender Way. However, 'the Lavender Way way' would hardly have the appropriate resonance – unless it was infused with conscious ironic humour combining the serious purpose of symbolizing the school's distinctiveness with an appreciation of the absurdity of the formulation). It is plausible that using the name of the school as a symbolic tool would be effective in enhancing a predisposition to identify with the school. But it would hardly convert the alienated. Similarly the widespread use by headteachers of the metaphor of the school as a 'family' would be an effective symbolization only if the school conformed to an idealized model of a closely-knit, mutually-supportive, value-sharing family (unless, by a reverse irony, the school was as conflictual, discordant and near-breakdown as many families are). Dissonance would arise if the headteacher was deploying the former connotation whilst the school, in fact, reflected the latter.

Willmott illustrates the gap between symbol and substance in his study of a primary school to which a new headteacher had been appointed:

> some of the changes introduced by the head were grounded in child-centred philosophy and practice, but contradictorily used by the head for explicit management aims. From day one, the management restructuring of the school was explicitly made top priority by the head. In the first morning of the term, an INSET [in-service training] session was provided for both teaching and non-

teaching staffs in which staffs were asked to talk about what they wanted from children. One of the key issues emphasized by the head throughout was 'we are not social workers'. This was the leitmotif throughout my time at Southside, and sat rather uncomfortably with the relatively high number of children on the 'at-risk' register: every weekly staff meeting and every morning briefing dealt with some issue of 'children requiring positive praise' for reasons stemming from home problems. (2002: 105)

As Willmott puts it: 'socio-economic factors are erased at a stroke'. Yet such socio-economic factors are powerful determinants of what happens in any school. Goal ambiguity was likely to be experienced by staff. They were faced with students having particular social and emotional needs in their classroom, alongside the stipulation of the headteacher that their goals should not extend to the kind of support that might be a precondition of these students being ready to learn.

The same headteacher proclaimed an openness to staff opinion, symbolized by inviting them to make their views known at staff meetings. But, as Willmott writes: 'Essentially, the democratic approach to meetings was more apparent than real.' At the end of September the headteacher announced a set of ground rules for staff meetings as follows:

1 Keep to the point
2 Don't interrupt
3 Start/end on time
4 No sidetracking.

Ten injunctions were listed in all. After announcing these rules she said, 'All in agreement?' Then she immediately requested that there be 'no grizzling if from time to time I have to remind you of the rules'. The rules governing democratic meetings were thus imposed without democratic consultation.

Second is the situational irony flowing from the use of *conservative means for radical purposes*. There is a deep logical ambiguity in the instrumental approach to cultural change, because it entails invoking the very features that promote and protect stability and continuity in order to achieve change. 'Planned cultural change' might even be thought to constitute an oxymoron. Culture is essentially conservative. Education is essentially a conservative institution, since it largely entails transmitting the cultural heritage. It is certainly a function of education to prepare pupils for the changing culture of the wider world but schools, as essentially adaptive organizations, are way underpowered to change the culture or 'build a new social order'. Strategies advocated by Deal of celebrating heroes and heroines, or engaging in ceremonies and rituals, are essentially conservative. They celebrate the past. In another context Weick (2000) writes of culture as 'how we *did* things round here' (emphasis added).

Deal is aware of the need for balance between innovation and tradition but other writers who invoke culture as a management tool are preoccupied with transformation. Reformers often accuse teachers as being unwilling to change. There are certainly teachers who are highly reluctant to make shifts in practice but the professional workplace literature suggests that there is a willingness among many teachers to promote change, within the constraints imposed by the very nature of schools. The problem is that the managerialist perspective on culture is a limited perspective. Its rituals are development plans, inspections, governors' meetings, league tables. But there is a school culture which entails harvest festivals, nativity plays, discos, swimming galas, community service, ways of moving about the school, reciprocal respect demonstrated between teachers and students, grouping arrangements in classrooms, and playground activities. For most headteachers and teachers, the latter is the lived culture of the school.

Third, there are *limits to consensus*. We have noted how school leaders are enjoined to create a 'strong' organizational culture, whose values and codes are universally shared, and yet a school culture has diverse components. The expectation that leadership is capable of achieving coherence between them is not very realistic: the endemic phenomenological ambiguity related to different interpretations of the same situation cannot be dissolved by words or deeds. The task of achieving such coherence as is feasible requires considerable skill and insight, and especially full recognition of the limited degree to which it is obtainable in principle. Ironies arise when a colonizing trend seeks to impose one culture on another, because consensus cannot be authentically manufactured through leadership activity alone.

Schein (1985) has pointed out that 'values' in organizations are inevitably contested. If agreement emerges as an outcome of contestation, the values become so deeply embedded that they are pre-conscious and observed without reflection. It is this level that Schein regards as the shared culture of an organization. The leadership and management literature is perhaps over-optimistic about reconciling incompatible values, and particularly in assuming that there can be a 'settlement' through accepting the values of leadership and management. The evidence is that teachers look elsewhere for their values, not least to their professional networks. Skilful school leaders are those who can achieve the minimal degree of consensus needed for the school to run smoothly whilst, as far as possible, enabling individual teachers to pursue their own values. This paradox is fruitfully explored by Nias et al. (1989: 53) whose study shows that successful primary school headteachers achieve a working consensus that tolerates difference and modulates school values in the teachers' interests. These authors also bring out the irony that perhaps the core value of a successful school is tolerance of the values of others. They write:

> the 'culture of collaboration' arises from and embodies a set of what may be broadly described as moral beliefs about the value of the relationship between individuals and groups. It does not grow from shared beliefs about the nature or organization of the curriculum, content or teaching methods, but it has an impact in several ways upon educational practice in the school. It leads in time to a broad curricular and pedagogical consensus, tolerant of difference and diversity. It is an instrument of moral education, through the hidden curriculum and especially through the attitude and behaviour of staff towards one another. It encourages a sense of team pride and so of hard work, and it facilitates relaxed, spontaneous co-operation over teaching and other professional responsibilities.

It should be noted, however, that the study was undertaken when value pluralism in teaching was still widely tolerated prior to the educational reform period.

We suggest that leadership and management theorists should not abandon the concept of culture altogether, but that an ironic perspective should be brought to bear. In the words of Hargreaves (1997: 1315): 'we should cultivate and learn from studies of teacher cultures that are tragic and ironic as well as the ones that are more epic and romantic'.

The learning organization

Learning has become a touchstone of educational policy. The inclusion of 'learning' in the titles of articles, research applications and policy documents is a notable trend. We have the 'learning organization', 'the learning school', the 'learning profession', the 'learning community' and the 'learning society'. As with culture, learning has a particular resonance for educationists. Since learning is the goal of education, there is promise of a happy isomorphism between the goals of education and the nature of the organizations in which it occurs. The metaphor of the 'learning organization' has provided a useful frame for understanding, and has stimulated valuable research in education (e.g. Leithwood et al., 1998; Marks and Louis, 1999). But again the learning organization is depicted as being both the means of transformation and the focus of transformation, and again the problem is one of excess whereby the unreflective sponsoring of the learning organization has potential for ironic consequences.

The idea of a learning organization goes back a long way. Approaches to organizational change in the 1960s were strongly influenced by the work of Miles (1964) whose concept of 'organizational health' embraced many of the characteristics now attributed to the learning organization.

119

Collective learning was also central to some approaches to organizational development (e.g. Schmuck and Runkel, 1971) and strongly influenced the approaches to what is now known as school improvement. *Learning organization* as a term emerged in the 1970s with the work of Argyris and Schon (1978). However, it came into greater prominence with the publication of *The Fifth Dimension: The Theory and Practice of the Learning Organization* by Senge (1990). Although mainly concerned with private sector organizations it became influential in the educational leadership and management literature.

The concept of the learning organization is multi-faceted. There is no agreed definition. It has been approached from various disciplinary perspectives as knowledge-for-understanding (including sociology and cognitive psychology) and as knowledge-for-action (including leadership and management and information technology) and has generated a substantial literature (see Huber, 1991). Embedded in the concept is a set of difficult epistemological and ontological issues centred on the question of whether organizations as such can be said to 'learn' (see Evers and Lakomski, 2000, for a sophisticated discussion). Theorists pursuing a knowledge-for-action intellectual project tend to reify organizations and hence organizational learning. Senge (1990: 6) claims that organizations can 'enhance their capacity to achieve their highest aspirations' – which raises the question: in what sense can an organization, as such, have aspirations?

Since we consider this assumption to be problematic, we distinguish between the learning organization and *organizational learning*. The latter term denotes the fact that organizations are contexts for a variety of forms of *individual* learning, including that which is achieved collectively through group activities. We fully support a policy of optimizing opportunities for teachers to learn in the context of their work situation. But we prefer to label this *professional learning* in order to indicate that it is focused on the core professional work of teaching, though it also includes a focus on leadership and management learning for teachers with or aspiring towards such responsibility.

Managerialist approaches to the learning organization

As used in the educational leadership and management literature 'the learning organization' is best regarded as a metaphor, or as a signifier of activities that we would term professional learning and the opportunities for such. But in some instances it connotes a collective learning model for transforming education. It is this connotation which is a potential source of irony and we explore some of its dimensions.

The model promotes *transformational* at the expense of *incremental* learning. We use 'transformational learning' to connote a process whereby the membership of an organization collectively 'learns' to transform its fundamental goals. We use 'incremental learning' to connote a process whereby members of an organization – as individuals or in groups – enhance their professional skills and learn how to improve the quality of their work. Key writers on the learning organization make similar distinctions. Argyris (1999) distinguishes between 'single loop' and 'double loop' learning. Whilst the former connotes improvement, the latter connotes the transformation of what Argyris refers to as the 'governing variables' of the organization. Weick and Westley (1996) treat the learning organization as an oxymoron. They write: 'To learn is to disorganize and increase variety. To organize is to forget and reduce variety.' March (1999) distinguishes between *exploitation* and *exploration*. Exploitation connotes the refinement of existing practice; exploration connotes the search for radically new alternatives.

Each of these writers is fully aware that both kinds of learning are essential, that transformational learning is the exception rather than the norm, and that learning emerges from work activities as well as through the learning opportunities structured by leaders and managers. But a problem lies in the way many writers have seized on transformational learning as a priority for leadership and management. For, although it might be possible, indeed sometimes essential, for members of private sector organizations to engage in transformational learning in order to survive, there is very little scope for such learning in such public services as education. For Argyris' 'governing variables' we should perhaps read 'government variables' in the context of contemporary education in the UK. Government intervention pre-eminently shapes and constrains learning, and may, unintentionally, be undermining the potential for learning that is genuinely transformational.

Ironies of the learning organization

What is done in the name of the learning organization is replete with ambiguities that generate situational ironies. First is the irony of *learning under constraint*. The learning organization idea is sponsored by policy-makers and promoted in the educational leadership and management literature at a time of very strong delimitation of learning, except within the narrow confines of external policy. Staff in schools are in effect still being 'taught a lesson' for the alleged deleterious consequences of earlier school-based innovation.

This lesson is being taught not just in Britain. Hargreaves with Giles report the poignant case of a Canadian school where staff had been developing the capacity for organizational learning, but were undermined by external pressures. Blue Mountain Secondary School in Ontario operated from its inauguration on 'the principles of a learning organization and a learning community' (Hargreaves, 2003: 98). The authors offer a clear account of its capacity to support learning as 'reflected in many different aspects of its creation, and its continuing operation; the nature and distribution of its leadership; its goals and vision; the organization of curriculum and teaching; its innovative structures and processes; and the teachers' orientation to personal and professional learning' (p.100). They go on to describe the deleterious impact of reformist government policies on organizational learning at Blue Mountain:

> Yet loss of time, overstretched leadership, recycled change, reduced support and a dispiriting climate of shame and blame that are all the results of market fundamentalism have taken the edge off Blue Mountain's most exciting programmes, hindered the maintenance of its technological capacity, undermined relationships, and put a dent in its learning community. (p.100)

The second irony relates to *learning under pressure*. There is a tendency for politicians to assume that failing schools need to be turned round through a visionary, transformational approach to developing a learning organization. New headteachers have been parachuted into such schools on that assumption. But failing schools may benefit more from an incremental approach to learning whereby staff learn, or relearn, how to do the basic things better. Some writers doubt whether what we have termed transformational learning is appropriate to schools where difficulties are being experienced. As Rait (1995: 73) put it: 'Organizations encounter situations that demand learning, which may be an arduous and disturbing process, when they are already weakened by stress and tension.' Staff in some schools may need to undertake incremental learning in order to establish a secure base for moving forward. There is perhaps an analogy here with Hargreaves' (2003) proposal for 'developmental school improvement'.

A third irony concerns *the proceduralization of learning* (the implementation of structures and procedures to ensure learning). An irony lies in the fact that this can actually constrain learning. One of the problems of managerialism is that it squeezes the life out of a good idea by institutionalizing it. Organizational learning is no exception. Many leadership and management texts shift from endorsing the value of organizational learning to advocating procedures whereby it should be programmed. Thus writers have proposed *criteria* (Pedler et al., 1997), *stages* (Jones and Hendry, 1994), *learning cycles* (Dixon, 1994) and *building blocks* (Pearn et al., 1995). Listing the building blocks approach gives a flavour of the institutionalization:

- examine the concept at top management level;
- analyse the current stage of learning;

- devise an implementation plan;
- equip managers to encourage learning;
- support learning;
- develop group and team learning;
- promote open learning;
- analyse jobs in terms of training needs.

One cannot quarrel with this list. It may be appropriate to learning where the focus is on learning to lead and manage. But in schools, where the core task is teaching and not leading or managing, if this 'building' enterprise were to be pursued vigorously and 'rationally', it could actually serve to limit learning and ensure that it is channelled solely within limits set down by senior staff.

We have no doubts about the continuing relevance of our connotation of 'organizational learning'. As Mulford (1998: 637) puts it: 'Organizational learning would appear to offer a way for a school to ride the "see saws" of change ... and to establish and maintain a sense of connectedness, direction and continuity. Organizational learning offers the potential of stability for change, an opportunity for schools to move ahead without losing their roots.'

Collaboration

Many terms are used to describe the aspect of organizational life that we are concerned with here. As well as collaboration they include participation, collegiality, empowerment, delegation, teamwork. We will consider the different connotations of these terms, but for the moment, we will adopt collaboration as our generic term. Collaboration figures strongly in the myth of transformation. The basic assumption is that organizations can be transformed by the collective will of the staff working collaboratively on the basis of shared beliefs and values. Collaboration is a key dimension of culture and the term 'culture of collaboration' is much used in the leadership and management literature. Writers, both those who are supportive of the reform movement and those who are critical, are unanimous on the benefits of collaboration. Rightly so. There is little doubt that effective organizations are characterized by a collaborative membership. However, the perspective on collaboration inhering in much of this literature is partial, allied to instrumental and integrationist values and driven by a leadership-determined version of culture discussed above.

Collaboration is perhaps the most generic of this family of concepts. Of the many meanings attached to it, we select one that is central to our argument. Collaboration can be used to connote those modes of working together – cooperation – that emerge from daily work practice. An ambiguity turns on the degree to which collaboration entails a genuine integration of work. The biggest barrier to integration is the value that teachers continue to place on their individual classroom autonomy. Little (1990) identified a continuum of collaboration ranging from relatively superficial 'story-telling' through 'aid and assistance' to the in-depth collaboration of 'joint work'. From her research, Little concluded that 'collaborations may arise naturally out of the problems and circumstances that teachers experience in common, but often they appear contrived, inauthentic, grafted on, perched precariously (and often temporarily) on the margins of real work' (p.507). Professional workplace studies report that opportunities for collaboration have been, for teachers, perhaps the major benefit of reforms. But they also reveal the continuing tension between voluntary and enforced collaboration.

We use *participation* to refer to the opportunities that staff members have for engaging in the process of organizational decision-making. Goal ambiguity turns on the relationship between teachers' opportunity to participate and their desire to participate. Control ambiguity arises in relation to the power available to teachers to make or affect decisions. *Empowerment* has become a term almost emptied of meaning, though it is still features in the rhetoric. The problem is that those who use the term rarely specify the nature of the power that is entailed in empowerment. The ambiguity is inflected in two forms of power: *authority* as the legal right to make the final decision and *influence* as the opportunity to have an impact on a decision by dint of expertise, persuasiveness, or opportunity (Bacharach and Lawler, 1980). While we can make this conceptual distinction the two forms are ambiguous at the level of practice (witness the discussion in Chapter 4 over which primary school role carries the greater authority over classroom practice – class teacher, curriculum adviser, leader of a group of classes, headteacher?).

Collegiality is the term that is least often defined in the literature. In origin it referred to the mode by which some professions made decisions. Lortie (1964) described collegiality as 'the way in which professional equals govern their affairs through democratic procedures'. However, decision-making in education has largely been overtaken by managerialism. Thus the term has come to have a variety of uses. As Brundrett writes:

> Professionalism has had the effect of allowing teachers to come together with respect for each other's professional ability, and the autonomous, indeed isolated, nature of teachers' work means the effective administrative functions of the complexities of school life actually necessitate some kind of collaborative

activity. Collegiality, however, takes matters further than mere collaboration in that it assumes that teachers have the right to take part in the decision-making process itself. (1998: 308)

Collaboration, participation, or collegiality are aspects of the dilemma of centralization–decentralization (see Table 2.2) and, as ever, their undoubted value can be vitiated through being pushed to excess.

Managerialist approaches to collaboration

Collaboration is both the subject and object of transformation. It is a tenet of the reformers that transformation will be best achieved through the collaboration of teachers and their participation in decision-making. However as we have defined the two terms, collaboration emerges from the communities of practice of teachers as they work together in matters of curriculum and pedagogy, whereas the scope and extent of participation in decision-making are matters that are ultimately determined by headteachers. Control ambiguity pervades both. On the one hand school leaders are enjoined to exercise their 'right to manage' but on the other hand they are enjoined, as a component of the transformational project, to involve staff in collaboration and participation.

The legal authority – and consequent accountability – of headteachers ensures that staff participation remains in their gift and understandably they are unlikely to establish or endorse patterns that threaten their control. In the final analysis, headteachers have authority and teachers have influence but the relationship between the two often remains ambiguous. What is presented as delegation may leave individuals or groups uncertain about, perhaps misled about, the degree of authority with which they have been invested. Delegation often turns out to constitute no more than consultation. Whilst the majority of headteachers and teachers live with this ambiguity and implicitly negotiate patterns of accommodation, those headteachers who have internalized the true belief are likely to so institutionalize both participation and collaboration that they become instruments of control. From this ambiguity ironies ensue.

Ironies of collaboration and participation

Let us look briefly at some ironies that flow from the attempt to meet the contradictory expectations of 'the right to manage' and the injunction to 'involve'. The first irony is *contrived collegiality*. This widely used term was introduced by Hargreaves to denote the practice whereby headteachers meet the injunction to be 'collegial' whilst ensuring that they retain control over teachers through involving them in decision-making:

> Collaboration can be a device to help teachers to work together to pursue and review their own purposes as a professional community, or it can be a way of redescribing administrative control within persuasive and pervasive discourses of collaboration and partnerships. Collaboration in this sense can be a burden as well as a blessing, especially once administrators take it over and convert it into models, mandates and measurable profiles of growth and implementation. (1994: 17)

Participation in the bureaucracy of decision-making generates phenomenological ambiguity for most teachers. Alongside the value of being offered a voice, the process transgresses the value of prioritizing their core function of teaching and associated activities. Participative decision-making consumes time that could be spent on more directly educational activities.

Desire and opportunity for participation. The ambiguity of participation is complicated by the likelihood that there are some areas in which teachers welcome increased participation but there are other areas in which they would prefer less participation – especially when it is contrived. The situational irony can ensue whereby teachers are encouraged to participate in decision-making in areas in which they have little desire for involvement but are excluded from areas in which they would like to have high involvement. This is the broad finding of a tradition of studies in teacher decision-making undertaken in a number of countries varying widely in the structure and culture of their education systems. Although there are some international variations, generally speaking teachers experience *decision-deprivation* (Bacharach et al., 1990) in areas which impinge directly on their classroom activities (curriculum, pedagogy, assessment, timetabling) but *decision-saturation* in administrative areas (staff appointments, planning, relationship with parent groups).

The institutionalization of collaboration. We use the term 'collaboration' to denote those patterns of professional interaction which emerge from daily practice. The professional workplace literature provides many examples of teachers collaborating informally in matters of pedagogy and curriculum. As noted above, teachers indicate that one of the positive effects of the reform period has been the increased opportunity for collaboration. However, it is clear that their preferences are for the informal, emergent and flexible forms of collaboration. Leaders and managers often seek to institutionalize these emergent developments in a formal structure with the consequent irony that they cease to be satisfying to teachers: they increase workload and reduce opportunities for spontaneity. Woods and colleagues (1997: 33) write: 'The institutionalization of formal discourse means more time spent in formal meetings to the detriment of classroom work. Collaboration becomes counterproductive.' Hargreaves sees the institutionalization of emergent collaboration among teachers as a variety of 'contrived collegiality':

> It occurs when spontaneous, dangerous and difficult-to-control forms of teacher collaboration are discouraged or usurped by administrators who capture it, contain it and contrive it through compulsory cooperation, required collaborative planning, stage managed mission statements, labyrinthine procedures of school development planning, and processes of collaboration to implement non-negotiable programs and curricula whose viability and practicality are open to discussion. (1994: 80)

Competitive collaborators. There is a euphoric tone in some leadership and management texts which treats collaboration as a solvent of all problems and particularly the problem of change. Such an approach acknowledges competition and conflict but sees these as aberrations which effective leadership will overcome. Not so. It may well be the case that the cooperation–competition balance is a contingency. We actually know rather little about this contingency in organizations, as opposed to experimental groups and groups in particular work contexts such as sports teams and string quartets. (It is widely known that the members of one of the most prestigious and most durable string quartets in the world cannot stand each other at a personal level.) We know far less about this contingency in educational settings (see Mulford, 1998, for a review).

The nature of the collaboration–competition balance as it emerges from the daily interactions of teachers remains unclear. But there is a widespread view that the competition specifically introduced by government, in an attempt to increase effectiveness through various forms of productivity pay, can have only a negative impact upon collaboration and (more fundamentally) on teacher satisfaction. A survey of teacher attitudes towards performance related pay (Farrell and Morris, 2004: 81) reported how 'teachers felt that it would be problematic to isolate the performance of individual teachers and deleterious to collegiality and teamwork in schools'. An irony that has been widely noted is that many who preach collaboration are in practice strongly committed to mandated competition.

Brundrett (1998) has adopted an ironic perspective towards collegiality. In response, Tomlinson (1998) has argued that there is considerable scope for genuine collegiality and participation in schools where headteachers are willing to encourage them and teachers willing to respond. We agree with both positions: collegiality and participation are desirable and possible but in circumstances which are managerially contingent.

Transformation: the benefits without the myth

The theme of this chapter has been that the strongest advocacy of a trans-formational approach to reform has come from those whose policies ensure that the opportunity for transformation is in fact denied to people working in schools. Headteachers and teachers are virtually allocated the role of lab assistants in the great government experiment that the reforms comprise. We have argued that this might have diverted attention from the important task for headteachers and teachers of incrementally improving what they already do. We have taken selected themes from the transforma-tional rhetoric and argued that although many researchers and theorists have sought to clarify these concepts, many writers continue to deploy them in an unreflective hortatory manner. In particular, many texts under-play the contingency aspects of these themes in their quite understandable enthusiasm for strengthening features of educational organizations that could, if implemented, generate ironies of excess.

However, it would appear from the professional workplace literature that these excesses are generated primarily by the true believers. Most headteachers and teachers handle the contingent balance through negotia-tion and accommodation. We must end by reaffirming that culture-building, organizational learning and staff collaboration have a sig-nificant role to play in school improvement and are important as emergent properties supported by a leadership that understands the dangers of excess.

7

Transmissional leadership for political transformation

The current primacy of 'leadership' over 'management' in the discourse of UK central government policy-makers and many academics is firmly linked with the interests of government politicians in transforming the public services, not least school education. The declared intention of politicians is radical change in the official goals of public service organizations and commitment to achieving them. The central government goal for modernizing the public services, to which organizations 'delivering' public services are invited to contribute, is spelled out below. The extracts are taken from the Prime Minister's foreword to a pamphlet setting out the central government ambitions and principles for public service reform (OPSR 2002: 2–3):

> Modernizing our public services is crucial to everything the Government wants to achieve for the country.
>
> Strong and high quality public services are essential if we are to achieve our central aim of spreading prosperity and opportunity.
>
> It needs us to play our part by providing an overall vision of where we must go and backing that with a real commitment to deliver that vision.
>
> I realize, as you do, how huge a task we face in transforming our public services.
>
> I know we have a lot more to do. Without your support, your advice and your leadership we won't be able to deliver.
>
> The goal is public services that give everyone, not just a few, real opportunity and security.

Government-led transformation of the public services is seen to depend on leaders of public service organizations (the 'you' to whom the foreword is addressed) supporting achievement of the goal of ministers to give 'everyone … real opportunity and security'. We noted in Chapter 1 how a characteristic of the complexity of change spanning administrative levels is that instigators depend on leaders and managers based at other levels to implement the instigators' envisaged change in organizations system-wide. The implicit logic underlying these extracts is that organization leaders are to adopt goals for their organization that contribute to achieving the overarching central government goal, and to harness the efforts of their members towards achieving these organizational goals. 'Re-forming' the public services by modernizing them is a means towards the long-term political end of radically enhancing public service efficiency and effectiveness.

So, in the statement above, *transforming* the public services refers to what government politicians are trying to do with and through organizational leaders. This conception of transformation rests on the assumption that the central government goal is substantially new, and that achieving it requires an equally substantial shift in the official goals of 'service delivery' organizations. Perhaps the rhetoric is new. But is the central government goal so different from what has gone before? Just how different is the adoption of 'modernizing' goals in service delivery organizations from the official goals about improvement espoused, say, in schools since the school-based innovation period of the 1960s? Central government transformation of the public services may be as mythical as the transformation of schools discussed in the previous chapter.

Whether transformation or more modest improvement is being pursued, it is down to organization leaders to bring about that shift on ministers' behalf (and ultimately, on behalf of the public who voted in the government and who consume public services). We will argue in this chapter that what central government politicians actually require of organizational leaders is, first, faithful *transmission* of externally specified organizational goals linked to the over-arching political goal of ministers for improving the public services. Second, the promotion of activity to implement the practices required to achieve these externally specified goals. In the Prime Minister's foreword, consider who has the leading role in providing the 'overall vision of where we must go', and by implication who is allotted the supporting role of following that vision. Organizational leaders are clearly required to be transmitters of a central government vision and associated reforms, not transformers of their organizations according to the diversity of their own beliefs and values and those of colleagues and other community members. Yet key ideas framing school leadership training, and associated academic texts following the knowledge-for-action and instrumentalist intellectual projects, are 'transformational leadership' and the notion that it is hierarchically 'distributed' across the organization.

There is a reasonably robust research base supporting the view that while classroom factors make more impact on student learning than school-level factors (Creemers, 1994), leadership and management can still make a significant difference through coordinating the work of staff (Hallinger and Heck, 1999). The fundamental situational irony to be examined here is that the central government promotion of what appears, on the surface, to be collective vision-based transformational leadership is misdirected. Central government public service reform amounts to a grand, decades-long experiment. By ministers' own account, the transformation they seek through public service modernization is without precedent. No tried-and-tested strategy exists: politicians are creating one as they go along. Unwittingly, ministers of successive governments have systematically removed much of what modest scope for radical transformation existed at school level during the time of school-based innovation. Their reforms are designed to ensure the achievement of their educational goals, and to rein-in any school-based innovation that might reflect values of which they disapprove. An unintended consequence is that the excessive leadership being externally fostered and evaluated generates ambiguities that may be doing more to hinder than to help learning and teaching – even to achieve this restricted set of externally-specified goals. Overled and undermanaged schools jeopardize precisely those improvements that well-intentioned politicians and educators are trying so hard to build.

A major difficulty lies in the contextual diversity of schools and classrooms, which affects what works effectively in them. It is not possible reliably to specify from a central administrative level precisely what will work in individual schools. Nor is it realistic to expect organizational leaders and managers to specify what will work effectively in individual classrooms. This problem is especially stark where new technologies (such as interactive whiteboards in classrooms) mean that no tried-and-tested technique exists. Even if it did, all teachers must have scope to learn for themselves how to adapt the technique and 'make it their own' in their classroom setting (Chapter 1). Centralized reform runs the risk of using yesterday's teaching techniques, developed in yesterday's environment, to prepare today's students for living and working in tomorrow's world. Yet as discussed in Chapter 6, organizational leadership can play a highly constructive part in creating and protecting sufficient scope for teachers to find out what will work for them, while also setting parameters bounding the diversity of practice.

Leadership inflation

Here we will examine ironies provoked by the domination of leadership over management in much UK government and academic discourse relating to school education. Historically, first administration, then management were the over-arching terms for achieving tasks with and through other adults to coordinate learning and teaching in schools (Chapter 4). Significantly, as earlier noted the term 'leadership' became prominent during the 1990s, perhaps because it connotes making change happen. The primacy of promoting change aligns with the orientation of 'top-down' reform policies to re-establish the strong boundaries that school-based innovation had challenged. Previously, leadership was widely conceived as that subcomponent of the over-arching notion of management concerned with influencing others' actions to secure change. Managing schools was seen as involving substantial coordination to run the organization from day to day, incorporating a modicum of leadership to promote desired change, especially when practitioners – supported by researchers, curriculum developers and teacher educators – developed an interest in school-based, or school-focused, innovation.

By contrast, in North America each concept has long been accorded equal status, as in this definition (Louis and Miles, 1990: 19–20): 'Leaders set the course for the organization; managers make sure the course is followed. Leaders make strategic plans; managers design operational systems for carrying out the plans. Leaders stimulate and inspire; managers use their interpersonal influence and authority to translate that energy into productive work.'

In short, leaders make new things happen while managers keep things going in the direction set by leaders (Egan, 1988). Innovation implies leadership of change – making new things happen – and management of change – keeping these new things on track. Leadership and management are seen as equally necessary to innovate and to run organizations. But leadership has a logical primacy over management when it comes to generating improvement. Restricting the definition of management to keeping old and new things on track means that the limited range of activities which then count as management cannot be enough to make a major improvement in practice. This is where leadership comes in, because new things must be made to happen if there are to be new things to keep on track in doing better things. The greater the improvement sought, the more new things must be made to happen, so the more leadership is needed. Hence radical transformation of practice implies extensive leadership, with management relegated to a supporting role.

Coinciding with interest in organizational leadership as a means of ensuring implementation of reforms in the UK was the cultural turn in leadership and management theory (Chapter 6). Leadership was a means of ensuring better performance through transforming the organizational culture. The idea that leadership can be transforming is associated with the

Table 7.1: *A continuum from transformational to laissez-faire leadership*

Form of leadership and associated factors	How leaders influence followers
Transformational leadership:	**leaders encourage followers to reach beyond their self-interest to embrace a collective goal advocated by leaders**
● idealized influence	leaders are charismatic, acting as a role model for followers, expressing high ethical standards that win followers' trust and respect, and providing them with a sense of collective purpose
● inspirational motivation	leaders communicate high expectations, engage followers in developing and committing themselves collectively to achieving a shared vision of a desirable future extending beyond their immediate self-interested concerns
● intellectual stimulation	leaders encourage followers to be creative and innovative, to challenge the assumptions of leaders and themselves, and to solve problems together
● individualized consideration	leaders create a positive climate and foster the development of followers, encouraging them to identify their individual needs and facilitating their efforts to meet these needs
Transactional leadership:	**leaders create situations where doing what leaders desire is in the self-interest of followers**
● contingent reward	leaders give specific rewards in exchange for the effort of followers, negotiating what they must do and the payoff for their support
● management by exception	leaders make corrective criticisms, proactively monitoring the extent of followers' compliance with their requirements, or reactively intervening after problems have occurred
Non-leadership:	**leaders adopt a 'hands-off' approach, providing no leadership**
● laissez-faire	leaders abdicate responsibility, avoid decisions, do not give followers feedback, and do not attempt to meet followers' needs

Source: Bass, 1985

American leadership theorist Burns (1978). His prescriptive theory entails leaders attending to followers' needs and motivating them to transcend their self-interest in order to pursue more altruistic, official organizational goals. Here is a clear instance of the assumption that an endemic internal organizational dilemma, here organizational goals versus individual needs and self-interests (Table 2.1) can be dissolved. Successful *transforming leadership*, by definition, implies self-interest being transcended, not subjugated, as individuals embrace together organizational goals that are more worthy and morally uplifting.

Transforming leadership is distinguished from what is often regarded as the less effective and perhaps amoral alternative of *transactional leadership*. Here leaders exchange rewards valued by followers in return for their support in achieving leaders' goals. Transactional leadership does not dissolve the organization–individual interests dilemma. However, it can sometimes be temporarily resolved where leaders make compromise deals: suiting sufficient self-interests of followers through rewards to 'buy' their support for organizational goals promoted by leaders.

Other theorists soon built on this foundation, Bass (1985) being particularly influential. Bass viewed transforming and transactional leadership not as alternatives but as lying along a continuum from transformational, through transactional to laissez-faire (Table 7.1). The emphasis on *inspirational motivation* is especially notable, proactively engaging other organization members in developing together and collaborating to achieve a shared, unifying vision. This is the essence of culture management (Chapter 4), a form of managerialism which is central to the vision promoted by central government politicians, leadership trainers and inspectors. But it is top-down transmissional leadership to implement a government vision that is actually being promoted, not organization-based transformational leadership to generate and implement the more diverse and possibly incompatible visions of members.

Transmissional leadership for public service modernization

Conceptions of transformational leadership were gradually applied to schools in North America (e.g. Leithwood et al, 1999; Starratt, 1995; Sergiovanni, 1996;) and the UK (Southworth, 1998). A consistent view of leadership has been adopted in the discourse of the National College for School Leadership. The statement of the NCSL's (2003) purpose echoes the radical tone of the Prime Minister's foreword: 'leadership has a central role to play in the transformation of education'. National training for aspiring and serving headteachers, subject leaders and special needs coordinators has become framed by national standards. They currently formulate the 'core purpose' of the headteacher as follows: 'The headteacher is the leading professional in the school. Working with and accountable to the governing body, the headteacher provides vision, leadership and direction for the school and ensures that it is managed and organized to meet its aims and targets' (DFES, 2004: 3).

In passing, we note again that the potential for headteachers to fulfil the role of 'leading professional' – as originally conceived by Hughes (1973) – has been severely constrained by the plethora of additional tasks (Table 4.4) now expected of them. The language is telling: 'the headteacher provides vision, leadership and direction' but must also ensure that 'aims and targets' are met. They are framed by central government national targets for key areas of the curriculum, and set in conjunction with LEA staff to reflect the local situation. Therefore, the vision, leadership and direction must encompass these externally specified aims and targets in any statement of official school goals. Part of the core purpose of the headteacher is to act as a transmitter of the central government vision underlying the aims and targets. This centralist tendency is similarly reflected in the six 'key areas of headship' (DFES, 2004: 6–11):

1 Shaping the future.
2 Leading learning and teaching.
3 Developing self and working with others.
4 Managing the organization.
5 Securing accountability.
6 Strengthening community.

Let us dwell on the transformational tone of 'shaping the future', implying that headteachers possess sufficient agency to be shapers. The elaboration states:

> Critical to the role of headship is working with the governing body and others to create a shared vision and strategic plan which inspires and motivates pupils, staff and all other members of the school community. This vision should express core educational values and moral purpose and be inclusive of stakeholders' values and beliefs. The strategic planning process is critical to sustaining school improvement and ensuring that the school moves forward for the benefit of its pupils.

Resonance with the transformational leadership factor 'inspirational motivation' is obvious (Table 7.1). Close behind comes 'idealized influence' through reference to 'moral purpose' expressed in the vision. The factor 'individualized consideration' is obliquely reflected in the key area 'developing self and working with others'. Headteachers are expected to support all colleagues through performance management and continuous professional development 'to achieve high standards' (which are externally framed). There is less resonance with the factor 'intellectual stimulation' in the proposals. Mention is made under 'creating the future' that the headteacher 'ensures creativity, innovation and the use of appropriate new technologies to achieve excellence', and under 'leading learning and teaching' that the headteacher establishes 'creative, responsive and effective approaches to learning and teaching'. But innovativeness is bounded by the vision and plan, and no mention is made of challenging anyone's assumptions.

There is unintended semantic irony in the language employed, likely to be reflected in training connected with the national standards. What initially appears transformational because of the visionary emphasis is actually more transmissional. Headteachers are to lead the visioning and associated planning process in compliance with central government-derived aims and targets. There is a hint of transactional leadership in the detail. Under 'developing self and working with others', the headteacher 'takes appropriate action when performance is unsatisfactory', consistent with the transactional leadership factor 'management by exception'. Implicitly, performance management sets conditions redolent of the 'contingent reward' factor, where performance-related pay is designed as an inducement directly linked to positive judgements of staff performance.

Thus transmissional leadership emphasizes those transformational leadership factors connected with promoting a vision aligned with the central government goal for transforming the public services. Transactional leadership is entailed where culture management designed to channel staff agency in the required direction has failed to lubricate transmission through satisfactory performance. 'Appropriate action' offers leaders a fall-back, delimiting the agency of those whose 'underperformance' threatens to inhibit faithful transmission.

As transmissional leaders, headteachers find themselves in a uniquely high-risk position, piggies-in-the-middle between central government and its agencies on the one hand, and their staff colleagues, governors and other community stakeholders on the other. Headteachers are legally responsible within the oversight of the governing body for leading and managing the school, and vulnerable to public 'naming and shaming' and even to forced resignation if an OFSTED inspection reveals transmissional leadership failure – whether to implement central government reforms or to reach stipulated targets for student achievement. The OFSTED criteria for judging leadership and management effectiveness (and now for judging separately leadership expressed by headteachers) have become a significant external means of channelling and delimiting headteachers' agency, and so

Table 7.2: OFSTED *criteria for judging school leadership and management effectiveness*

Characteristics of effective leadership	Characteristics of effective management
there is a clear vision, with a sense of purpose and high aspirations for the school, combined with a relentless focus on pupils' achievement	the school undertakes rigorous self-evaluation and uses the findings effectively
strategic planning reflects and promotes the school's ambitions and goals	the school monitors performance data, reviews patterns and takes appropriate action
leaders inspire, motivate and influence staff and pupils	performance management of staff, including support staff, is thorough and effective in bringing about improvement
leaders create effective teams	a commitment to staff development is reflected in effective induction and professional development strategies and, where possible, the school's contribution to initial teacher training
there is knowledgeable and innovative leadership of teaching and the curriculum	the recruitment, retention, deployment and workload of staff are well managed, and support staff are well deployed to make teachers' work more effective
leaders are committed to running an equitable and inclusive school, in which each individual matters	approaches to financial and resource management help the school to achieve its educational priorities
leaders provide good role models for other staff and pupils	the principles of best value are central to the school's management and use of resources

Source: OFSTED, 2003b: 7–10

that of their colleagues. These criteria are likely to reinforce, through external 'management by exception', the internal 'management by exception' that headteachers are expected to express. The OFSTED criteria are listed in Table 7.2 as characteristics of effective practice that inspectors are required to assess.

Leadership is differentiated from management. Characteristi~ tive leadership tally with the national standards, as on(They are strong on 'inspirational motivation' and 'ideal\

extending here to leaders as role models. But there is no indication of 'intellectual stimulation' and only a nod towards 'individualized consideration' implicit in the characteristic: 'running an equitable and inclusive school, where every individual matters'. Transactional leadership turns up under 'management' through school self-evaluation and monitoring of performance data. Within 'management by exception' such activities are potential precursors to corrective action, depending on what monitoring and evaluation reveal.

Management is subordinated to leadership. It is judged mainly according to whether procedures like performance management, brought in as a reform but now constituting normal practice, have been faithfully implemented – down to 'best value' as a guiding principle for efficient and economic resource expenditure. These procedures form part of the transmission mechanism, directed towards achieving the 'school's ambitions and goals' in line with the overall goal of central government. For transmission, the creativity, innovation and challenging of assumptions associated with 'intellectual stimulation' and the attention to potentially diverse individual needs of 'individual consideration' could be a hindrance. Beyond quite narrow limits, fostering locally-initiated innovation and tolerating diverse practices would risk reconstituting the dilemmas and underlying value diversity that culture management attempts to dissolve.

There is a strong emphasis on 'creating effective teams'. Headteachers are viewed as the 'top leader' in their organization. There is also clear acknowledgement in the national standards and in training provision of the contributory leadership role for subject leaders and other 'middle managers'. The notion of *distributed leadership* has rapidly entered the discourse of national-level trainers, inspectors and academics. It was stimulated in part by the theoretical work of Gronn (2000: 72), who comments that past researchers have long identified how leadership may be distributed in various ways, and that 'distributed leadership has not so much been "discovered" as "rediscovered", due to the awareness that interdependence, rather than follower-dependence, provides the empirical foundation for leadership'. Transmissional leadership reflects the unequal interdependence between central government politicians and staff in public service organizations. There is little sense in which government ministers are followers of school staff, except where unanticipated responses of practitioners stimulate ameliorative policy-making (Chapter 1). But Gronn's formulation highlights how politicians depend on practitioners to implement their public service modernization policies. Conversely, practitioners depend on politicians for support and resources.

Transformational leadership as conceived by Burns and Bass is individualistic, with little account of collective leadership. We discussed in Chapter

4 how an implicit structure for hierarchically distributed leadership and management was established in all but name when posts of special responsibility in UK schools became reinterpreted as a management hierarchy. The distribution of leadership is now differentiated through this hierarchy, with deputies and subject leaders in subordinate and specialized roles. But even allowing for the distribution of organizational leadership, it remains transmissional, framed by central government politicians as contributing to the realization of their over-arching goal for modernizing the public services.

Any vision you like, as long as it's central government's?

Perhaps the greatest ambiguity generated by the gap between transmissional leadership and the rhetoric of collective vision-based leadership relates to the time and energy required for vision-building and associated planning for improvement, when the goal for doing so is either unclear or appears inauthentic to busy practitioners. Conditions are ripe for policy pathos if visionary leadership becomes perceived as just another instrumental, externally-imposed, and unnecessary requirement. If taken seriously in schools, it may even demotivate staff because of the designed-in implementation gap between their practice and the 'could do better' visionary expectation to which their attention is perennially drawn.

We have indicated how the professional workplace literature gets close to the perspective of practitioners. However, we are not aware of knowledge-for-understanding research into vision-building in UK schools. We leave readers to evaluate whether our account resonates with their experience. (Readers working in organizations may care to reflect whether they are aware if their organization has a vision or mission statement; if it has, whether they were consulted over its formulation and their values are reflected in the statement; if so, whether they can recall what is stated; if so, whether it accurately summarizes the views of organization members about improvement; and if so, whether they refer to it regularly to guide their practice.)

What renders vision-building necessary and worthwhile from the standpoint of practitioners? Central government expectations are enshrined in legislation, some quantified as targets (Chapter 4). Even where local diversity is promoted, central requirements make it clear what staff must do (as in the policy to establish 'specialist' secondary schools, which specialize in a particular subject while still catering for the full National Curriculum). Any vision or mission statement and associated plan must be consistent with the aspiration to meet these expectations and requirements if they are to satisfy OFSTED inspectors. It is unsurprising to find extensive isomorphism among school mission statements. Indeed, our conversations with school staff suggest that there has been much copying of what is thought to be required. The internet has many uses. A vision statement or plan may function symbolically more as a signal of compliant transmission for the purpose of external accountability than as an internal device for securing unified staff commitment. The discipline of brevity for vision statements forces them to be so general that most mean all things to all people and so challenge nobody's educational values. Take this compilation vision statement, gleaned from internet sources:

> We aspire to provide a welcoming, happy, caring and secure learning environment, offering all students stimulating, challenging, enjoyable and equal educational experiences. We hold high expectations of every student, encouraging them to develop their talents to the full. We value them as individuals, developing their positive self-image and giving them respect for others. The school offers a broad and balanced curriculum which meets National Curriculum requirements. Our aim is to work in close partnership with parents and the wider community to prepare our students for work and citizenship in the twenty-first century.

We suspect that few would quibble. It would be difficult to justify rejecting any sentiment while still perceiving oneself as an educator or responsible citizen.

Vision-building in the UK school context seems hardly necessary as a starting point for improvement planning and action. More than enough information to operationalize the school-level response to central government expectations is contained in National Curriculum guidance and materials, national assessment documentation, OFSTED inspection criteria and commercial publications. Local circumstances, say status as a church school, or a school catering for students from diverse ethnic groups, will be well-known to school staff. In this context we wonder whether the implicit goals of vision-building are, at most, operationally to offer a locus for keywords acting as reminders to staff and members of the local community, and instrumentally to provide a rhetorical statement for OFSTED inspections. Is this goal worth the effort?

A related source of ambiguity that vision-building exacerbates is logical, and potentially time-consuming. When is the vision ever built? If vision-building is a process of rallying staff round the educational values that they share, a vision statement is simply a device for encapsulating whatever they shared at a particular time. Must the process be revisited whenever contributors to the vision (staff and often parents, governors and others in the local community) come and go? If new staff are appointed from elsewhere, should they be expected to 'buy in' to the present vision or to contribute to its reformulation as the foundation for their commitment?

Yet another source of ambiguity is phenomenological. We noted in Chapter 6 the limits to consensus over values constraining managerialist attempts at culture management. Vision-building cannot dissolve value dissent. Potential conflict can be avoided by keeping the activity of vision-building separate from the activity of teaching, and by keeping the sentiments expressed vague enough to be capable of multiple interpretation. The compilation vision statement above illustrates this point. If it specified teaching practices, say a particular approach to teaching reading or setting homework, staff or parent hackles would be more likely to rise. Vision-building is widely acceptable only to the extent that the vision statement stops short of indicating how it will be operationalized. Because it is at a high level of abstraction, room to manoeuvre remains for staff to operationalize it according to their diverse curricular and pedagogic codes. What, in our example, might 'equal educational experiences' mean? Equal in time of study? Equal in the level of prior attainment required? Equal opportunity to demonstrate readiness as a condition for being offered more advanced educational experiences? The phrase could mean all these interpretations and more, leaving space for diverse approaches.

Situational ironies are not hard to find. 'What works' about vision-building within transmissional leadership is that it doesn't actually need to work as a culture management technique. Practice is strongly delimited anyway by central government directives, national assessment of student learning, and OFSTED surveillance. Vision-building does work as a symbolic device for reassuring outsiders that staff are working in the best interests of the students and in compliance with national requirements. But it takes time that could have been spent on more pressing educational matters and so risks alienating staff who already know what they have to do. The very brevity of vision statements means that they are in effect a collection of slogans, their meaning is assumed rather than defined, and so they may appear trite and unconvincing to staff who are expected to adopt them. Or once a vision-building exercise is over, the outcomes risk becoming ossified as slogans for the outside world – committed to memory by staff only when preparing for an inspection.

Distributing leadership: the risk of being damned if you do, damned if you don't

We noted earlier how the OFSTED criteria include the characteristic of effective leadership that 'leaders create effective teams'. But what if leaders 'create' teams in name that are later judged as ineffective in practice? Who will be held to account? Team members for failing to fulfil their responsibility to t╵

team, or leaders for failing to fulfil their responsibility for creating an effective team? OFSTED inspection reports are not overflowing with judgements about effective headteachers responsible for ineffective senior staff teams (SMTs or SLTs), effective headteachers responsible for ineffective subject leaders, or effective subject leaders responsible for ineffective subject departments. As one of us put it when reporting research into SMTs: 'It is hard to see inspectors taking the view: "Great SMT; pity about teaching and learning"' (Wallace and Huckman, 1999: 3). Headteachers are placed in a uniquely high-risk position because as 'top leader' they have responsibility for the practice of all their team colleagues. There is an asymmetry of external accountability. Other team members are unlikely to be held to account for failing to play their part in enabling a team to perform effectively. It is seen as the responsibility of leaders to get them to contribute fully.

Yet there is a control ambiguity with teams in hierarchically structured organizations that the emphasis on asymmetrical accountability increases. Leaders are generally higher in the management hierarchy than the rest of their team membership. They tend to be assumed to possess, in principle, sufficient authority to control the actions of colleague members. If they fail, their poor leadership must be to blame. But the interdependence that Gronn highlighted between all involved in organizational leadership and management means that all are reliant on each other. Even those at the bottom of the management hierarchy possess sufficient agency to use influence covertly by dragging their feet or overtly by resisting the overtures of leaders. Strong hierarchically-ordered external accountability makes it risky for leaders to share leadership and management through team approaches, and certainly more risky than it is for others to become members of teams. When called to account for team failure, the leader is most vulnerable to condemnation (damned if you do distribute leadership). Equally, operating hierarchically and refusing to delegate leadership tasks risks the condemnation of inspectors for failing to create effective teams (damned if you don't distribute leadership).

On top of external accountability, staff shoulder a heavy burden of organizational tasks that must be achieved, and which leaders depend on their colleagues to carry out because they themselves do not have the time or expertise. The endemic internal organizational dilemma of hierarchy (centralization versus decentralization of decision-making – Table 2.1) becomes acute. It appears to have been generated by the central government-induced context combining strong, asymmetrical external accountability with intensification of work through multiple reforms. During the 1990s one of us researched secondary school and large primary school SMTs. In secondary schools, SMTs originated with the larger organizations created by comprehensivization (Chapter 3). Most SMTs in primary schools emerged after the onset of central government reforms in the late 1980s. Here headteachers faced responsibility for an unprecedented profile of mandated innovations, and were forced to delegate responsibility for their implementation to colleagues. The latter rapidly became more expert on particular innovations than headteachers, who increasingly depended on their support. The dilemma for headteachers over how far to share decision-making over leadership and management tasks was summarized as follows:

> their greater dependence on professional colleagues draws them towards sharing management tasks through some kind of team approach; in a climate of increased external accountability, however, they may be wary of sharing in ways that might backfire if colleagues turn out to be empowered to act in ways that produce low standards of pupil achievement, alienate parents and governors, bring negative media attention, or incur negative judgements by inspectors. In short, how much sharing dare they risk? (Wallace and Huckman, 1999: 3)

SMT practices also reflected an endemic phenomenological ambiguity, already extended by the emergence of promoted posts as a management hierarchy during the 1960s. Belief in a *management hierarchy* topped by the headteacher sat uneasily alongside an egalitarian belief in the entitlement to participate equally in decision-making. This belief had surfaced during the years of school-based innovation (Wallace, 1989), had been advocated by academics and trainers in the USA and UK (e.g. Blase and Anderson, 1995; Southworth, 1995), and was reinforced by the adoption of team approaches to leadership and management. Team members are widely believed to have an *equal contribution* to make to decisions, whatever their position in the management hierarchy: in an SMT headteachers are the team leader but they do not have all the best ideas. The main justification for team approaches lies in maximizing the range of ideas that contribute to difficult decisions – many heads are better than one (see Evers, 1990). Hence the idea of all team members, including the team leader, contributing as equals.

The SMT research indicated that all leaders and their team colleagues were found to subscribe to *both* beliefs, even though they were mutually incompatible. It is impossible to operate at the same moment as if all team members are equal, but leaders are more equal than the others. It is very possible to act at different times according to one belief, then the other. Potential for the fullest contribution of every team member was realized where all, including the headteacher, habitually operated according to their shared belief in making an equal contribution. All team members were aware that the headteacher was uniquely vulnerable as SMT leader to being held externally accountable for efforts of the SMT. So if the headteacher

..... uncomfortable with the majority view on a particular decision, all team members other than the headteacher were ready to defer according to their shared belief in a management hierarchy. The capacity to operate as equals, with contingent regression to hierarchical operation, was a sophisticated way of dealing with the endemic limits to consensus (Chapter 6). It could develop only gradually. Willingness of all members to work in this way depended on accrued experience of working with and coming to trust each other. Under such conditions, the headteacher was willing to share leadership as the normal way of operating, while other team members were prepared to hand it back occasionally when the headteacher wanted to over-rule them as top leader in the management hierarchy.

The professional culture in these teams conforms to our view of culture as endemically ambiguous, containing contradictory elements. The dilemma of centralized decision-making by the headteacher, as team leader, versus decentralized decision-making by working consensus could be resolved. Doing so required all team members to operate according to one pole of the dilemma or the other at any time, and to be willing to swing from one to the other. But the dilemma was ever-present. It could not be dissolved.

The central government managerialist policies of ratcheting up external accountability while imposing an ongoing innovation and improvement burden on school staff have unintentionally augmented the endemic ambiguity of team operation within a hierarchical organization. School leaders are externally accountable for the extent to which they 'create effective teams'. But the situational irony follows that central government politicians have created conditions in which it is highly risky for leaders to distribute leadership equitably through team approaches. Where headteachers, subject leaders and others with leadership and management responsibility play safe by operating hierarchically, they incur the cost of losing the benefits of pooling ideas and shared commitment to shared decisions. The primary school SMT study suggested that playing safe was a strong temptation for headteachers. Where they succumbed, their team colleagues felt excluded. They had more to offer than 'acting as the headteacher's sounding-board'.

The managerialist high-risk organizational environment created by central government reforms militates against extensive sharing of leadership and management. Paradoxically, extensive sharing fosters the modest experimentation needed to operate effectively in the changing reform environment. It is also necessary if staff capacity to transmit reforms into practice through implementation in their organizations is to be maximized. But of course extensive sharing and experimentation carry the risk, from central government politicians' perspective, of practices emerging in schools that transgress the very boundaries (Table 4.2) that they and their predecessors have been painstakingly re-erected over the last two decades.

Planning to distraction

One distinction between leadership and management drawn by Louis and Miles (1990) in the definition we quoted earlier is that 'leaders make strategic plans; managers design operational systems for carrying out the plans.' In the national standards for headship, establishing a shared 'strategic vision' leads into strategic planning, the process being viewed as critical for improvement efforts. The logic seems impeccable: first gain commitment to a shared aspirational vision, next specify organizational goals to operationalize the vision, then work out how to implement action to achieve these goals. An important element of transmissional leadership is for organizational leaders to steer the translation of externally specified goals into implementation activity on the ground.

However, this logic is overly rationalistic for the contingent, relatively turbulent environmental circumstances in which planning is forced to take place. Circumstances where highly rationalistic planning approaches cannot work effectively have arisen partly as a consequence of central government reforms in general, and the managerial innovation of development planning in particular. It is worth rehearsing the development planning story because this innovation has generated such an enduring ironic legacy. It was introduced into UK schools in the early 1990s (Wallace, 1998a), in a climate of unprecedented central government demands for planning administered through LEAs:

- staff in schools were expected to produce an annual National Curriculum development plan to frame the academic year-by-academic year implementation of each subject;
- they were also expected to produce an annual budgetary plan under the local management of schools initiative, and an annual staff in-service training plan, both based on the financial year because they were connected with financial resources.

Two overlapping annual planning cycles were thus imposed by different central government reforms. Development planning was conceived by Hargreaves and Hopkins (1991) as a managerial innovation to support the implementation of multiple reforms, including the National Curriculum. Their ideas for the development planning process and associated plan document grew out of development work, pursuing the instrumentalist intellectual project and funded by central government, with staff in LEAs and schools during 1989 and 1990. They conceived development planning as consisting of four sequential processes or stages within an annual cycle (DES, 1989: 5):

1 *Audit*: a school (sic) reviews its strengths and weaknesses.
2 *Plan construction*: priorities for development are selected and then turned into specific targets.
3 *Implementation*: of the planned priorities and targets.
4 *Evaluation*: the success of implementation is checked.

Detailed plans are made for the coming year, and the next two in outline. As the first year ends, new detailed plans are made for the year ahead with reference to the outline plan made the previous year. The outline projection is taken forward to cover two years beyond what is now the coming year. So the plan rolls forward annually.

The year of the fieldwork is significant. The landmark 1988 Education Reform Act was coming into force, but most of the mandated innovations had yet to be implemented. It proved to be a lull before the reform storm. Staff in schools still possessed sufficient agency to plan a restricted number of improvements at the beginning of the year. They could realistically expect to implement them without further central or LEA interruption and to evaluate what they had achieved by the year's end.

An unwitting situational irony with lasting effects was generated by the fact that the external demands on school staff for implementing innovations and other changes were still moderate when the fieldwork was done. By the time the development planning innovation was disseminated to staff in all schools through advice documents (DES, 1989, 1991), the number and pace of reforms, and ameliorative central government policy-making where implementation was proving problematic, had become frenetic. By then, as now, school staff possessed much less agency and so had less control over the innovation profile and unplanned changes for which they had to plan a response. The development planning framework was already outdated by the time it was implemented in the majority of schools.

While not a formal central government requirement, development planning soon became one in effect because of the OFSTED inspection regime established in the mid-1990s. In addition, responsibility for 'Education Development Planning' was imposed on LEAs. National targets for improving student standards of literacy and numeracy were adjusted in negotiation with school staff and governors, and became another basis for judgement in OFSTED inspections. By the mid-1990s, research in primary schools (Cuckle et al., 1998) revealed a 'typical pragmatism' on the part of headteachers in complying with the many external contenders for priorities in school development plans. Headteachers were not so much responding to 'key issues' for improvement identified through an inspection, as pre-empting them. Many facing an inspection anticipated what key issues the inspectors were likely to identify and incorporated them into the school development plan before the inspection. (One might question why compiling a development plan was necessary if headteachers could already guess what inspectors would wish prioritized. Or why the inspection was necessary if headteachers already knew what inspectors would find wanting.)

At the time of writing, inspectors expect to see development plan documents and to assess the extent to which they are reflected in practice. They also require an 'action plan' to be formulated by the governors and staff to indicate how any shortcomings revealed by a school inspection are to be addressed. This document, too, is then subject to OFSTED scrutiny. So development planning constitutes an annual ritual that school staff and governors cannot afford to ignore.

Research conducted by one of us in the early 1990s (Wallace and McMahon, 1994) indicates why development planning is ill-suited to guiding planning for improvement and unplanned changes in a relatively turbulent environment. It may contribute to managerialist excess, taking up time that could be used more profitably on other tasks. A root cause of endemic logical ambiguity in organizational planning lies in the contradictory pressures for long-term coherence and for short term flexibility. Planning based on annual cycles can work for promoting coherence, reducing ambiguity by enabling priorities to be established and a consistent direction for long-term development to be sustained. It offers a basis for saying no to additional possibilities in order to keep activity manageable. However, in unpredictably evolving circumstances, planning based on occasional cycles can prove overly rigid, with outdated plans becoming increasingly irrelevant to the current press – to which the response must be yes, so increasing ambiguity. More continual, incremental planning offers flexibility to reduce ambiguity whenever evolving circumstances require existing plans to be modified or new ones created. But it does little for coherence beyond the short term, and can unnecessarily increase ambiguity in circumstances which are stable enough for longer-term planning to be feasible.

There is no logically coherent middle way to operate which keeps cyclic planning for long-term coherence and incremental planning for short-term flexibility in stable balance. Many prescriptive planning frameworks, including strategic planning, lean towards the sequence of activities that works for long-term coherence planning (see Mintzberg, 1994; Steiner, 1979;), at most allowing for a temporary switch to a more incremental approach where extremely turbulent circumstances force it.

This logical ambiguity has been exacerbated by the imposition of development planning in a relatively turbulent environment for which it was scarcely designed. Such turbulence sharpens the external dilemma of persistence – organizational certainty versus adaptation to the external environment (Table 2.2). Staff in schools are expected to develop medium-to long-term plans to operationalize their shared vision, increasing the element of organizational certainty about the direction for internal improvement efforts. But they are also expected to adapt to the external environment by implementing the evolving profile of innovations connected with central government reforms. Retaining a coherent direction for improvement and unplanned changes is very difficult in the face of often unpredictable and ever-evolving demands from the external environment.

A sense of the factors that may promote environmental turbulence or stability and their impact on planning may be gained from the list identified in the research by Wallace and McMahon (Table 7.3). Some creating turbulence were beyond school-level control, yet had to be addressed. Others could be reduced by staff action. The balance between environmental turbulence and stability was found to be critical for the planning process. The more the balance lay towards turbulence, the more incremental planning was dictated. The more the balance lay towards stability, the more feasible planning based on occasional cycles became, though it was optional. Incremental planning, incorporating longer-term goals, was logically just as feasible. A model of 'flexible planning' was put forward which explicitly reflects the logical ambiguity of pursuing coherence and flexibility. It consists of three components, acknowledged as coexisting in unresolvable tension (Wallace and McMahon, 1994: 28):

- response to spasmodic shifts in information about external innovations and unrelated crises and issues, affecting
- the continual creation, monitoring and adjustment of plans for the short and medium term within a long-term vision, linked to
- cyclic planning for the academic and financial years.

Coherence and flexibility are to be reconciled as far as possible through a rolling planning process, coping with all three components day-by-day, with occasional pre-specified formal reviews and incremental informal 'rapid reaction' reviews whenever evolving circumstances require them. There is no tidy logic in this model. But it was derived inductively from the way headteachers and their colleagues in primary schools facing a high degree of turbulence actually coped with planning for change.

As a seemingly permanent feature of transmissional leadership connected with vision-building, we note three situational ironies to which

Table 7.3: *Impact of factors promoting environmental turbulence and stability on the planning process*

Factors promoting turbulence or stability	Impact on the planning process in schools
Factors promoting environmental *turbulence*	
Abundance of externally initiated innovations, mostly compulsory	Coping with multiple, simultaneous goals and overload for staff
Low school-level control over externally initiated innovations	High proportion of reactive planning in response to external demands
Initiation by the headteacher of major innovations	Contribution to multiple goals and the staff workload
Crises and issues indirectly connected with innovations	Requirement for a planned response, often requiring alteration of existing plans
Ambiguity over and unpredictable changes in the characteristics and implementation requirements of externally initiated innovations	Frequent adjustment of plans
Inadequate resources to achieve goals	Adjustment to reduce the scale of activity, inhibition of the implementation of innovations
External monitoring of progress with innovations	Planned response to deal with criticisms
Routine management activity affected by externally initiated innovations	Adjustment of plans for managing routine activity
Externally initiated innovations affecting the management of planning (e.g. LMS, in-service training)	Creation of new tasks for managing planning and considerations that planning must take into account
External imposition of two overlapping planning cycles (academic year and financial year)	Adjustment of plans according to the stage reached in each cycle
Conflict at school level over the direction of development (especially among governors, or between governors and the headteacher)	Inhibition of planning, coping with a lack of commitment to implementation
Innovatory approaches for managing planning for change (development planning), sometimes mandated	Creation of new roles and tasks, implementation of formal procedures, sometimes to an externally determined timetable

Table 7.3: *Continued.*

Factors promoting turbulence or stability	Impact on the planning process in schools
Factors promoting environmental *stability*	
Availability of clear and consistent information about externally initiated innovations	Facilitation of detailed planning
A high level of control over innovations originating in school	Facilitation of detailed planning within available resources
Adequate resources to achieve goals	Facilitation of detailed planning
Lack of external monitoring of progress with innovations	Control over the degree and timing of implementation
Consensus at school level over the direction of development	Facilitation of detailed planning, commitment to implementation
Institutionalization (building into normal practice) of innovations	Termination of planning for implementation, reduction of staff workload
Routinized and flexible procedures for adjusting plans	Ease of response to changing circumstances
Support among governors and parents for, or passivity towards, the direction of development	Facilitation of implementation

Source: Wallace and McMahon, 1994: 68–9

development planning has given rise. The first is short term and probably long gone. When development planning was introduced, it constituted an innovation in itself which contributed to the very turbulence that its advocates intended it to reduce (see Table 7.3).

The second is more enduring: the one-sidedness of development planning based on sequential annual cycles in providing a framework for establishing coherence. The framework offers little support for dealing with the need to retain flexibility in the turbulent times that modernizing the public services perpetuate. This flexibility extends to adopting new priorities during the year in response to new central government initiatives and other changing circumstances that could not have been predicted when the plan was constructed. In Wallace and McMahon's research schools, headteachers dutifully led the development planning process and compiled the development plan document. But they worked round development planning much more incrementally (hence the primacy given to continual creation, monitoring and adjustment in the flexible planning model). Development planning and incremental planning occupied parallel universes, with the latter providing the bulk of ongoing guidance and located in people's minds rather than being committed to paper. Completing the development plan document was regarded as a temporary distraction. Once written up it tended to remain in a drawer, to be dusted off next year when the time came for it to be evaluated and a new one constructed.

The third irony relates to the very occasional but nevertheless significant bureaucratic function of the development plan document as a source of information for OFSTED inspections. An unintended consequence of OFSTED inspectors expecting to see a development plan is that what they are shown may be an artifice that is unfit for its purpose in guiding incremental updating of operational plans in a turbulent environment. Also the flurry of activity that can be imposed at any time of year to prepare for an OFSTED inspection contributes to the temporary turbulence that inhibits normal educational activity.

Leadership as a managerialist transmission device

We have examined several leadership ambiguities and the situational ironies they produce which militate against realistic efforts to improve learning and teaching. First, the transformational rhetoric–transmissional reality gap created by a particular conception of leadership underlying prescriptions for practice, promoted through government-sponsored training and scrutinized in practice through OFSTED surveillance. Second, the overemphasis on visionary aspects of transformational leadership, largely for external consumption. Third, the pressure placed on headteachers to share leadership while making it ever more risky to do so. Fourth, imposing a time-consuming framework for planning improvement activity which is insufficiently flexible to support ongoing adaptation to contingent and evolving circumstances. The root cause of these ironies is the disjunction between the transformational role of organizational leadership in the rhetoric of public service transformation and the reality that faithful transmission is actually sought. Leadership in 'service delivery' organizations like schools offers a means for central government politicians to tighten control over public service provision through their organizational leadership and management. The over-arching vision and goal belongs to central government. Present and aspiring leaders in schools are being groomed to transmit externally specified official goals in implementing government reforms and thus contribute to realizing the over-arching political goal.

We reiterate that leadership and management have a very positive contribution to make in supporting teachers' efforts to improve the learning and teaching process. But excessive emphasis on transmissional leadership, unhelpfully portrayed as promising transformation, is fuelling endemic ambiguities. In turn, these ambiguities are creating conditions for situational ironies that undermine transmission by directly or indirectly detracting from the all-important learning and teaching focus. The deepest irony is that the managerialist central government promotion of excessive leadership for unrealistically high central control, rather than leadership and management as such, is inhibiting the improvement that central government politicians, and many teachers and headteachers desire. But easing up on external control, not attempting to increase it further, is needed to create conditions favouring incremental improvement rather than mythical transformation.

PART FOUR: THE IRONIC RESPONSE AND THE FUTURE OF MANAGERIALISM

8

Patterns of ironic response

Part Four takes our argument forward to its conclusion. So far we have employed the ironic perspective to show how the excesses of managerialism have exacerbated the ambiguities and consequent ironies which are endemic in the educational enterprise. The potential for excess has been illustrated in central government policies for the reform of schooling through the conduit of leadership and management, and in practices influenced by current leadership and management theory pursuing the knowledge-for-action and instrumentalist intellectual projects. The present chapter draws upon a number of professional workplace studies suggesting that most headteachers and teachers, in their responses to managerialism, are to varying degrees deviating from the stated intent of policy-makers and holding to their professional beliefs and values. In Chapter 9 we reach beyond the reported behaviour of headteachers and teachers to propose that an ironic orientation underlies practitioner response to managerialism. We endorse such an orientation as a legitimate response to the ironies generated by managerialism: an ironic response to ironic situations. Finally, in Chapter 10, we consider some of the features of what we term 'temperate leadership and management': a legitimate and ethical response to the managerialist excesses of our time based on the proposition that education is likely to flourish if not over-led.

There are two major ways in which headteachers and teachers can respond to the excesses of managerialism: through political strategies and through organizational strategies. Political strategies entail engagement with educational issues, outside schools, through party political activity or through participation in such groups as teacher unions or associations with a specific political agenda. However, it is difficult for teachers as a group to mobilise for collective action over educational issues for several reasons: the diversity of views within the profession, personal career interests, and prevailing limitations on union power. Thus teachers only rarely resort to overt resistance.

Responses to excess are more likely to be found at the level of the school with teachers, individually and in groups, modifying reforms in the perceived interests of students. As we have already noted, the irony of school-level response is that it does not take the form of outright rejection but constitutes a principled effort to make unrealistic reforms viable in contingent conditions: to make plans that shouldn't work, work. Although we are positing an organizational frame for these activities some may actually transcend the organizational boundary and have their source in professional interest groups and inter-school collaboration. We now explore some of the strategies that headteachers and teachers have adopted to adapt policies.

Modes of adaptation

Reform is a process not an event. We noted in Chapter 7 how headteachers and teachers in post at the beginning of the reform period found that they had continually to adjust their work in response to successive policies and policy U-turns. Adjustment has also been necessary for teachers entering the profession as they discover that their motivations for becoming teachers are not wholly congruent with current expectations of the teaching role. We propose that there are three major modes of adaptation: *compliance, mediation* and *non-compliance*. This simple list has been informed by several detailed typologies. A general typology of adaptation is that proposed by Merton (1957: 132–133) based on the relationship between goals and institutional means in North American society. Goals are 'the things worth striving for' and institutional means are 'the acceptable modes of reaching out for these goals'. We also draw on typologies of teacher responses from the professional workplace literature.

Pollard et al. (1994) propose three types of response to the National Curriculum: compliance, mediation and resistance. We here use a similar terminology but for our purposes we prefer the broader term 'non-compliance' to 'resistance' for three reasons. First, we wish to include in our category more passive forms of response than the active forms connoted by resistance. Second, we prefer to reserve the term resistance for quasi-political activities that are undertaken outside the school. Third, strategies which some observers have regarded as negative resistance we would regard as 'mediation': not root and branch resistance but ways, possibly quite radical, of ensuring that the best interests of students remain a central concern.

Before discussing patterns of response we should emphasize that our purpose is heuristic. The typology which we use, and the typologies on which we draw, are not necessarily fixed categories. Although teachers in each category may generally act in accordance with the definition of that category, in certain circumstances they may respond in other ways. Osborn et al. (2000: 67) note that their own categories 'represent role configurations or strategies which individual teachers might adopt and move through at different times and in different ways'.

Compliance

This response entails the acceptance of both the goals and the means of a given society or institution: what Merton termed *conformity*. The reports of the PACE (Primary Assessment, Curriculum and Experience) research project used the term *compliance* to connote 'acceptance of imposed changes and adjustment of teachers' professional ideology accordingly, so that greater central control was perceived as acceptable, or even desirable' (Osborn et al., 2000: 68; Pollard et al., 1994: 100). We interpret this category as including a range of responses from 'true belief' in both the goals and the means of reformist policies to 'getting by': accepting the goals and means of reform without enthusiasm or positive commitment. We would include here what Merton refers to as *ritualism* whereby the individual rejects the goals inherent in the reforms but ritualistically pursues the means. It is acceptance of the means of reform that makes this an essentially conformist response.

Woods et al. (1997: 60) identified a category of *compliant* teachers who 'accommodate, concur, and allow changes to impinge on them'. Within this category they identified a diversity ranging from 'supporting', through 'surviving', to 'disturbed' conformists. These are the teachers whose efforts are diverted from teaching towards coping efforts that vary considerably from positive conformity to strategic compliance. Compliance would also cover the response of those infant teachers described by Evans et al. (1994: 104) as 'going by the book' which 'represented an uncompromising rigidity towards delivering the contents of the subject documents to the last letter'. These teachers clearly conformed to the means if not the official goals of the National Curriculum.

In a study of the ambiguities faced by middle managers in further education colleges, Gleeson and Shain (1999) identified a category of 'willing compliers' who were 'typically ambitious and have either been recently promoted, or are seeking promotion within the organization. Often they were pursuing further management qualifications to aid their promotion prospects'. The researchers also found a category of 'unwilling compliers'. They write: 'Paradoxically, those values and challenges which most excite the willing compliers are those which unwilling compliers find most difficulty in relating to.' They also identify a group of 'strategic compliers'. 'This response is perhaps best explained as a form of artful pragmatism which reconciles professional and managerial interests.'

Non-compliance

The rather general term of non-compliance conveys a range of responses that are non-accepting of the reforms. They range from a defiant rejection to a passive opting out. We can locate Merton's *retreatism* in our non-acceptance category. This response entails rejecting both goals and means. By using strategies of avoidance, retreatists are able to remain disengaged, keep their heads down and thus get by. Perhaps the 'head-in-the-sand' teachers identified by Evans et al. (1994) fall into this category since they carry on as far as possible doing what they have always done and hope that the reforms will go away. Pollard and his colleagues have also identified a response that they refer to as *retreatism* whereby teachers submit to the imposed changes without any change in their professional ideology. This response leaves them with deep-seated feelings of resentment, demoralization and alienation. Woods and his associates identify a category that they term the *diminished* teacher which they apply to those who feel devalued or disillusioned and who are 'leaving' the system or 'sinking' beneath it.

There appear to be few if any non-compliant headteachers. However, there is considerable evidence, from many sources, of headteachers opting for early retirement – often a result of stress and burn-out. This is a form of *retreatism* but the term does not exactly capture the position of many headteachers who have left, and we prefer Hirschmann's (1970) term *exit*. Or we can perhaps use the term *principled retreatism* since for many it is not a 'cowardly' act but a principled rejection of the goals and means of education as incorporated in the reforms. Woods (1995: 156) wrote of one headteacher retiree, 'for him this was a positive move, almost a triumphant act'.

Although we have presented our *non-compliance* category as ranging from active rejection to passive resistance it would appear that very few teachers are assertively non-compliant, and the PACE researchers found no headteachers who had adopted this response. The evidence from professional workplace studies suggests that there are more examples of teachers leaving the field than offering defiant opposition. One of Merton's response categories is *rebellion*, which entails an effort to transform the goals and means of society as a whole. As we are exploring responses to the goals and means of a sub-system of society – education – rebellion in this context would entail an attempt to transform the goals and means of education. Here the subsystem is the target of change from without, rather than from within. Thus rebellion is not particularly relevant to our argument since, for reasons outlined earlier, schools tend not to be sites of revolt.

Nevertheless, studies suggest that there are some indications of non-compliant responses. An example is the PACE project resistance category: 'resistance to the imposed changes in the hope that the sanctions available to enforce them would not be sufficiently powerful to make this impossible' (Pollard et al., 1994: 100). Teachers seeking to change the educational system in a root and branch way must do so through political parties, unions and interest groups, or through establishing alternative forms of schooling. But there is far less scope for the latter response now than during the 1960s period of school-based innovation which saw an efflorescence of alternative schools. Few now exist. Recently one longstanding alternative school, Summerhill, only just avoided closure following OFSTED inspections, illustrating how far central specification of acceptable practice extends beyond state education into the independent sector.

Mediation

This term captures various responses, constituting positive attempts to transform prevailing goals and means in education within the constraints of policy imperatives and school structure. These headteachers and teachers are our heroines and heroes. They are possessed of the ironic orientation which we outline in the next chapter. They are ironists because they recognize the contradictions in policy and the disjunctions between policy and practice. They are also principled. They neither opt out nor rebel but seek to 'work round' policies and structures. We have noted how the views among headteachers and teachers are diverse, so there is no consensus about educational goals and means among those who respond in this way. But the principle that they share is to do their best, as they see it, for students in the contingent circumstances in which they teach. Thus *mediation* seeks to transform policies into practicalities. Mediation also implies achieving continuity. This is the connotation which dominates the use of the term by the PACE team whose respondents 'emphasized the continuity between their existing practice and what is required of them' (Pollard et al. 1994: 73).

We will characterize many teachers as practising what we will term *principled infidelity*. A fidelity model of educational change is one whereby teachers are expected to implement externally-determined innovations in curriculum and pedagogy exactly as their originators intended. This approach to change has something in common with the earlier idea of a 'teacher-proof curriculum'. We use the term *infidelity* to convey the notion that teachers do not always slavishly adhere to the expectations embodied in educational policies but, whilst 'keeping up appearances', adapt mandated changes to the needs of their situation. We use the term principled to indicate that these adaptations are not simply subversive but are consistent with the professional values of teachers. There is also considerable evidence of such *principled* infidelity among headteachers, keeping up the appearance of meeting the demands of managerialism whilst sustaining their professional educational values (e.g. Wallace and Hall, 1994; Wallace and Huckman, 1999).

In this category we would include several of the strategies identified in the PACE project: *incorporation* and *creative mediation*. The team states that over the eight-year period of the PACE study the predominant response of teachers was *incorporation*. This entailed adopting the National Curriculum, but adapting its requirements to existing ways of working which incorporated the educational beliefs of headteachers and teachers. As one teacher in their sample put it: 'I'll accept the changes, but I won't allow anything I consider to be really important to be lost' (Osborn et al., 2000: 68). A smaller group adopted the strategy of *creative mediation*. As the term implies, this strategy was more creative than incorporation. Osborn and her colleagues identified several types of response. *Protective mediation* was adopted as a strategy by those teachers who sought to protect children from the pressures arising from, for example, new national assessment arrangements. They sought to routinize testing in order that the pupils did not see the national tests as out of the ordinary. However, as they comment (Osborn et al., 2000: 76): 'It is ironic that this strategy operated by teachers at the upper end of the primary school with the aim of protecting the children and enabling them to do their best was likely to result in increasing the climate of instrumentalism already developing.'

Innovative mediation entails teachers initially internalizing the statutory requirements of the National Curriculum but, on the basis of the confidence gained, going beyond these requirements by developing particular aspects in ways which more closely accorded with their values. Several contributors to the professional workplace literature have noted the phenomenon of creative mediation even though they have not used the term.

As Osborn and her co-researchers point out, it is a strategy that would encompass those teachers identified by Galton (1995) and Woods (1995) who were able to be highly creative whilst working within the constraints of the National Curriculum. We would classify the *enhanced* teachers (Woods et al., 1997) as displaying an ironic response since they are innovative in pursuing their educational goals notwithstanding the constraints under which they work. Evans et al. (1994) identified a *common sense* approach entailing conscientious efforts to do one's best, tempered by the recognition that the unrealistic expectations which were being imposed necessitated compromise.

One widespread manifestation of the ironic response of principled infidelity occurred in relation to the Technical and Vocational Education Initiative (TVEI) that ran from 1983 until the introduction of the National Curriculum in 1988. The purpose of this initiative was to replace the existing 'liberal' curriculum with a technical and vocational curriculum, more attuned to the economic needs of society. Significantly this pilot initiative was sponsored not by the Department of Educational and Science but by the Manpower Services Commission (MSC) which, policy-makers felt, was better able to overcome the 'providerist' orientation of the educational establishment. However, since the MSC had no power to impose this curriculum its adoption by teachers was voluntary. After an initial negative response from teachers, enthusiasm grew as it became clear that participation in the scheme brought additional resources into schools. Teachers were able to develop progressive teaching methods within the broad TVEI framework, what Helsby (1999) called 'the paradox of TVEI'. We would classify this unintended consequence for policy-makers as an example of irony: teachers were in a position to use government funds to reintroduce some of the very aspects of curriculum and pedagogy, such as interdisciplinary studies and discovery methods, that became the targets of reform.

Helsby summarizes her own findings as follows:

> Despite the unpromising framework, there were examples of both heads and managers striving to work their way round the new organizational paradigm and refusing to play the roles allotted to them by the educational reforms. Thus some school managers sought both to protect their staff from what they saw as the worst features of the changes and to maintain a commitment to educational, as opposed to managerial, values. (1999: 149)

This finding was widespread. No survey data exist which would enable us to suggest what proportion of headteachers and teachers fall into the *mediation* category generally, or any of its subdivisions, but case-studies indicate that a substantial number could be included.

Tactical forms of mediation

Let us narrow our focus, and concentrate on mediatory responses which we regard as meeting irony with irony. They involve coping with the ambiguities, dilemmas and pressures inherent in situational irony by ostensibly meeting formal expectations whilst modifying external demands with integrity. The tactics which we discuss here are those of individuals, groups and entire school staffs. We begin by considering what can be regarded as a meta-strategy which is to some extent adopted across all schools.

Protective colouration

Animals and plants adopt shapes and colourings to convince predators that they are something other than what they are. School staff have this capacity. It is a capacity that was undermined by the accountability demands of educational reforms intended to render the internal activities of schools more transparent. But, ironically, the reforms themselves have induced staff in schools to adopt protective colouration.

We note at several points in this book that education is essentially an adaptive social institution. By this we mean that people associated with schools as organizations have only limited agency in relation to the much more powerful constituents of their environment that delimit their room for manoeuvre: politics, the economy, culture, the media and technological development. Reforms have resulted in the boundaries of the school becoming much more permeable than in the past, increasing the pressures towards adaptation. But in order to sustain beliefs and practices which are generally held by teachers but are at odds with external expectations, they 'present' an appearance of conformity to the outside world whilst sustaining their beliefs internally. This is made possible because schools as organizations have an unclear technology and diffuse goals – issues that we have already considered – and thus it is difficult to establish a clear relationship between goals, means and outcomes.

Institutional theory offers an approach to understanding organizations that throws light on adaptive colouration (see Rowan and Miskel, 1999). The early application of institutional theory was almost entirely concerned with schools in the USA, and it preceded the UK reforms. The chief protagonists of this approach argue that it was possible for school staff to sustain a rationalized myth: 'rules specifying procedures to an outcome that are based on beliefs that are assumed to be true or taken for granted' (Hoy and Miskel, 1996: 221). Meyer and Rowan (1988) emphasize the importance of what they call 'ritual classifications': of teachers and their accreditation, of the curriculum, of student grouping, and of student categories. These classifications represent standardized activities which are not necessarily linked to outcomes:

> The classifications of education, however, are not rules to be cynically manipulated. They are sacred rituals that give meaning to the whole enterprise, both internally and externally. These categories are understood everywhere to index education. They are not understood to be education, but they are also not understood simply to be alienating bureaucratic constraints. So the decoupling that is characteristic of school systems must be carried out in the utmost good faith. (1988: 104–5)

As long as they are recognized by the public and sustained in the school these classifications generate what Meyer and Rowan term the 'logic of confidence'. To put it in a British context: politicians and the public had confidence in schools as long as there was a recognizable curriculum: traditional subjects, formal methods of examining these subjects, nationally-accepted credentials, qualified teachers, and students grouped according to age and ability. In the past such confidence has diverted detailed enquiry into the relationship between goals, processes and outcomes.

The logic of confidence vested in British schools had evaporated by the mid-1970s (Chapter 4). Ritual classifications in schools had to some degree been abandoned in the course of innovations in curriculum, pedagogy, student grouping and modes of assessment. Policy-makers bent on reform did not seek to restore the old classifications by government decree, but sought to tighten the coupling between schooling and outcomes through various forms of accountability. Thus the existing protective colouring of schools was removed and concealment was no longer an option. However, although the reforms did demonstrably strengthen the links between schooling and measurable outcomes, they nevertheless led to different forms of ritual classification. They included prescribed curricula, a testing regime, action plans, standardized inspections, codified school policies, mission statements and the like. These requirements certainly changed the nature of education but, ironically, they also became the new rationalized myths and indices which stood as a proxy for education. They enabled headteachers and teachers to develop new forms of protective colouration. The logic of confidence was far from fully restored but headteachers and teachers developed new forms of camouflage, some of which are discussed below.

The professional workplace literature, and studies which focus on the work of headteachers, frequently report them as attaching far greater importance to the *presentation* of the school to various external audiences than in the past. The motives underlying such presentations can range from professionally dubious self-aggrandizement to the protection of staff from external pressures. An interesting account of a 'reluctant image constructor' by Woods et al. (1997: 108–20) neatly illustrates some of the consequences – intended and unintended – of the role.

Strategic compliance

This term has some affinities with mediation but merits a separate discussion. It was developed to account for a phenomenon observed in the study of students in a medical school in the US (Becker et al., 1961). Students entered the medical school with a sense of idealism. It gradually declined as they experienced a gap between their ideals and the requirements of the course in terms of tests and exams and later, in terms of their interaction with patients. Their idealism was put on hold in favour of 'making the grade': strategic compliance with the requirements of the course in order to pass (see also Becker et al., 1968). Students were able to separate their cynicism about the course from their continuing idealism which strengthened, in a specific form termed 'professional idealism', an idealism now informed by the realities of practice. In a study of students on initial teacher training courses in English universities, Lacey (1977) also found evidence of strategic compliance. Students adapted their behaviour and assignments to the expectations of the university staff in order to 'make the grade'. However, Lacey also identified a different form of adjustment which he termed 'strategic redefinition'. Here students did not merely comply with requirements and expectations, but sought to change them: 'They achieve change by causing or enabling those with formal power to change their interpretation of what is happening in the situation' (p.73). Woods (1995: 73) found evidence of strategic redefinition among a set of creative teachers who 'sought to redefine the National Curriculum through their own values'.

Creative accountability

The analogy here is with 'creative accountancy': the ability of an accountant to present financial data in ways that are most likely to be helpful to a client. However, the generally tolerant view of creative accounting has shifted somewhat after recent business scandals, notably the Enron case. School staff and governors must now publicly account for their activities in a variety of forms – sometimes, literally, 'forms'. Perhaps the greatest opportunity for 'creativity' is in the school brochure which, hardly surprisingly, tends to present the school in the best possible light. The brochure is largely a marketing device and, as marketing now has a key place in school leadership and management, creativity here is admired (unless it is seriously misleading). There is less opportunity for 'creativity' in the documentation of 'hard' data such as balance sheets, national test scores and examination results. We actually know very little of the creativity, if any, which goes into the presentation of these data. There is a notional line between ironic and cynical data presentation. We do not, of course, condone the practice of intervening to 'improve' student test and examination scores that has occasionally been reported in the press. This is not ironic – it is illegal.

Perhaps the greatest opportunity for creative accountability occurs in the documents presented as part of an OFSTED inspection. Studies of the inspection process have suggested that preparing the necessary documentation is time consuming for two reasons. One is that the required material may be non-existent, out of date, or in a drawer and out of the consciousness of staff (as we noted with development planning). The other is that the writing, or rewriting, of this documentation requires a great deal of thought and imagination.

Collusion

Whereas *principled infidelity* can be an individual response, collusion is inherently a collective ironic response. Two of the coping mechanisms identified by Osborn and her colleagues can be included here. *Collaborative mediation* occurred where teachers worked together to offset the overload created by the National Curriculum and to compensate for the weaknesses of individual teachers in particular areas. These wholly informal arrangements enabled teachers to derive satisfaction from continuing to meet most of the requirements of the National Curriculum whilst minimizing the stress entailed in teaching aspects where they felt less competence. *Conspiratorial mediation* is seen by Osborn and her co-researchers as a more subversive form of collaborative mediation since it represents a partial, rather than a total, resistance to the reforms. It was evident in one of the inner-city schools in their sample that teachers worked together to implement the National Curriculum selectively in order to avoid student overload. Thus, with the tacit support of the headteacher, they ignored the history and geography programmes of study except where they fitted naturally into topics being covered. Teachers of seven-year-olds in the same school, again with the collusion of the headteacher, decided in 1995 not to implement new national tests, although they agreed to use the assessment materials in ways of their own choosing.

Collusion can also occur between schools. Market accountability is designed to ensure competition for students between schools. But on professional grounds collusion can occur between staff in different schools, minimizing competition in some areas. Wallace (1998b) has explored the 'counter-policy' adopted in seven different collaborative groups of schools. Vann (1999), from a headteacher's perspective, noted that headteachers have been successful in resisting pressures to compete and have worked collaboratively.

Despite the prevailing enthusiasm for staff collaboration, it would seem that such collaboration is not always approved by senior staff if it appears to be beyond their control. In such cases collaboration can be construed as 'collusion'. Gleeson and Shain reported that in some further education colleges middle management group meetings may be held without the knowledge of senior managers. In one college middle managers met as a separate group to develop innovative strategies for dealing with the pressures of work. Gleeson and Shain (1999: 485) noted: 'Paradoxically [we would say ironically], such action posed a threat to the dominant management culture and was swiftly halted by the principal.'

Performance

We use the term *performance* to draw the analogy between the rites of accountability and the conventions of the theatre. Mangham (1978) and others have applied a dramaturgical frame to understanding leadership and management in general. There is obviously an irony embedded in the fact that people not only continuously 'play roles' but they may on occasions 'play at roles'. Strengthened accountability has probably created more occasions, and greater imperatives, than in the past for headteachers and teachers to play at roles (as in the instance mentioned in Chapter 1 of the supply teacher who acted the part of a parent helper).

A play is an appropriate metaphor for the presentations which constitute such accountability events as OFSTED inspections and teaching quality visits in higher education. Anyone who has been involved in any such event will have been struck by the ironies entailed. This is perhaps particularly true for those who at different times have been in the 'cast' of the visited in their own institution and in the 'cast' of visitors to other institutions. Established procedures act as scripts. But, as with actors in the theatre, teachers and headteachers bring different interpretations to the role, within the limits on role variations that are possible. Helsby (1999: 129) quotes a former Labour MP and educationalist as saying that 'the OFSTED people are trained ... to keep blank, impassive faces'. Studies of the OFSTED inspection process suggest that enormous efforts lasting over a lengthy period go into preparation for the 'production' and rehearsals are often held. Reports are the equivalent of 'reviews' of books, plays and films and parties are sometimes arranged to coincide with the publication of the report – which may be convivial or otherwise depending on its content. Reversion to normal everyday life follows the production, often bringing a depressed period of 'post-OFSTED blues', whatever the content of the report.

Woods and colleagues discuss the case of Chris, a primary school headteacher, who commented that preparing for an OSTED visit was like 'preparing for a wedding'. Sustaining Chris's own metaphor they note that she played the role of 'mother of the bride', planning everything as carefully as she was able. Yet for Chris, it was not just a 'performance'. It was also 'for real'. The purpose of the performance was not to mislead but to ensure that the work of the school was presented in the best possible light. The success of the inspection strengthened Chris's professional confidence.

Woods et al. (1997: 127) also report that at the school where Theresa was a teacher, there was an initial assumption that nothing would change during the inspection period and life would go on as normal. But as the inspection approached the need for a 'performance' emerged. They write: 'For Theresa, she and her colleagues had the skills to put on whatever performance was demanded – to manipulate the reality.' After the inspection Theresa would appear to have returned to normal 'despite feelings of deprofessionalization during inspection week'. Clearly, for her, professional acting was no substitute for professional teaching. A paper by Case et al. (2000) on primary school inspection, with the neatly ironic title 'Please Show You're Working', reports that the teachers in their study were self-reflexive and actually used a theatrical metaphor, with its associations of performance, staging and 'inauthenticity', in relation to their responses to OFSTED inspection.

The irony of responses to managerialism

Managerialism promoted by central government policy-makers appears to have yielded more unintended than intended responses in schools. The professional workplace research implies that most headteachers have offered enthusiastic or less-than-enthusiastic compliance, consistent with our assertion in Chapter 7 that they actually provide leadership which is transmissional, despite the transformational rhetoric. Fewer teachers appear to have responded enthusiastically to all the reforms. But many have welcomed those that have facilitated greater collaboration with colleagues, while retaining considerable doubts about other aspects. There is little evidence of school-level rebellion. Non-compliance has taken the form of opting out as far as possible and, in the case of many headteachers and teachers, taking early retirement.

Significantly, the evidence suggests that the majority of headteachers and teachers have adopted some form of mediation whereby accountability requirements are ostensibly met but the full impact of the reforms has been buffered. For school staff, the purpose of this mediation has been to sustain educational beliefs that are at odds with the goals and the means of central government reforms. Headteachers have also sought to protect their educational role (as 'leading professionals' who are educators – see Chapter 4) against the growing demands of the managerial or 'chief executive' role. They have protected themselves by various forms of dissembling, for the most part principled dissembling. In particular the majority of headteachers have apparently sought to mediate between external demands and the traditional work patterns of teachers.

The professional workplace literature on which we have drawn has suggested various patterns of teacher and headteacher response to recent educational reforms. They should be regarded as no more than heuristic. They have been inferred largely from a literature where the emphasis tends to be more on teachers than on headteachers. Much of this literature deals with primary schools, and responses in secondary schools may be significantly different. It has drawn little on studies dealing exclusively with school leaders and managers because they do not generally evoke accounts of how headteachers and teachers 'work round' (as opposed to coping with) the demands which the reforms impose. While the responses to managerialism conveyed in this chapter are tentative, we believe that they indicate a widespread ironic response to the reforms which can be taken as an indicator of the *ironic orientation*, to be discussed next.

9

The ironic orientation and professional practice

In this chapter we hypothesize a congruence between professional practice and what we shall term an *ironic orientation*. On the face of it, this would appear to be an implausible linkage. The public image of professionals has been one of reassuringly confident and ethical practitioners solving client problems on the basis of a high level of expertise, founded in a recognized body of valid knowledge. On the other hand, an ironic orientation:

- recognizes the contingency of professional practice;
- is initially sceptical of theoretical knowledge;
- takes a pragmatic approach to problem-solving;
- constructs solutions from a combination of theory, experience, intuition and common sense;
- recognizes the need to reflect on which elements of practice appear to have been successful and which appear to have been less successful.

The traditional model of a profession now commands little political or public support (Chapter 5). It is being replaced by a new professionalism emphasizing the expressed needs of clients – including the state-as-client – with practitioners required to demonstrate competence in delivering an externally-determined service. The underlying purpose in this change in attitude towards the professions has been to reduce ambiguity. We have already indicated our acceptance of the need for greater professional accountability targeting professional incompetence and idiosyncratic practice and ensuring attention to client wishes. But we also believe that professional practice is, to a significant extent, endemically indeterminate. The present attempt to reduce the scope for judgement, levels of risk and professional responsibility (a more fundamental concept than accountability) is in danger of impoverishing the quality of professional practice and inhibiting the very incremental innovation that is vital for improving its effectiveness.

We also agree that professional practice can be enhanced through enlightened leadership and management. But we are concerned that there are dangers in assimilating the norms of professional practice into the norms of managerialism. We believe that an ironic orientation is appropriate to professionals, including those who move into leadership and management positions.

Changing concepts of a profession

Historically, medicine and law succeeded in establishing a particular conception of a profession. At the root of this conception was the claim that professional practice was different from other kinds of work in being endemically indeterminate. Although it was accepted that many aspects of professional practice were routine, there was, on the other hand, much in professional practice that entailed working in uncertain and contingent situations. From this position it was argued that the quality of professional work could be guaranteed only if professionals were granted a high degree of autonomy at the level both of individual practitioners and of the profession as a whole – particularly in relation to the state. For their part, professionals would acquire through a lengthy period of education not only a set of appropriate competences but also a body of knowledge which would form the basis of judgements made in uncertain situations. The integrity of professionals would be guaranteed by self-governing professional bodies, ensuring conformity to ethical standards that gave priority to client interests. This traditional model became the touchstone of the many occupations whose practitioners sought to achieve professional status during 'the rise of professional society' that lasted approximately from the 1870s to the 1970s (Perkin, 1989).

There have long been criticisms of this traditional model and its underpinning ideology – George Bernard Shaw famously referred to the professions as 'a conspiracy against the laity'. In the 1960s there emerged a body of sociological criticism of the professions which challenged the basic assumptions of the model. It was argued that the lengthy training and the academic knowledge which professionals had to acquire were largely a matter of self-aggrandizement, that the claim to autonomy was a means of avoiding accountability to clients, and that ethical codes were interpreted less in the interests of clients than in the self-interest of professionals.

The political origins of this critique were of the radical left, though it was the emergence of the market-orientated political right that precipitated a major change in the concept of a profession. The professions were seen as monopolies that inhibited the operation of the market, restricted consumer choice, and gave priority to provider interests over consumer concerns. Ensuing policies challenged the autonomy of individual practitioners and the autonomy of the profession as a collectivity. Accountability was increasingly centralized through greater state involvement, while simultaneously decentralized by increasing opportunities for consumer choice through the operation of the market. An internal market was created in such public services as education and health, whereby practitioners in neighbouring organizations competed with each other for clients and public resources. The policy switch was precipitated by the growing costs of the provision of public services in conditions of increased stringency as a result of the oil crisis of 1973, the growth in the number of public service professions and the proliferation of specialisms, and, in addition, the publicity given to scandals arising from a lack of accountability and the reluctance of professional bodies to deal with derelictions.

Education was the profession perhaps most affected by this change, which came during the period of school-based innovation in Britain. The enhancement of professional status had been a major project of teachers since the nineteenth century. Through combining a professional rhetoric with a political strategy, teacher unions had been quite successful in achieving changes in the teaching profession in terms of credentials, length of training, practitioner autonomy and influence on national policy. Studies of the teaching profession in England and Wales (e.g. Dale, 1989) have shown how, between the 1870s and 1970s, teacher professional bodies had achieved an accommodation with the state that Dale referred to as 'licensed autonomy'. This settlement ended in the 1970s when the view developed that an excess of teacher autonomy had led to such diverse provision, fuelled by school-based innovation, that educational quality was declining unacceptably. Subsequent legislation undermined the autonomy of teachers and rendered them much more accountable to central government and, through the introduction of greater parental choice and an internal market, to consumers. The school became the unit of account, with the headteacher becoming uniquely accountable for the performance of colleagues (including other SMT members – Chapter 7), and student learning outcomes.

These developments precipitated the concept of 'the new professionalism'. This term has no single connotation and there is far from unanimity about the nature of the phenomenon. However, the element common to all approaches was a shift away from a focus on institutional issues relating to status, governance and political influence to a primary focus on professional practice and its leadership and management. This was signalled by a semantic shift whereby 'professional' – as noun and adjective – became uncoupled from the idea of a 'profession' and took on a 'detached', 'hard', 'tough', instrumental', 'practical' connotation akin to the everyday connotation of 'leadership and management'.

Hence 'to be professional is to have acquired a set of skills through competency-based training which enables the practitioner to deliver, according to contract, a customer-led service in compliance with accountability procedures collaboratively implemented and managerially assured' (Hoyle, 1995: 60, adapted). This somewhat overstated and provocative distillation of prevailing political attitudes towards the professions conveys the shift from the earlier concept of professionalism, which put such a high value on autonomy. The new connotation is of a professionalism which entails rule-following practice, whether through the observance of prescribed procedures or the internalization of a particular set of cultural norms.

The drive to change the nature of professions brought to an end not only the old settlement between the teaching profession and the state but also its manifestation at the school level: the balance between autonomy and constraint. In the 1960s the issue of control was represented in the USA as a conflict between two patterns of organizing work: the bureaucratic and the professional. (In the UK the issue is more appropriately expressed in terms of the tension between teacher autonomy and the 'traditional' power – in Weber's term – of the headteacher.) Writers on schools as organizations and on teachers as professionals noted how an accommodation between the two organizing principles was achieved in many schools by a partial segregation of administration and teaching: Bidwell (1965) noted 'the structural looseness of the school' and Weick (1976) described educational organizations as 'loosely coupled systems'. The settlement that saw an implicit acceptance of the existence of largely distinct teacher and headteacher 'zones' (Hanson, 1979) was ended by government moves to increase the accountability of the professions.

Currently there exists a somewhat messy situation in schools. Institutionalization of the management hierarchy (Chapter 4) and the government strategy for policy implementation mean that teachers are increasingly involved in leadership and management. There are also pressures to professionalize educational leadership and management as a distinctive occupation (Chapter 5). Nevertheless, as we saw in Chapter 8, the professional workplace literature implies that most headteachers continue to regard themselves more as professional educators than as professional leaders and managers. We therefore avoid drawing an overly strong distinction between headteachers and teachers as professionals in our discussion of the appropriateness of an ironic orientation.

Components of an ironic orientation

We hypothesize an ironic orientation that has five components. Though we consider these separately here, they constitute, in combination, a general orientation to professional work. We are aware that the names we have attached to these components are not necessarily those that headteachers and teachers might use. We have chosen them as labels for phenomena reported in professional workplace studies and related literature. We are conscious that each term has several levels of connotation. One is the *general* connotation, contained in definitions offered by concise dictionaries, representing the everyday meaning attached to the concept. This level of connotation will be the main focus of our discussion of each component. Another is the *professional* connotation: one or more specialized usages that are deployed in theory and research relating to professional practice. Where appropriate, we briefly discuss these connotations. Each component also has a more profound *philosophical* connotation, raising issues relating to, for example, the objectivity of knowledge or the universality of values.

We will consider such issues later in the chapter where we seek to justify our endorsement of the *ironic orientation*. But to give an indication of how the three levels of connotation inter-relate we will very briefly refer to one component: pragmatism. At a general level *pragmatism* connotes 'practicality', 'what works'. At a professional level in teaching pragmatism connotes a pedagogical strategy that is rooted in action, experiment and discovery. Pragmatism in leadership and management similarly connotes a flexible administrative strategy for coordinating teaching work based on trying things out and learning through experience, rather than being driven by a restricted set of principles. At a philosophical level pragmatism connotes a particular view of knowledge advanced by such American philosophers as Peirce, James and Dewey. We have assumed that the general meaning is most central to our argument though, as a result of the growing sophistication of teachers and headteachers, the professional level of connotation has come to shape their thoughts about practice. For some, this might also be true of connotations at the philosophical level.

Contingency

Teachers tend to be strongly aware of the limitations of over-rational approaches to learning, whether embodied in national policies or in research laying claim to a high degree of prediction. They are aware of what Jackson (1968) termed the 'immediacy' of classroom events, as are leaders and managers of the myriad interactions in daily organizational life. They continually confront complexity, chance and the adventitious nature of the teaching process. They are conscious that there may be several equally viable ways of achieving the same learning or coordination outcome – 'equifinality' in the language of systems theory. They are also ever-conscious of the need to take advantage of such opportunities for promoting learning or smooth coordination as present themselves, even if it means adapting the 'script'.

This orientation ensures teachers and headteachers constantly appreciate the significance of *contingency* in the sense of the particular set of circumstances in which they work. Every school is like all other schools, like some other schools and like no other school. This is true of classes, of students, of staff and communities. Although there are some general principles relating to effective teaching, the teaching profession has not been strong on generating agreed bodies of practice. Some writers, including Lortie (1975), have rightly pointed to individualism in the culture of teaching as the reason. We most definitely do not interpret the contingency component of the ironic orientation as one of 'anything goes'. But it is the unique and contingent nature of their setting and their tasks which teachers and headteachers tend to emphasize. Thus national policies and generalized research findings are scrutinized for their applicability to a contingent situation. Such an orientation can be seen as inimical to building a body of good practice. Teachers or headteachers who are inattentive to contingencies wider than their own classroom or school can be seen to be limited as professionals. But the orientation towards contingency appears to be one of adaptation, not rejection. Teachers and headteachers seek a degree of order and predictability, the issues of classroom control or ensuring sufficient coordination alone ensuring that such is the case. They welcome policies that will support order and predictability. But their welcome is guarded.

Jackson (1968) reported that teachers valued their autonomy, a finding that is near-universal in studies of teacher satisfaction. However the US elementary school teachers he studied did not reject 'curriculum guides' in favour of complete autonomy over what and how they taught. They were content for the guides to be available as long as they were free to adapt them to the contingent circumstances of their own classrooms. Recent British professional workplace studies also suggest that teachers are far from unequivocally opposed to the National Curriculum, but they view it through the lens of their school and classroom circumstances. Nor are teachers wholly scornful of the relevance of educational research to practice. Here again, the contingency test is applied. Are the findings and their practical implications appropriate as they stand to my subject, my school, my class?

Teachers' attitudes towards research are actually somewhat paradoxical. They express a wish for unequivocal findings as guides to practice and are disappointed by the equivocation which researchers often express. At the quasi-technical level, there has been a move to build contingency assumptions into research design. They include varieties of teacher research and collaborative research pursuing the knowledge-for-action and reflexive action intellectual projects that are intended to inform professional practice in specific contexts rather then produce generalisations.

Scepticism

One dictionary definition of *scepticism* is 'a mistrust of ideas' (Collins, 2001). It comes close to the connotation that we believe represents the orientation of teachers towards their professional work. However, we would add that although teachers and headteachers may have an *initial* mistrust of ideas, they are willing to adopt them if they appear to be beneficial.

Teachers have traditionally been sceptical of the theory to which they have been exposed during their initial training. In particular, they have been sceptical about the existence of a tight relationship between theory and practice. This scepticism was often reinforced in young teachers by those more experienced. The theory component of initial teacher education courses was one target of reforms to establish greater uniformity in teacher education, with an increased emphasis on the practical problems of teaching and a switch in the balance of courses from being university-located to being school-located. It also led to new routes into teaching which were essentially school-based. Although the scepticism of teachers and headteachers towards educational theory persists, ironically their scepticism appears now to be more often directed at government policies. Many see such policies, in whole or in part, as non-viable. One mathematics teacher dismisses them as 'mostly mad-cap ideas on the back of envelopes at dinner parties' inducing, as he expresses it, 'professional impotence' (Bottery, 1998: 85).

Scepticism should not be equated with cynicism. On the contrary, scepticism appears to motivate teachers and headteachers to adapt unrealistic policies as best they can to the realities of their classrooms and schools. We have noted the fundamental irony earlier that teachers, through principled infidelity and often with headteacher support, are adapting government policies that would be unworkable if implemented according to the strict letter of the policy document.

Pragmatism

We have already offered a general connotation of pragmatism as 'what works'. One dictionary definition is 'an action or policy dictated by consideration of practical consequences rather than theory' (Collins, 2001). Teachers and headteachers are undoubtedly pragmatic in this sense. The initial question posed in relation to any theory or policy is: 'Will it work for me?' The behavioural correlate of this orientation is 'making the best of things'. Where a policy or theory does not 'work' when implemented with fidelity, pragmatism entails adapting it to achieve a satisfactory balance between the generalized intention and contingent constraints. We have seen in Chapter 8 how teachers have been particularly adept at such adaptation.

Moore et al. (2002) have also identified pragmatism as a response of headteachers to managerialism. In a study of eight schools they found that headteachers could not be located in the oppositional categories of 'headteacher tradition' and 'managerialist' but that most drew eclectically on both traditions using, where appropriate, managerialist strategies to sustain an educational vision. They write: 'This kind of 'pragmatism-with-principles' (what we might call 'strategic pragmatism') was evident in the majority of our headteachers' stated views on management and leadership' (p.185). Pragmatism-with-principles means that headteachers might conform to, or appear to conform to, aspects of managerialism (such as accepting the importance of league-table position in a market context), while holding on to a personal vision which included other values such as social justice and equality of opportunity. We would regard this as an ironic professional orientation.

Pragmatism also has a professional connotation with reference to learning and teaching. The pragmatic approach to learning entailing activity, experiment and discovery was an option for much of the last century and was widely debated in educational circles. However, it was an orientation that perhaps appealed more to teachers than to parents and politicians and opinion remains divided within the teaching profession itself. There was a boundary-crossing efflorescence of pragmatism in the curriculum and pedagogy of the 1960s (Chapter 4) which probably contributed to the backlash leading to successive central government reforms. Yet this orientation still shapes the professional ideas of many teachers and headteachers. As discussed in Chapter 8, it has recurred in various contexts including the TVEI scheme and the National Curriculum.

Constructivism

Constructivism (or *constructionism*) does not have a canonical definition. But it can be nevertheless used to connote an orientation which many teachers and headteachers bring to their work. They construct their own pedagogies or administrative approaches from a variety of 'materials' including experience, theories-in-use, research evidence, and reports of effective practice and formal requirements. As we have noted above, teachers and headteachers would generally appear to take an 'equifinality' approach to teaching, rejecting the alleged 'one true path' to success in favour of a combination of methods and approaches. The constructivist approach is frustrating to those theorists who believe that they have identified the most effective approach to, say, the teaching of reading or to the building of a shared vision of school transformation. It is also frustrating to those politicians who yearn for a definitive approach which all teachers and headteachers should adopt. Kenneth Clarke, when Secretary of State for Education, stated that the best way of teaching reading was clear enough to him and thus should be clear to, and implemented by, all teachers.

The professional connotation of constructivism rests on a growing body of research into learning and teaching associated with the theories of Vygotsky (see Prawat and Peterson, 1999). The constructivist approach to professional practice has also been endorsed by those who have researched 'communities of practice'. This concept refers to groups of people who engage collaboratively on a set of tasks. Wenger (1998: 7) writes: 'Communities of practice are an integral part of our daily lives. They are so informal and pervasive that they rarely come into explicit focus, but for the same reasons they are quite familiar. Although the term may be new the experience is not.' He notes the diversity of communities of practice but the communities of practice at work are of most interest to us. He states:

> Workers organize their lives with their immediate colleagues and customers to get their jobs done. In doing so, they develop or preserve a sense of themselves they can live with, have some fun, and fulfil the requirements of their employers and clients. No matter what their official job description may be, they create a practice to do what needs to be done. Although workers may be contractually employed by a large institution, in day-to-day practice they work with – and in a sense, for – a much smaller set of people and communities. (1998: 6)

Wenger's account relates to work in general. Communities of professional practice conform to this account but, without reverting to the old model that presented professions as qualitatively different from other occupations, we can note that there are some characteristics that are more likely to be found in professional work. Such communities share with most occupations a strong element of routine. But the ambiguity and indeterminacy of their work puts a premium on judgement, guided by knowledge and principles, exercised in contingent circumstances. For service professionals such contingency is powerfully shaped by the fact that their work entails sustained interaction with their clients (students and their parents in the case of teachers, and students, parents and a wider range of stakeholders in the case of headteachers). The interaction between most teachers and other professionals is less sustained than with their classes because the basic work unit is the teacher-and-students. Teachers' communities of practice are therefore strongly shaped by this structure.

Teacher professionalism is embedded in local communities of practice. As Talbert and MacLaughlin put it:

> Teacher professionalism depends to a significant degree on the extent and character of the local teacher community ... teachers who participate in strong professional communities within their subject area departments or other teacher networks have higher levels of professionalism, as measured in this study, than do teachers in less collegial settings. (1996: 141–2)

In contrast to managerialist attempts to create collaboration (Chapter 6), collegiality in communities of practice is not 'contrived' but arises out of collaborative engagement with professional problems. It is important to note that communities of practice are relatively independent of the formal organisational structures and procedures. They are contexts of mediation between the autonomous teacher and the formal structure (and its policy context). They are emergent in that they arise from practice. They are small: typically with not more than a dozen members, and face-to-face interaction is relatively easy and frequent. They may be temporary, forming, dissolving or reconfiguring according to their significance for members. They may transcend organizational boundaries, as with communities of teachers of different subjects in the same school, or teachers of a particular subject from different schools. Leadership is informal, emergent and exercised on the basis of expertise, experience or access to resources. Given these characteristics, one can see communities of professional practice as sites that support an ironic orientation.

Reflexiveness

Underlying the notion of *reflexiveness* is the idea that professional practice is improved to the degree that practitioners reflect on its apparent successes and failings with a view to future improvement. We cannot estimate how far teachers or headteachers in the past have reflected on their practice, or in what ways. The general notion of reflexiveness has been overtaken by Schon's (1983) conception of 'the reflective practitioner', which has had a considerable influence on initial and continuing professional education. The idea of the reflective practitioner is predicated on the recognition that professionals, and perhaps particularly teachers, have a considerable degree of tacit knowledge (Polanyi, 1971).

A discussion of the professional connotation of reflexiveness takes us to the threshold of a philosophical discussion well summarized by Egan:

> The central constituent of irony is a high degree of reflexiveness on our own thinking and a refined sensitivity to the limited and crude nature of the conceptual resources we can deploy in trying to make sense of the world. That is, irony involves sufficient flexibility to recognize how inadequately flexible are our minds, and the languages we use, to the world we try to represent in them. Ironic, really. (1997: 155)

We believe that the ironic orientation long informed professional practice but was not made explicit. The interests of the professions in protecting the power, status and work conditions of members were well-served by overstating the capacity of professionals to handle client problems, whilst stressing the indeterminacy of professional practice. Now that the focus has swung away from professional institutions to professional practice it is desirable to be explicit about the limits to accountability and the endemic indeterminacy of professional practice. Our idea of an ironic orientation offers a label for acknowledging how professionals, including those with leadership and management responsibility for other professionals, actually approach their work.

In defence of the ironic orientation to professional practice

We are aware that many objections can be made to the idea that an ironic orientation correlates with professional practice. They stem largely from its relativist cast that could be held to undermine a universalistic approach towards knowledge and to dilute the moral mission of education, so inhibiting the optimism and enthusiasm of teachers and headteachers, and destroying the confidence of clients in teachers as professionals. We accept the cogency of these objections. However, we suggest that the premises on which they are based do not obtain in the sub-optimal conditions of contemporary professional practice. To counter some of these objections we will offer some observations, while stopping far short of a full philosophical discussion.

Relativism in knowledge

In considering knowledge first, we dive in at the deep end. It could be argued that the approach to knowledge that we endorse in the ironic orientation puts us among those who Williams (2003) termed the 'truth deniers' or even those who Haack (2000) has called 'the new cynics'. However, we neither accept the total relativity of knowledge nor embrace an extreme subjectivism. We fully endorse the pursuit of objective knowledge in the natural and social sciences. But professional practice cannot afford to wait for the holy grail of complete objectivity before the practitioner can act. Egan encapsulates our position:

> Objectivity in the old sense is unattainable because we cannot determine whether the versions of the world and of experience capture how things are. The liberal ironist conceives of objectivity rather as a term useful to refer to those things about which it is relatively easy to achieve the widest intersubjective agreement. Knowledge is not discovered, Descartes-style, by sitting alone, and getting it right, but rather constructed in dialogue and out of agreement. The old distinction between knowledge and opinion is redrawn to distinguish between those claims or perspectives about which wide agreement is easy to achieve and those about which it is hard to achieve. Truth is reconceived as a commendatory reference to beliefs that are widely and easily shared, not as corresponding to reality. (1997: 153)

We accept that there are some 'facts', especially in relation to the physical world, that command such near-universal agreement that one could safely remove the scare quotes and simply term them facts. There is a facticity about being able to land people on the moon and we agree with the comment that 'there are no constructionists at thirty thousand feet' – relativism doesn't keep aeroplanes in the air. We also agree that there is near universal agreement on many geographical facts and, perhaps to a lesser degree, on historical facts where there is a rather greater degree of interpretation.

However, we are not concerned here with knowledge in general but with professional knowledge. There are some aspects of professional knowledge that command virtually universal agreement, especially professional knowledge that is grounded in the natural sciences. This is less so in the case of those professions such as teaching whose work is underpinned by the social sciences in which objectivity is more problematic. There is not a one-to-one correspondence between the social world and its interpretation through one's senses and the concepts of language. Different people understand what may be the same social world in different ways. They may use a variety of terms to interpret and evaluate their experience, as illustrated by our endeavours stipulatively to define the key concepts of our argument so as to ensure clarity of communication.

We nevertheless believe that it would be unwise to move too far from what Merton (1957) termed the 'organized scepticism' of the natural sciences. The scientific community requires claims to new knowledge to be adequately supported by what is understood to be credible evidence, as tested by such institutions as peer review, whilst appreciating that values, interests, and careers are entailed in the interpretation and implementation of research findings. Moreover, prescriptions for practice can rarely be simply 'read off' from the data. Although total objectivity is a criterion too far in relation to the profession of teaching – and of leadership and management – there is no case for abandoning research in those fields in conditions of organized scepticism. But it has to be accepted that research evidence will constitute only one kind of contribution to an agenda for professional practice.

Relativism in values

There is considerable overlap between the debate about the objectivity of knowledge and the debate about the existence of transcendental values. Our position on values thus parallels our position on knowledge, and will doubtless evoke criticism from the protagonists of a values-driven leadership in education. We take the view that not only should teachers bring their values to the task of teaching and leaders and managers to the task of running schools, but that they can do no other. Nor can writers avoid bringing their values into their publications. This book is positively dripping with values. Some values will receive near-universal support, but there are many values which are incommensurable. The ironic orientation might be criticised as a relativistic approach to values which is therefore ethically rudderless. But an ironic orientation does not mean abandoning all values: it means abandoning the search for external, incontestable, universal values. Pluralism rules. More importantly, it means making comparative judgements whereby we make a case for our values against the different values of other groups, on the basis of argument backed by evidence.

The ironic orientation recognizes that one is usually seeking a balance between incommensurable values in a temporal context, resulting in accommodation, negotiation and, ultimately, an agreement to differ. The irony is that if one was to envisage a shared fundamental value it would be that of tolerating values other than one's own. If to suggest this is to invite the charge of relativism, so be it. We are not engaging in a debate about the possibility of transcendental values, not least because we are concerned with one small area of human activity: professional practice. Values are central and are well worth articulating. There is no way of avoiding them.

But it is vital to acknowledge the range of values involved, including those connected with providing a professional service and furthering one's career.

For the ironist, acknowledging the centrality of values entails accepting that one's own values are neither universal nor incontestable. We follow Berlin (1969) in recognizing that ultimately some value positions are incommensurable but that one is not thereby inhibited for arguing the case for one over another. On this issue Berlin cites Schumpeter (1942): 'To realize the relative validity of one's convictions and evidence and argument yet to stand for them unflinchingly, is what distinguishes a civilized man (sic) from a barbarian.' To which Berlin adds: 'To demand more than this is perhaps a deep and incurable metaphysical need, and more dangerous, moral and political immaturity' (p.170).

Parochialism in scope

It can be argued that the ironic orientation to contingency, action and social construction of meaning contravenes the universalistic aspiration of science and the need to build a shared body of professional knowledge whose applicability reaches beyond the purely local. Although Schon's concept of the reflective practitioner has greatly influenced thinking about professional education and the role of the professional in relation to knowledge, action and reflection, the concept has been criticized for parochialism. Barnett (1997: 76) has argued that 'Schon goes too far in running action and reflection together ... He downplays the role that pure reflection can play in evaluating and critiquing action.' Others have criticized the notion of the reflective practitioner for its failure to build a body of shared professional knowledge. A similar charge is levelled against communities of practice: the professional knowledge they generate does not transcend the immediate in time, space and membership and may, in fact, perpetuate poor practice.

There is cogency in the charge that teaching in particular has not been good at building a body of valid knowledge either in terms of research evidence-informed practice or in the dissemination of demonstrable good practice. It may thus be that the ironic orientation could reinforce parochialism among teachers and headteachers. But this need not necessarily be the case. We do not see an ironic orientation as incompatible with an extended professionalism that entails reflecting on the wider context of an immediate problem.

Demotivation of practitioners

An ironic orientation might be regarded as incapable of providing the appropriate motivational base for professional practice. We have conceded that it is unlikely to set the blood racing. Setting aside the vast and equivocal literature on motivation, common sense suggests that people are more likely to be motivated if they can see a direct link between goals, methods and outcomes. But achieving this in professional practice is possible in only limited circumstances, and the limits are especially narrow in such a diffuse field as education. This is a fact with which professionals have to come to terms with in professional schools. Merton and Barber make the point in relation to medicine:

> doctors are often capable of specifying the conditions under which certain kinds of therapy will succeed, and in such situations they may obtain positive or negative results without knowing why. In addition, therefore, to the defences that doctors must acquire to meet predictable failures – the inevitable loss of patients for whose ills medical science simply has no remedies – doctors must learn to cope with situations in which they think they know what can or cannot be done, and what consequently will happen, but which turn out better or worse than their expectations. It is only if doctors become familiar with the problem of structured uncertainty in the course of their medical education, if they learn to work as well as possible within the limits set both by the development of medical science and human fallibility, that they can avoid becoming demoralized by accusations and self-accusations of incompetence and quackery. (2004: 155–6)

Studies of 'the fate of idealism' in medical schools (Chapter 8) show that students can become disenchanted by the fact that 'making the grade' becomes a priority, that they have to acquire a substantial amount of codified knowledge which appears to have little relevance to practice, and that there is less certainty about the efficacy of one form of practice over another than they had expected. The problem is even more pronounced in university and college education departments where the social science base has less legitimacy than the natural science base of medicine, where the teaching staff are no longer practitioners, and where there has been a strong emphasis on constructivism.

Students undergoing initial teacher education demonstrate a degree of ambiguity concerning the relativity of practice. On the one hand they want 'answers' to problems of method, on the other hand they want freedom to develop their own methods. So in effect they want guides to practice that they are free to ignore. The professional workplace research suggests that experienced teachers welcome the structure of the National Curriculum but also want the freedom to adapt it in the light of conditions that they increasingly come to recognize as contingent, as we noted earlier.

Public confidence

The charge of contributing to the growing loss of public confidence in the professions might be laid against an ironic orientation. It is generally agreed that there has been a decline of public trust in the professions (Bottery, 2004; O'Neill, 2002). This stems, in part, from members of the public becoming much more sophisticated in their approach to professional practice, encouraged by increased media interest and the growing political emphasis on 'choice'. The political drive for accountability has curbed the excesses of professional incompetence and malpractice, with undoubted benefit to clients. However, the accountability 'solution' has become – ironically – part of the problem. In stripping away the self-protective devices of the professions, accountability measures have also revealed the indeterminacy of professional practice that had been concealed by the habit of deference. Professionals are found wanting when the general public wants them to demonstrate command of certain knowledge. Many parents are exercised by academic and professional equivocation about educational 'facts'.

If the ironic orientation does contribute to a public loss of confidence, we see this as a dilemma with no solution. It is on the whole better that professionals should be up-front about the indeterminacy of practice than to conceal this within a cloak of pseudo-omniscience. Therefore the public, too, have to accept that they cannot expect unequivocal answers. While accountability procedures rightly protect the public against professional dereliction, excessive accountability is no solution to a problem that has such deep epistemological roots. We can only urge constant professional reflection and debate, attention to the potentiality of evidence-informed practice, and the exercise of judgement within the constraints of accountability procedures and acceptable levels of risk. It is ironic that the greater accountability which has opened professional practice to greater public scrutiny has also encouraged a much higher level of litigation against practitioners. In response, professionals are becoming much more risk-averse, thereby inhibiting the innovativeness that is held to be a characteristic of professionalism.

This unintended consequence is well illustrated in Britain by a debate over school students going on educational visits. Several high-profile cases of alleged negligence have led many school staff to review their policies on school visits and their risk-assessment procedures. The outcome in some instances has been the abandonment of school visits. Yet headteachers in other schools have declared that the educative value of such visits is such that the decision has been made to accept the risk.

Irony and the professional domain

We have argued that the traditional concept of a profession is not, and probably never was, an appropriate model for teaching and its leadership and management. But the conflation of professionalism and managerialism implied in certain conceptions of the new professionalism is equally inappropriate. Professional practice has its own virtues, but they differ from the transcendental values that some of the current rhetoric urges school leaders and managers to adopt. These virtues are captured in what we have termed the ironic orientation to professional work. We have acknowledged that there is no transcendental ethic which would support this orientation. But we assert that there is a suitably contingent ethic that can be invoked. In this connection we strongly endorse the five constituents of a professional ethic set out by Bottery (1998: 166–169) that applies equally to teaching and to leadership and management (though we must emphasize that Bottery would not necessarily endorse our ironic perspective).

1 The ethic of provisionality: 'Each individual must recognize the limits of his or her own judgements, his or her values. Nevertheless a rejection of an absolutist objectivity does not entail the acceptance of its opposite.'
2 The ethic of truth searching: 'To say that an ethic of provisionality is required does not necessarily imply an acceptance of relativism. We have to accept the Sisyphus quality of much endeavour...'
3 The ethic of reflective integrity: 'Each professional must recognize the limits of personal perception, of the need to incorporate many understandings of the situation.'
4 The ethic of humility: 'Each professional must realize that such provisionality means that personal fallibility is not a failing but a condition of being human.'
5 The ethic of humanistic education: 'The duty of professionals is to help clients to help themselves.'

We have argued for the continuing distinctiveness of a professional educator domain which interacts with a leadership and management domain, but which should not become subservient to it (a threat detailed in Chapter 5). The function of leadership and management is to create and sustain the conditions in which professional educational practitioners can be accountable but can also flourish. The traditional model of a profession, once the benchmark for many occupations including teaching, had serious conceptual limitations. Where it informed practice the interests of clients were not necessarily well served. This model was never going to be achievable by teaching, nor would its achievement be of benefit to students and their families. We doubt whether, in the case of teaching, the model extended much further than the rhetoric of occupational leaders. Teachers have always been concerned with status and have traditionally felt that their status was 'too low' in comparison with the major professions. Nevertheless, as we have noted above, the evidence of professional workplace studies suggests that teachers have never been too preoccupied with 'being a professional' in terms of the traditional discourse but have tended to focus on 'acting professionally' (Helsby, 1999).

10
Temperate leadership and management: living with irony

In the late nineteenth century Thomas Yates built a highly successful business selling wine relatively cheaply to the working class. Ironic, one might think, as Yates was a leading figure in the temperance movement. But Yates reasoned that he was more likely to wean people away from drinking noxious gin by offering them a more wholesome alternative at a reasonable price in his 'wine lodges'. Every bottle of Yates' wine carried the legend: 'Moderation is true temperance'. We have sought to establish a link between irony and moderation. Irony is an antidote to excess. Moderation is our prescription for what we regard as the excesses of managerialism. Of course, we recognize that moderation is hardly a rousing slogan. It clearly lacks the 'can do' appeal of many of the current texts on leadership and management. Our advocacy of compromise, tolerance, negotiation, contingency and balance is a far cry from the popular transformational rhetoric, and it would surely be ironic to unfurl a banner that read: 'Moderates of the world unite!' Moreover, we are not advocating any major transformation of educational leadership and management but, rather, endorsing the orientation that appears to be held by many teachers and headteachers. We simply aim to bring the ironic perspective and temperate leadership and management from their present *samizdat* status into the arena of professional debate.

We make the assumption that most headteachers and teachers prefer a temperate climate to the extremes of desert and tundra. There will always remain, we hope, the explorers who will have their sights set on radical transformation. But the evidence presented in this book suggests that there is no case for all headteachers and teachers, or even the majority, to be pressured into 'thinking outside the box' or 'pushing the envelope' (as the prevailing clichés have it) since the opportunity for radical transformation is currently not an option in education. The case is no stronger for the source of this pressure – the grand political experiment in public service transformation pursued by successive governments – to continue in its present form.

Exploitation versus exploration

To explain why we think that more temperate leadership and management facilitated by more temperate policy-making promises greater educational improvement for less ironic cost, we return to March's (1999) distinction cited in Chapter 6 between *exploitation* (refining existing practice) and *exploration* (looking for new alternatives). We earlier used this distinction to argue that state education is underpowered to transform itself through a major emphasis on exploration, rather than exploitation.

We surmise that the push for transformation of services will recede, as politicians come to recognize that the public funds currently being spent on one initiative after another are having only a marginal effect in relation to the size of the investment. The vicious cycle of policy initiative, unintended consequences, ameliorative policy initiative, unintended consequences, and so on, is neither very effective nor efficient. Educational reforms have certainly led to improvements but a perpetual revolution in education is alienating rather than motivating. The time might well soon come when government ministers learn to trust teachers and headteachers to a greater extent, whilst sustaining the minimum of accountability procedures required to identify those (probably few) teachers who are professionally unsatisfactory and those methods (also probably few) that are clearly unsuccessful. Today's accountability procedures are a hammer to crack a nut.

March implies that there is no definable, stable and cost-free 'best balance' between exploitation and exploration (which is also the case for the organizational dilemmas discussed in Chapter 2). There is an equivalent dilemma for policy-makers over how far their system-wide strategy for improving public service effectiveness should rely on exploration – trying out radical new alternatives through the multiple policy initiatives of system transformation, and on exploitation – applying, consolidating and further developing incrementally what has been tried and found to work in the past.

Whatever mix of exploitation and exploration is attempted constitutes a political gamble. Policy-making inherently means risk-taking, but the size of the risk is relatively controllable. Over-reliance on exploitation risks costing policy-makers dear through outmoded practices that no longer work in today's situation and are even less likely to do so in tomorrow's world. Policy-makers find themselves leaning towards the opposite pole of exploration because new alternatives are needed to cope with new situations. But over-use of exploration equally risks costing policy-makers dear through failing fully to harness existing know-how that may be applicable to not-so-new situations. Exploration can generate the ineffectiveness of failed grand experiments because, as March (1999) comments, it is likely that most new ideas will turn out not to work, even though a few may bring big gains. Compounding endemic ambiguity with that added by radical change precludes explorers from reliably predicting which of their ideas will turn out to be the few that make a transformative difference, or the many that produce ironic consequences undermining the transformational endeavour. Highly exploratory policy-making means big risk-taking. In our terms, policy-makers stand to generate ironic unintended consequences of their own making because of the high failure rate that is an endemic cost of exploration. They then find themselves leaning towards the opposite pole of exploitation.

Ogawa and colleagues (1999) used the metaphor of a pendulum to capture the vacillation that occurs between actions relating to one or other pole of organizational dilemmas. The parallel here is for policy-makers to vacillate between exploitation and exploration. Too big a swing towards one generates a pull to swing towards the other. There is no 'rest' position: the pendulum cannot be stopped. But policy-makers do have some control over the size of the swing they give to the pendulum. The bigger the swing towards either pole, the bigger the risk of ironic unintended consequences. Conversely, the smaller the swing, the smaller the risk.

We suggest that a temperate, low-swing, primarily exploitative approach to fostering incremental experimentation and consolidation in service organizations is a much lower risk strategy than the last two decades of high-risk, high-cost government reliance on exploration. Temperate policy-making implies a less directive approach than exploration, emphasizing the facilitative policy instrument of capacity-building (Chapter 3), and expanding the scope for the service dimension of professional practice embodying an ironic orientation (Chapter 9). It also implies delimiting the extremes of professional agency through modest accountability mechanisms to minimize consensually unacceptable malpractice or incompetence – but without penalizing the moderate majority. It further implies maximizing moderate agency and channelling it to facilitate professionals giving of their best in the contingent circumstances of each service organization, fostering diversity within the bounds of consensually acceptable practices.

Temperate leadership and management

We will discuss seven characteristics of temperate organizational leadership and management which could be promoted and supported through temperate policy-making for gradual improvement. These are:

- reducing leadership and management;
- contingent leadership and management;

- fostering professionalism;
- incorporating emergence;
- developing trust and accepting risk;
- sponsoring local improvement;
- seeing schools as institutions.

These characteristics will strike those committed to transformation as timid and even pessimistic. However, they capture what headteachers and teachers are attempting to achieve in stress-inducing times and are infused with both a spirit of scepticism about political grand educational experiments and, paradoxically, with a spirit of optimism about the possibility of incremental, local achievements.

Reducing leadership and management

One paradox of temperate leadership and management is that a major task is to reduce current levels of leadership and management. The ultimate purpose of doing so is to free teachers to concentrate on their core tasks of teaching and preparing to teach. The key function of temperate leadership and management is to take the strain and absorb the stress. They take the strain through structures and routines that relieve teachers of non-teaching tasks and create spaces in which teachers can maximize their professional contribution. Temperate leadership and management also absorb stress. There is ample evidence that much teacher stress arises from a required participation in accountability procedures, particularly those that include completing paperwork and attending meetings. The reduction of these activities is likely to reduce stress, increase satisfaction and thereby enhance the quality of teaching.

We recognize that we are asking much of headteachers, many of whom are also experiencing stress. We also recognize that accountability procedures are putting them under considerable pressure to extend rather than reduce leadership and management activities and to involve teachers to an ever greater degree. But we suggest that, rather than go with the drift of setting up ever more committees and pushing out ever more paperwork, temperate leadership and management entail questioning the symbolic and ritualistic nature of many of these activities and negotiating agreed levels with colleagues. This endeavour may well involve issues of autonomy, trust and risk, to be considered below.

We are encouraged by the suggestion in the professional workplace literature that the job satisfaction of headteachers still stems largely from achieving educational goals in relation to which leadership and management are tools. We take an 'adjectival' view of educational leadership and management. It may be that in the private sector leadership and management can be perceived as generic activities and that job satisfaction is to be derived largely from achieving specific and measurable output goals. This is attested by the fact that senior business managers move readily from leadership and management roles in one sector of industry or commerce to another. But in education, though some headteachers may derive their job satisfaction from the instrumentalities of leadership and management, the majority apparently look to more diffuse sources of satisfaction. Thus on grounds of satisfaction alone headteachers are likely to be attracted to working with the emergent properties of schools arising from the daily activities of teachers as fellow professionals.

Contingent leadership and management

In an early recognition of the contingency of leadership Machiavelli (1979: 382) wrote: 'Just as Rome once had Fabius as the best leader in times requiring that the war be drawn out, so later she had Scipio in times suitable for winning it.' The Fabius referred to is Fabius Maximus, known as Cunctator, whose name has given two words to the English language: *Fabianism* and *cunctation*. Members of the Fabian Society believe in evolutionary rather than revolutionary socialism, hence fabianism connotes that slow and steady wins the race. Cunctation is 'the action of delaying' (OED, 1971) and hence, similarly, connotes incrementalism. On the other hand Scipio was the heroic leader in the conventional sense. The Grand March from Handel's *Scipio*, though slow and stately, stirs the blood. But Fabius as well as Scipio should be regarded as a hero, though not dashing or 'transformational'. Machiavelli remarks on Rome's luck in having a match between circumstances and leadership style. There are contexts in education in which heroic leaders might be contingently appropriate. Some schools are in such a parlous condition that only heroic leadership can 'turn them round' and the literature reports instances of such leaders. But for many (we suspect most) schools effective leadership is much more appropriately Fabian, marked by the long haul towards improvement and an awareness of the negative unintended consequences of excess for morale.

Temperate leadership is not an abrogation of leadership. It presents a challenge just as great in its own way as aggressive transformation. Education needs its Scipios, but it probably has greater need for its Fabiuses. What it does not need is over-confident Scipios. Education is not a battle and the military metaphors employed in many leadership and management texts are inappropriate. The challenge is not to draw the sword of transformation but to think, discuss and negotiate as part of action. Contingency and incrementalism are somewhat un-utopian and contrary to the transformational *zeitgeist*. But they are congruent with the awareness that changes in the framework of education probably have only a marginal impact on learning and teaching quality as a whole. They also recognize that greater improvements are more likely to flow from head-teachers and teachers making improvements to their prevailing practices at the school level. Whilst we admire those educational explorers who are the Scipios of the system and make bold moves, we also value those Fabians who steadily improve existing methods.

Fostering professionalism

The essence of temperate leadership and management is the nurture of pro-fessionalism and, in particular, the nurture of its service dimension. In relation to the provision of a quality service, temperate leadership and management have both a default function and a support function. The default function entails ensuring that teachers are *doing things profession-ally*. This involves good classroom organization, ascertaining that essential routines are observed: that work is regularly marked and that essential paperwork is completed promptly and accurately. Another aspect entails ensuring that teachers *act professionally* in the sense of maintaining appro-priate relationships with other teachers, with pupils and with parents. These relationships are often articulated in policies or codes of practice that cover such areas as rights, respect and mutual support. Despite the existence of codes and the operation of widely-understood norms, profes-sional behaviour entails a considerable degree of judgement. Temperate leadership and management would essentially rely on this judgement and intervene in those exceptional cases of obvious dereliction and where 'mat-ters of principle' arise. Here the function of temperate leadership and management is essentially to foster debate on these issues with individuals and groups.

However, temperate leadership and management entail a much more positive approach to sponsoring, supporting and modelling professional-ism. Central to this function is the encouragement of professional learning. In Chapter 6 we discussed how organizational learning can too easily become over-systematized and lead to listing recipes for 'building a learn-ing organization'. At that point we indicated our preference for professional learning in the sense of learning how to improve the knowl-edge of content, the skills of transmission and an awareness of the context of learning and teaching. Whilst not wishing to diminish systematic approaches to professional development we note that many areas of learning are relevant to teaching, and temperate leadership and management will convey a general expectation of learning without over-specification.

Another key function in fostering professionalism involves taking autonomy seriously. The link between autonomy and professionalism is perhaps the central dilemma for the leadership and management of professionally-staffed organizations. We can refer briefly to some of the problems entailed. One is the operational meaning of autonomy. Complete autonomy is neither possible nor desirable. Autonomy is always relative. The sources of relativity are diverse. They include the socio-political context, where change brought by reforms has reduced the degree of autonomy enjoyed by teachers. Another issue, drawing on Berlin's well-known distinction, is whether an expressed desire for autonomy represents 'freedom to' or 'freedom from'. Whilst we endorse aspects of 'freedom from' – managerial coercion for example – our enthusiasm is for autonomy that constitutes 'freedom to', especially in relation to pedagogy. A third issue is autonomy as a source of job satisfaction. Virtually all studies of teacher satisfaction indicate teachers' preference not for total autonomy, which is in any case unrealizable, but autonomy within supportive structures and guidelines. A fourth issue is that professional collaboration is a constraint on autonomy, but teachers appear to be willing to accept this form of constraint if collaboration is of their own construction and not contrived.

Achieving a balance between these competing forces is the task of school leaders and managers in association with colleagues. This task is difficult, not only because achieving a balance entails vacillation between the poles of endemic dilemmas, but also because it entails achieving a balance in an individual school where a headteacher's preferred leadership and management style and the preferences of the majority of teachers may well diverge. However, we urge the case for optimizing autonomy largely because the balance appears to have been struck in recent years more in favour of control. The preference for autonomy is also partly pragmatic. There is really no alternative. As long as the basic technology of teaching remains centred on the teacher-and-learning-group, conceding a substantial degree of autonomy to teachers within the acceptable parameters of surveillance and its costs is inevitable.

Incorporating emergence

Temperate leadership and management will be particularly concerned with developing – without over-institutionalizing – ideas, techniques and interactions emerging from practice. Much of the leadership and management literature tends to adopt a top-down perspective and presents organizational activity as a function of the actions of those in leadership and management roles. This perspective overshadows the fact that organizational properties also emerge from the daily activities of members who do not necessarily hold formal leadership and management positions. There are various bodies of literature that emphasize the importance of emergence. The tradition of organizational studies of which March is a leading figure has long emphasized that organizations 'run backwards' in the sense that actions precede structures, decisions and choices. A related perspective is that of Weick who emphasizes organizing as an ongoing process rather than organization as a fixed set of structures and procedures. Within leadership theory there is growing attention to distributed leadership, which gives due attention to the leadership acts occurring in all parts of the organization (Gronn, 2000; Harris, 2001). There is the literature on communities of practice (e.g. Wenger, 1998) which describes how work groups collaborate to control their own practice. Finally, there is the emphasis placed on emergence in complexity theory.

Discussions of emergence have, in some instances, led to excessive claims for alternatives to formal leadership and predetermined structures. But generally the need is recognized to achieve a balance between emergence and predetermination. We argue that temperate leadership and management would not only recognize the phenomenon of emergence but also actively seek to encourage it. The role of leadership and management in relation to emergence is identification, support and achieving congruence between emerging forms and established, authoritative forms.

Developing trust and accepting risk

Promoting the autonomy of teachers and putting reliance on emergent innovations is predicated on *trust* and entails *risk*. The case for autonomy is closely related with the case for trust. Trust is widely viewed as being in decline in society generally (Bottery, 2004: O'Neill, 2002), and in Chapter 9 we noted the loss of trust in the professions, particularly on the part of politicians (ironically, survey data suggest, at present one of the least trusted 'professions' in society). In relation to teaching some writers have held that politicians have gone beyond a passive loss of trust and have adopted what Ball (1990: 18) has termed a 'discourse of derision'. These wider changes have undoubtedly had an impact on the degree of trust among staff within a school including, particularly, the extent to which headteachers trust their colleagues.

Not all teachers are to be trusted. Individual teachers may not deserve trust at either of two levels. It may be that they are not to be trusted to meet the basic demands of the job in terms of time-keeping and undertaking routine tasks. It is clear from the proceedings of appeals against dismissal, from cases of prosecution and from other sources that a few teachers betray trust in terms of client and colleague relationships. Others may lack the competence, or are unwilling or unable to acquire the competence, to be effective practitioners – let alone acquire the higher levels of professionalism. Thus some teachers clearly need close surveillance and control, not in relation to dereliction but in terms of their lack of basic competence.

Notwithstanding the fact that some teachers betray trust, a general climate of mistrust is a matter of concern. We therefore argue that headteachers should adopt an initial presumption of trust on two grounds. First, behaviour is influenced by the expectations of others. People will generally be trustworthy to the degree that they are trusted. Second, there is no alternative to trusting teachers to behave responsibly. Accountability is important but has its limits. The nature of professional practice is such that without a prohibitively expensive and draconian form of surveillance, the potential for accountability is restricted. Professional practice involves responsibility. Responsibility is more fundamental than accountability since it is too deep and diffuse to be amenable to procedural control. Langford (1985) made the useful distinction between *agent-for-another* and *principal*. As agent-for-another a professional seeks to achieve a set of predetermined goals. As principal a professional is responsible not only for achieving but also for setting the ends of his or her action. We regard a professional as both accountable *and* responsible in the latter sense. It follows that trust is not only desirable but is inevitable. We see professional leadership and management as orientated towards responsibility and hence high trust. We see managerialism as orientated towards accountability measures that are predicated on low trust.

There are factors which make it difficult for school leaders and managers to have a presumption of trust since trust entails risk. It can take many forms, including career risks for the headteacher. These are entailed in failing to meet targets, receiving negative inspection reports, and becoming the object of litigation by parents. We recognize that such factors may militate against trust, but also that headteachers possess sufficient agency to work on avoiding a climate of mistrust and obtrusive surveillance of the kind that can amount to bullying (fortunately rare), as inferred from professional workplace studies.

Sponsoring local improvement

We have noted in preceding chapters that 'school improvement' can sometimes be equated with managerialism. This is unfortunate. *Improvement* is an eminently suitable term for the major task of headteachers and teachers that follows from our analysis: to enhance educational quality in their contexts by steadily improving on what they already do, through a primary (but not exclusive) emphasis on exploitation. Although it will not bring fame, it will bring professional satisfaction. The aspiration of 'true believers' in managerialism to bring about a high-speed transformation through a primary emphasis on exploration invites the irony of negative unintended consequences – directly proportional to the amount of ambiguity that radical change inherently generates.

There is less scope for exploration in education than in business, except perhaps in the area of educational technology which is driven by business incentives rather educational needs. Within a context of service accountability, however moderate in its scope, greater success is likely to come through doing the traditional things better than through attempting high-risk innovation. Recent educational history shows that some of the best-known explorers in the period of school-based innovation, when a strong emphasis on exploration was feasible, encountered negative reactions which often led to dismissal or transfer to another school. The evidence over the past 40 years is that schools which have been highly exploratory have rarely survived in their innovative form (witness the demise of the individualized middle school curriculum discussed in Chapter 2). In education the costs of heavy investment in exploration are high, not necessarily in terms of direct and quantifiable costs but in terms of the hidden costs of time and stress among teachers and the opportunity costs entailed in diverting the efforts of teachers away from their core tasks.

Seeing schools as institutions

Temperate leadership and management entail a recognition of the nature of education as a social institution and, particularly, that as an institution it differs in fundamental ways from business. We earlier noted (Chapter 5) how the problem of managerialism in schools stems in part from political insistence that practice in the public services has much to learn from the disciplines of private sector leadership and management. It is undoubtedly the case that school leadership and management can be, and has been, sharpened considerably through the adoption of techniques developed in the private sector, particularly since schools have been required to become 'self-managing', competitive and market responsive. But there is a distinction to be drawn between techniques and goals. It is the adoption of the prevailing goals of the private sector organizations (assumed, incidentally, to be more clear and specific than is actually the case) that has generated leadership and management to excess.

Education and business are institutions with quite different purposes, cultures and functions. The two institutions certainly intersect to some degree other than simply in terms of basic leadership and management techniques. State funded education transmits some of the generic skills required by the workforce of a competitive economy, it differentiates broadly between categories of students including those entering the workforce, and it bestows credentials. However, there are also fundamental differences that at root can be expressed in the language of innovation and conservation. Members of private sector organizations must respond to changes in the market, create new markets, or risk demise (or, at least, the departure of senior managers). Market criteria have certainly imposed changes on the system of schooling, as discussed in previous chapters – including school types, admission policies, credentials. But it is frequently noted, and often regretted, that despite the massive changes that have occurred at this level the core educative processes, sometimes called 'the technical core', of education have remained relatively impervious to market policies. The transmission of culture, one of the key, and inevitably conservative, functions of education has remained unchanged. The educational core is so persistent that politicians will eventually come to realize that the continuous transformation they espouse can easily degenerate into a situation where no value is given to 'heritage, continuity, consolidation and tradition (which are all vital ingredients of schooling) where only incurable change addicts prosper and survive' (Hargreaves, 1994: 11–12).

The term *institution* has many connotations but we use it here as defined by March (1999: 54): 'The core notion is that life is organized by sets of shared meanings and practices that come to be taken as given for a long time.' As the phrasing indicates, institutions are not immutable but their basic forms appear to have a degree of tenacity. It is not necessary to invoke some sort of Platonic essence to make the case that schooling is readily identified as such whatever the local context, whether a Hong Kong high rise school or a corrugated iron hut deep in the African bush. There is a teacher, a group of students and recognizable codes governing the interaction between teacher and students and between students that are both formal and informal. There are also relatively unchanging ceremonies and rituals that are central to the culture of all schools. We do not go as far as affirming that these characteristics are invariants or that they will remain forever beyond the change process, since it is possible to conceive of changes in the fundamental codes of schooling driven by new technology. But we do regard them as having a degree of persistence which must be respected.

Thus a number of writers have noted that schools have a 'deep structure' or a 'grammar' (Mulford, 1998; Pentland and Rueter,1994; Tyak and

Cuban, 1995). These deeply embedded institutional forms are not easily reached by change efforts, and especially not through leadership and management. A persistent theme in studies of educational innovation and the management of change is that, despite massive change efforts and considerable expenditure, teaching has remained relatively unaffected, to the despair of the protagonists of transformation. The absence of expected impact cannot be wholly attributed to the Luddite teachers. But it can be attributed to the recognition by headteachers and teachers of the 'rightness' of the relatively enduring characteristics of schools as institutions.

Of particular help here is the distinction drawn by March (1999) between the 'the logic of consequence' and 'the logic of appropriateness'. The former entails an orientation towards consequences: effects, outcomes, and so forth. It is this logic of consequence that has come to dominate action in education as a result of reforms. On the other hand: 'Action is taken on the basis of the logic of appropriateness associated with roles, routines, obligations, standard operating procedures and practices' (1999: 55). In addition: 'Actions are expressions of what is exemplary, natural, or acceptable behaviour according to the (internalized) purposes, codes of rights and duties, practices, methods, and techniques of the constituent group and of the self' (p.57). It is the importance of the logic of appropriateness that we wish to affirm.

Although schooling will always have its logic of consequence, including the conservative function of transmitting elements of the culture to successive generations, there will always be a non-consequential aspect to schooling. Despite the alternatives that information technology can even now provide, it is likely that children will continue going to school since participation in schooling is valued as a natural activity in its own right. The act of participating in the daily rituals and practices of schools has great significance for the lives of children. The logic of appropriateness is not being invoked here as a version of child-centred romanticism. Consequences, in the form of measurable cognitive outcomes, are vital to individual children as well as to the state. But in the dilemma presented by the two forms of logic, we believe that the significance of the logic of appropriateness needs to be reaffirmed. In the face of policies dominated by consequence it falls to headteachers and teachers to maintain a contingent balance that enables teachers to engage in the valued rituals and practices that are appropriate as well as consequential.

Coda: the fundamental spirit of optimism

At the beginning of this book, we offered a summary of the current orthodoxy of leadership and management, especially as inflected in school improvement texts. Our alternative view offers a stimulus for debate about moving in a more realistic direction. The essence can be captured in a few statements:

1 School improvement entails the exploitation and development of teaching and associated skills and a cautious approach to exploring new ways of doing things.
2 It is encouraged by school leaders who value teacher autonomy, display trust with acceptance of related risks, and sponsor innovations that emerge from communities of professional practice.
3 Teachers in these communities take seriously their responsibilities towards clients and their own ongoing learning.
4 Teachers are supported by temperate leadership and management which take the strain and minimize the stress that may otherwise ensue where external policies are insensitive to contingent circumstances in individual settings.

Because we have not subscribed to the myth of transformation and been carried along by the enthusiasm of its protagonists, we may be accused of having a limited vision and even of being over-pessimistic. If so, we are in the company of probably the majority of headteachers and teachers who, the professional workplace literature implies, whilst welcoming some aspects of the reform movement have generally found its effects oppressive. However, although managerialism connected with reforms has generated considerable dissatisfaction, headteachers and teachers appear to have maintained a degree of satisfaction and optimism. We believe they have done so by adopting an ironic orientation towards the situation and achieving a mediation between policy and practice. There have been relatively few believers in the myth of transformation in the sense of radical change: headteachers and teachers have generally focused much more on limited, local but nevertheless satisfying changes.

There is a deep discrepancy between the current aspirations of many policy-makers and the perennial aspirations of teachers. The 'frame' of policy-makers is society. They seek to create education systems that are more competitive or more equal or, somehow, both more competitive *and* more equal. Teachers may have the same aspiration in their role as political actors but they are in a position to know, as professional actors, the difficulties entailed in shaping education to these ends. The 'frame' of teachers is different from that of policy-makers and is limited to success with individual pupils, groups and classes where 'success' is more than (but obviously includes) examination success and embraces personal success in making incremental improvements to their teaching. As March (1999: 361) puts it: 'One can imagine pessimism without despair or an acceptance of irrelevance without loss of faith, but perhaps the greatest tradition of education is that of optimism without hope, a commitment to the joyful unconditional obligations of participation in education.'

In our terms, the commitment of ironists to optimism without hope means living comfortably with the endemic ambiguities and situational ironies of organizational life, without hope of eliminating them. In the face of radical transformation, it means coping with additional ambiguities and ironies through mediation, bringing to bear an ironic orientation and an ironic humour, without hope that grand political experiments will be eschewed. It means a temperate approach to leadership and management, fostering teachers' freedom to teach within broad consensually established limits.

Most fundamentally, it means teachers and headteachers, without hope of achieving a radical transformation of society, being eternally optimistic about their ability to make things marginally better for those students who are in a particular school at a particular time.

References

Alexander, R. (1984) *Primary Teaching*. London: Cassell.

Alexander R. (1995) *Versions of Primary Education*. London: Routledge.

Alexander, R. (1997) *Policy and Practice in Primary Education*. (2nd edn) London: Routledge.

Amis, K. (1997) *The King's English: A Guide to Modern Usage*. London: Harper Collins.

Argyris, C. (1999) *On Organizational Learning*. (2nd edn) Oxford: Blackwell.

Argyris, C. and Schon, D. (1978) *Organizational Learning: A Theory of Action Perspective*. London: Addison-Wesley.

Bacharach S. B., Bamburger, P., Conley, C. and Scott, B. (1990) 'The dimensionality of decision-making in educational organizations', *Educational Administration Quarterly*, 26 (2): 126–67.

Bacharach, S. B. and Lawler, E. S. (1980) *Power and Politics in Organizations*. San Francisco: Jossey-Bass.

Ball, S. (1990) *Politics and Policy-making in Education*. London: Routledge.

Ball, S. (1998) 'Educational studies, policy entrepreneurship and social theory,' in R. Slee and G. Weiner with S. Tomlinson (eds) *School Effectiveness for Whom?* London: Falmer.

Barber, M. (ed.) (1996) *The National Curriculum: A Study in Policy*. Keele: Keele University Press.

Barnett, R. (1997) *Higher Education: A Critical Business*. London: SRHE/Open University Press.

Baron, G. and Taylor, W. (eds) (1969) *Educational Administration and the Social Sciences*. London: The Athlone Press.

Bass, B. (1985) *Leadership and Performance Beyond Expectations*. New York: Free Press.

Becker, H., Geer, B., Hughes, E. and Strauss, A. (1961) *Boys in White: Student Culture in Medical School*. Chicago: University of Chicago Press.

Becker, H., Geer, B. and Hughes, E. (1968) *Making the Grade: The Academic Side of College Life*. New York: Wiley.

Berger, P. and Luckmann, T. (1967) *The Social Construction of Reality*. Harmondsworth: Penguin.

Berlak, A. and Berlak, H. (1981) *The Dilemmas of Schooling*. London: Methuen.

Berlin, I. (1969) *Four Essays on Liberty*. Oxford: Oxford University Press.

Bernstein, B. (1967) 'Open schools, open society?', *New Society*, 10: 152–4.

Bidwell, C. (1965) 'The school as a formal organization', in J. G. March (ed.) *Handbook of Organizations*. New York: Rand McNally. pp. 927–1022.

Blase, J. and Anderson, G. (1995) *The Micropolitics of Educational Leadership*. London: Cassell.

Board of Education (1937) *Handbook of Suggestions for Teachers*. London: Her Majesty's Stationery Office.

Bolam, R. (ed.) (1982) *School-focused In-service Training*. London: Heinemann.

Bolman, L. and Deal, T. (1984) *Modern Approaches to Understanding and Managing Organizations*. San Francisco: Jossey-Bass.

Bottery, M. (1998) *Professionals and Policy: Management Strategies in a Competitive World*. London: Cassell.

Bottery, M. (2004) *The Challenges of Educational Leadership*. London: Paul Chapman.

Bower, M. (1966) *The Will to Manage: Corporate Success through Programmed Management*. New York: McGraw Hill.

Brundrett, M. (1998) 'What lies behind collegiality: legitimation or control?', *Educational Management and Administration*, 26 (3): 305–16.

Brunsson, N. (1989) *The Organization of Hypocrisy*. Chichester: Wiley.

Bucher, R. and Strauss, A. (1961) 'Professions in process', *American Journal of Sociology*, 65: 325–34.

Burns, J. (1978) *Leadership*. New York: Harper & Row.

Caldwell, B. and Spinks, J. (1988) *The Self Managing School*. London: Falmer.

Caldwell, B. and Spinks, J. (1992) *Leading the Self Managing School*. London: Falmer.

Callahan, R. (1962) *Education and the Cult of Efficiency*. Chicago: University of Chicago Press.

Carter, R. (1992) 'The LINC project: the final chapter?', mimeo. Nottingham: University of Nottingham.

Case, P., Case, S. and Catling, S. (2000) 'Please show you're working: a critical assessment of the impact of OFSTED inspections on primary teachers', *British Journal of the Sociology of Education*, 21 (4): 605–27.

Central Advisory Council for Education (England) (1967) *Children and their Primary Schools*. (The Plowden Report). London: HMSO.

Chambers, W. and R. Ltd (1998) *The Chambers Dictionary*. Edinburgh: Chambers Harrap Publishers Ltd.

Chubb, J. and Moe, T. (1990) *Politics, Markets and America's Schools*. Washington, DC: The Brookings Institute.

Cicourel, A. and Kitsuse, J. (1963) *The Educational Decision Makers*. New York: Bobbs Merrill.

Clark, B. (1960) *The Open Door College*. New York: McGraw Hill.

Collins (2001) *Collins Concise Dictionary*. Glasgow: HarperCollins.

Coopers and Lybrand (1988) *Local Management of Schools*. London: HMSO.

Creemers, B. (1994) *The Effective Classroom*. London: Cassell.

Cuckle, P., Hodgson, J. and Broadhead, P. (1998) 'Investigating the relationship between OFSTED inspections and school development planning', *School Leadership and Management*, 18 (2): 271–83.

Daily Telegraph (1991) '"Progressive" teaching was a £14m failure,' 2 August.

Dale, R. (1989) *The State and Educational Policy*. Milton Keynes: Open University Press.

Davison, C. and Kemshall, T. (1998) *OFSTED Exposed!* Instead: Walsall, UK.

Deal, T. (1998) 'The symbolism of effective schools', in A. Westoby (ed.) *Culture and Power in Educational Organizations*. Milton Keynes: Open University Press. pp. 198–222.

Department for Education and Employment (1998) *Teachers Meeting the Challenge of Change*. Cm 4614. London: DFEE.

Department for Education and Skills (2004) *National Standards for Headteachers*. London: DFES.

Department of Education and Science (1972) *Teacher Education and Training*. (The James Report). London: HMSO.

Department of Education and Science (1989) *Planning for School Improvement*. London: DES.

Department of Education and Science (1991) *Development Planning: A Practical Guide*. London: DES.

Dimmock, C. and Walker, A. (2003) 'Developing comparative and international educational leadership and management: a cross-cultural model', in M. Preedy, R. Glatter and C. Wise (eds) *Strategic Leadership and Educational Improvement*. London: The Open University in association with Paul Chapman Publishing. pp. 77–92.

Dixon, N. (1994) *The Organizational Learning Cycle*. London: McGraw Hill.

Egan, G. (1988) *Change Agent Skills: Assessing and Designing Excellence*. San Diego: University Associates.

Egan, K. (1997) *The Educated Mind: How Cognitive Tools Shape our Understanding*. Chicago: University of Chicago Press.

Elster, J. (1978) *Logic and Society*. New York: Wiley.

Empson, W. (1930) *Seven Types of Ambiguity*. London: Chatto and Windus.

Enright, D. (1984) *The Alluring Problem: An Essay on Irony*. Oxford: Oxford University Press.

Evans, L., Packwood, A. and Neill, S. (1994) *The Meaning of Infant Teachers' Work*. London: Routledge.

Evers, C. (1990) 'Schooling, organisational learning and efficiency in the growth of knowledge', in J. Chapman (ed.) *School Based Decision Making and Management*. London: Falmer Press.

Evers, C. and Lakomski, G. (1996) *Exploring Educational Administration*. Oxford: Pergamon.

Farrell, C. and Morris, J. (2004) 'Resigned compliance: teacher attitudes towards performance-related pay in schools', *Educational Management, Administration and Leadership*, 32 (1): 81–104.

Firestone, W. and Louis, K. S. (1999) 'Schools as cultures', in J. Murphy and K. S. Louis (eds) *Handbook of Research on Educational Administration*. (2nd edn) San Francisco: Jossey-Bass. pp. 297–322.

Fullan, M. (2001) *The New Meaning of Educational Change*. (3rd edn) New York: Teachers College Press.

Galton, M. (1995) *Crisis in the Primary Classroom*. London: Fulton.

General Teaching Council (2003) Keynote speech by Carol Adams to the North of England Education Conference. http://www.primaryheands.org.uk/documents/doc9html Accessed 31 December 2003

Giddens, A. (1979) *Central Problems in Social Theory*. Berkeley: University of California Press.

Giddens, A. (1984) *The Constitution of Society*. Cambridge: Polity.

Glatter, R. (1972) *Management Development for the Education Profession*. London: Harrop.

Gleeson, D. and Shain, F. (1999) 'By appointment: governance, markets and managerialism in further education', *British Educational Research Journal*, 25 (4): 545–62.

Greenfield, T. (1975) 'Theory about organizations: a new perspective and its implications for schools', in M. Hughes (ed.) *Administering Education: International Challenge*. London: Athlone Press. pp. 71–99.

Gronn, P. (2000) 'Distributed properties: a new architecture for leadership', *Educational Management and Administration*, 28 (3): 317–38.

Gronn, P. (2003) 'Distributing and intensifying school leadership', in N. Bennett and L. Anderson (eds) *Rethinking Educational Leadership*. London:Sage. pp. 60–73.

Guardian (2003) 'Schools cash for rail crash enquiry firm,' 28 April.

Haack, S. (2000) *Manifesto of a Passionate Moderate: Uncomfortable Essays*. Chicago: University of Chicago Press.

Hallinger, P. and Heck, R. (1999) 'Can leadership enhance school effectiveness?' in T. Bush, L. Bell, R. Bolam, R. Glatter and P. Ribbins (eds) *Educational Management: Redefining Theory, Policy and Practice*. London: Paul Chapman. pp. 178–190.

Hanson, E. M. (1979) *Educational Administration and Organizational Behaviour*. (2nd edn) Boston, MA: Allyn and Bacon.

Hargreaves, A. (1983) 'The politics of administrative convenience', in J. Ahier and M. Flude (eds) *Contemporary Education Policy*. London: Croom Helm. pp. 23–57.

Hargreaves, A. (1994) *Changing Teachers, Changing Times*. London: Cassell.

Hargreaves, A. (1997) 'The cultures of teaching and educational change', in B. Biddle, T. Good and I. Goodson (eds) *International Handbook of Teachers and Teaching*. London: Dordrecht: Kluwer. pp. 1287–1319.

Hargreaves, A. (2003) *Teaching in the Knowledge Society*. Maidenhead: Open University Press.

Hargreaves, A. and Tickle, L. (1980) *Middle Schools: Origins, Ideology and Practice*. London: Harper and Row.

Hargreaves, D. and Hopkins, D. (1991) *The Empowered School: The Management and Practice of Development Planning*. London: Cassell.

Harris, A. (2001) 'Distributed leadership and school improvement', *Educational Management and Administration*, 32 (1): 11–24.

Helsby, G. (1999) *Changing Teachers' Work*. Buckingham: Open University Press.

Hirschman, A. (1970) *Exit, Voice and Loyalty*. Cambridge, MA: Harvard University Press.

Hodgkinson, C. (1991) *Educational Leadership: The Moral Art*. Albany NY: SUNY Press.

Hoy, W. and Miskel, C. (1996) *Educational Administration: Theory, Research and Practice*. (5th edn) New York: McGraw Hill.

Hoyle, E. (1965) 'Organizational analysis in the field of education', *Educational Research*, 7 (2): 94–114.

Hoyle, E. (1974) 'Professionality, professionalism and control in teaching', *London Educational Review* 3 (2): 13–19.

Hoyle, E. (1975) 'Leadership and decision-making in education', in M. Hughes (ed.) *Administering Education: International Challenge*. London: Athlone Press. pp. 30–44.

Hoyle, E. (1986) *The Politics of School Management*. London: Hodder & Stoughton.

Hoyle, E. (1994) 'Organization theory', in T. Husen and N. Postlethwaite (eds) *International Encyclopaedia of Education*. New York: Pergamon Press. pp. 6224–6227.

Hoyle, E. (1995) 'Changing concepts of a profession', in H. Busher and R. Saran (eds) *The Management of Professionals in Schools*. London: Longman. pp. 59–70.

Hoyle, E. (2001) 'Teaching: esteem, status and prestige', *Educational Management and Administration*, 29 (3): 139–152.

Hoyle, E. and John, P. (1995) *Professional Knowledge and Professional Practice*. London: Cassell.

Huber, G. (1991) 'Organizational learning: the contributing processes', *Organizational Science*, 2 (1): 124–62.

Huczynski, A. (1993) *Management Gurus: What Makes Them and How to Become One*. London: Routledge.

Hughes, M. (1973) 'The professional-as-administrator: the case of the secondary school head', *Educational Administration Bulletin*, 2 (1): 11–23.

References

Hughes, M. (ed.) (1974) *Secondary School Administration: A Management Approach.* (2nd edn) Oxford: Pergamon Press.

Jackson, P. (1968) *Life in Classrooms.* New York: Holt, Rinehart and Winston.

Jones, A. and Hendry, C. (1994) 'The learning organization, adult learning and organizational transformation', *British Journal of Management,* 5: 153–62.

Kuper, A. (1999) *Culture: The Anthropologists' Account.* Cambridge, MA: Harvard University Press.

Lacey, C. (1977) *The Socialization of Teachers.* London: Methuen.

Langford, G. (1985) *Teaching as a Profession: An Essay in the Philosophy of Education.* Manchester: Manchester University Press.

Lawton, D. (1984) *The Tightening Grip: Growth of Central Control of the Curriculum.* Bedford Way Paper 21. London: University of London Institute of Education.

Leithwood, K., Jantzi, D. and Steinbach, R. (1999) *Changing Leadership for Changing Times.* Buckingham: Open University Press.

Leithwood, K., Leonard C. and Sharratt, L. (1998) 'Conditions fostering organizational learning in schools', *Educational Administration Quarterly* 34 (2): 243–76.

Little, J. W. (1990) 'The persistence of privacy: autonomy and initiative in teacher professional relations', *Teachers College Record* 91 (4): 508–36.

Lortie, D. (1964) 'Suggestions for long-term research on team teaching', in J. Shaplin and H. Olds (eds) *Team Teaching.* Boston, MA: Allyn and Bacon. pp. 270–305.

Lortie, D. (1975) *Schoolteacher.* Chicago: University of Chicago Press.

Louis, K. S. and Miles, M. (1990) *Improving the Urban High School.* New York: Teachers College Press.

MacGilchrist, B., Myers, K. and Reed, J. (1997) *The Intelligent School.* London: Paul Chapman.

Machiavelli, N. (1979) 'The discourses', in P. Bondarello and M. Musa (eds) *The Portable Machiavelli.* London: Penguin.

Maclure, S. (1970) 'The control of education', in *The History of Education Society: The Government and Control of Education.* London: Methuen.

Maclure, S. (1998) 'Through the revolution and out the other side', *Oxford Review of Education,* 24 (1): 5–24.

Mangham, I. (1978) *Interactions and Interventions.* New York: Wiley.

March, J. (1999) *The Pursuit of Organizational Intelligence.* Oxford: Blackwell.

March, J. and Olsen, P. (1976) *Ambiguity and Choice in Organisations.* Bergen: Universitetsforlaget.

March, J. and Simon, H. (1958) *Organizations.* New York: Wiley.

Marks, H. M. and Louis, K. S. (1999) 'Teacher empowerment and the capacity for organizational learning', *Educational Administration Quarterly,* 35 (Supplement): 707–50.

Martin J. and Frost, P. (1996) 'The organizational culture war games: the struggle for intellectual dominance', in S. Clegg, C. Hardy and W. Nord (eds) *Handbook of Organizations.* London: Sage. pp. 599–621.

Mcdonnell, L. and Elmore, R. (1991) 'Getting the job done: alternative policy instruments', in A. Odden (ed.) *Education Policy Implementation.* Albany, NY: SUNY Press. pp. 157–83.

McGovern, C. (1991) 'Very peculiar practice for state schools,' *The Mail on Sunday,* 4 August.

McLaughlin, M. (1991) 'The RAND change agent study: ten years later', in A. Odden (ed.) *Education Policy Implementation.* Albany, NY: SUNY Press. pp. 143–55.

McLaughlin, K., Osborne, S. and Ferlie, E. (eds) (2002) *New Public Management: Current Trends and Future Prospects.* London: Routledge.

Merton, R. (1957) *Social Theory and Social Structure.* (2nd edn) New York: Free Press.

Merton, R. and Barber, E. (2004) *The Travels and Adventures of Serendipity.* Princeton: Princeton University Press.

Meyer, J. W. and Rowan, B. (1988) 'The structure of educational organizations', in A. Westoby (ed.) *Culture and Power in Educational Organizations.* Milton Keynes: Open University Press. pp. 87–112.

Miles, M. (ed.) (1964) *Innovation in Education.* New York: Columbia University, Teachers College, Bureau of Publications.

Mintzberg, H. (1994) *The Rise and Fall of Strategic Planning.* New York: Free Press.

Moore, A., George, R. and Halpin, D. (2002) 'The developing role of the headteacher in English schools: management, leadership and pragmatism', *Educational Management and Administration,* 30 (2): 175–98.

Morgan, C., Hall, V. and Mackay, H. (1983) *The Selection of Secondary School Headteachers.* Milton Keynes: Open University Press.

Morrison, K. (2002) *School Leadership and Complexity Theory.* London: RoutledgeFalmer.

Muecke, D. C. (1969) *The Compass of Irony.* London: Methuen.

Mueller, D. (1989) *Public Choice* Vol II. Cambridge: Cambridge University Press.

Mulford, W. (1998) 'Organizational learning and educational change', in A. Hargreaves, A. Lieberman, M. Fullan and D. Hopkins (eds) *International Handbook on Educational Change.* London: Kluwer.

National College for School Leadership (2003) *Prospectus 2003/04.* Nottingham: NCSL.

Nias, J., Southworth, G. and Yeomans, R. (1989) *Staff Relationships in the Primary School.* London: Cassell.

Odden, A. (ed.) (1991) *Educational Policy Implementation.* New York: SUNY Press.

OED (1971) *Oxford English Dictionary.* Oxford: Oxford University Press.

Office for Standards in Education (2003a) *Inspecting Schools.* London: OFSTED.

Office for Standards in Education (2003b) *Leadership and Management: What Inspection Tells us.* Document No. HMI 1646. London: OFSTED.

Office of Public Service Reform (2002) *Reforming our Public Services: Principles into Practice.* London: OPSR.

Ogawa, R., Crowson, R. and Goldring, E. (1999) 'Enduring dilemmas of school organisation', in J. Murphy and K. S. Louis (eds) *Handbook of Research on Educational Administration.* San Francisco: Jossey-Bass. pp. 277–95.

O'Neill, O. (2002) *A Question of Trust.* Cambridge: Cambridge University Press.

Organisation for Economic Cooperation and Development (2003) *Education at a Glance 2003.* Paris: OECD.

Osborn, M., McNess, E., Broadfoot, P. with Pollard, A. and Triggs, P. (2000) *What Teachers Do. Changing Policy and Practice in Primary Education.* London: Continuum.

Osborne, D. and Gaebler, T. (1992) *Reinventing Government.* Reading, MA: Addison-Wesley.

Parkinson, C. N. (1985) *Parkinson's Law or the Pursuit of Progress.* London: Penguin.

Pearn, M., Roderick, C. and Mulrooney, C. (1995) *Learning Organizations in Practice.* London: McGraw Hill.

Pedler, M., Burgoyne, D. and Boydell, T. (1997) *The Learning Company.* (2nd edn) London: McGraw Hill.

Pentland, B. and Rueter, H. (1994) 'Organizational routines and the grammar of action', *Administrative Science Quarterly*, 39 (3): 484–510.

Perkin, H. (1989) *The Rise of Professional Society*, London: Routledge.

Perutz, M. (1998) *I Wish I'd Made You Angry Earlier: Essays on Science, Scientists and Humanity*. Cold Spring Harbor: Laboratory Press.

Peters, T. and Waterman, R. (1982) *In Search of Excellence*. London: Harper and Row.

Polanyi, M. (1971) *Personal Knowledge*. London: Routledge and Kegan Paul.

Pollard, A., Broadfoot, P., Croll, P., Osborn, M. and Abbott, D. (1994) *Changing English Primary Schools? The Impact of the Education reform Act at Key Stage One*. London: Cassell.

Popper, K. (1963) *Conjectures and Refutations*. London: Routledge and Kegan Paul.

Powell, C. and Paton, G. (eds) (1988) *Humour in Society: Resistance and Control*. London: Macmillan.

Prawat, R. S. and Peterson, P. L. (1999) 'Social constructivist views on learning', in J. Murphy and K. S. Louis (eds) *Handbook of Research on Educational Administration*. (2nd edn) San Francisco: Jossey-Bass. pp. 202–36.

PriceWaterhouseCoopers (2001) *Teacher Workload Study: Interim Report*. London: PriceWaterhouseCoopers.

Primary Needs Independent Evaluation Project (1987) *The PNP Coordinator: Opportunities and Ambiguities*. (Interim Report No 5) Leeds: University of Leeds.

Rait, E. (1995) 'Against the current: organizational learning in schools', in S. B. Bacharach and P. Mundell (eds) *Images of Schools: Structures, Roles and Organizational Behaviour*. Thousand Oaks, CA: Corwin Press. pp. 71–107.

Rhodes, R. (1997) *Understanding Governance: Policy Networks, Governance, Reflexivity and Accountability*. Buckingham: Open University Press.

Rowan, B. and Miskel, C. G. (1999) 'Institutional theory and the study of educational organizations', in J. Murphy and K. S. Louis (eds) *Handbook of Research on Educational Administration*, (2nd edn) San Francisco: Jossey-Bass. pp. 359–83.

Schein, E. (1985) *Organizational Culture and Leadership*. San Francisco: Jossey-Bass.

Schmuck, R. and Runkel, P. (1971) *Handbook of Organisational Development in Schools*. Palo Alto, CA: Mayfield Publishing Co.

Schon, D. (1983) *The Reflective Practitioner*. New York: Basic Books.

Schumpeter, J. (1942) *Capitalism, Socialism and Democracy*. London: Allen and Unwin.

Senge, P. (1990) *The Fifth Discipline: The Art and Practice of the Learning Organization*. New York: Doubleday.

Sergiovanni, T. (1996) *Moral Leadership*. San Francisco: Jossey-Bass.

Sergiovanni, T. and Corbally. T. (eds) (1984) *Leadership and Organizational Culture*. Newbury Park, CA: Sage.

Smircich, L. (1983) 'Concepts of culture in organizational analysis', *Administrative Science Quarterly*, 28: 339–58.

Southworth, G. (1995) *Looking into Primary Headship*. London: Falmer Press.

Southworth, G. (1998) *Leading Improving Primary Schools*. London: Falmer Press.

Starratt, R. (1995) *Leaders with Vision: The Quest for School Renewal*. Thousand Oaks, CA: Corwin Press.

Steiner, G. (1979) *Strategic Planning*. New York: Free Press.

Stoll, L. (1999) 'Realising our potential: understanding and developing capacity for lasting improvement', *School Effectiveness and School Improvement*, 10 (4): 503–32.

Swidler, A. (1986) 'Culture in action: symbols and strategies', *American Sociological Review*, 51 (2): 273–86.

Talbert, J. and McLaughlin, M. (1996) 'Teacher professionalism and local school contexts', in I. Goodson and A. Hargreaves (eds) *Teachers' Professional Lives*. London: Falmer. pp. 127–53.

Tan, C. H. (2000) 'High-performance human resource strategies in learning schools', *The Learning Organization*, 7 (1): 32–9.

Taylor, F. W. (1911) *The Principles of Scientific Management*. New York: Harper and Brothers.

Taylor-Gooby, P. and Lawson, R. (1993) (eds) *Markets and Managers: New Issues in the Delivery of Welfare*. Buckingham: Open University Press.

Tomlinson, H. (1998) 'A response to Brundrett', *Educational Management and Administration*, 26 (3): 317–9.

Tyak, D. and Cuban, L. (1995) *Tinkering Towards Utopia: Reflections on a Century of Public School Reform*. Cambridge, MA: Harvard University Press.

Vann, B. (1999) 'Minorities in the United Kingdom: can principals ever be one of us?', *School Leadership and Management*, 19 (2): 201–4.

Wallace, M. (1986) 'The rise of scale posts as a management hierarchy in schools', *Educational Management and Administration*, 14: 203–12.

Wallace, M. (1989) 'Towards a collegiate approach to curriculum management in primary and middle schools', in M. Preedy (ed.) *Approaches to Curriculum Management*, Milton Keynes: Open University Press. pp. 182–94.

Wallace, M. (1996) 'When is experiential learning not experiential learning?' in G. Claxton, T. Atkinson, M. Osborne and M. Wallace (eds) *Liberating the Learner: Lessons for Professional Development in Education*, London: Routledge. pp. 16–31.

Wallace, M. (1998a) 'Innovations in planning for school improvement: problems and potential', in A. Hargreaves, A. Lieberman, M. Fullan and D. Hopkins (eds) *International Handbook of Educational Change*, Dordrecht, Netherlands: Kluwer Academic Press. pp. 1181–202.

Wallace, M. (1998b) 'A counter policy to subvert educational reform: collabration among schools and colleges in a competititve climate', *British Educational Research Journal*, 24 (2): 195–215.

Wallace, M. (2003) 'Managing the unmanageable? Coping with complex educational change', *Educational Management and Administration*, 31 (1): 9–29.

Wallace, M. and Hall, V. (1994) *Inside the SMT: Team Approaches to Secondary School Management*. London: Paul Chapman.

Wallace, M. and Huckman, L. (1999) *Senior Management Teams in Primary Schools: The Quest for Synergy*. London: Routledge.

Wallace, M. and McMahon, A. (1994) *Planning for Change in Turbulent Times: The Case of Multiracial Primary Schools*. London: Cassell.

Wallace, M. and Pocklington, K. (2002) *Managing Complex Educational Change: Large-scale Reorganisation of Schools*. London: RoutledgeFalmer.

Wallace, M. and Poulson, L. (eds) (2003) *Learning to Read Critically in Educational Leadership and Management*. London: Sage.

Wallace, M. and Wray, A. (2002) 'The fall and rise of linguists in education policy-making: from "common sense" to common ground', *Language Policy*, 1: 75–98.

Weick, K. (1976) 'Educational organizations as loosely-coupled systems', *Administrative Science Quarterly*, 21: 1–19.

Weick, K. (2000) *Making Sense of the Organisation*. Oxford: Blackwell.

Weick, K. and Westley, F. (1996) 'Organizational learning: confirming an oxymoron', in S. Clegg , C. Handy and W. Nord (eds) *Handbook of Organizational Studies*. London: Sage. pp. 440–58.

Wenger, E. (1998) *Communities of Practice: Learning, Meaning and Identity*. Cambridge: Cambridge University Press.

Weston, P., Barrett, E. and Jamison, J. (1992) *The Quest for Coherence: Managing the Whole Curriculum 5–16*. Slough: National Foundation for Educational Research.

Whitty, G., Power, S. and Halpin, D. (1998) *Devolution and Choice in Education*. Buckingham: Open University Press.

Williams, B. (2003) *Truth and Truthfulness: An Essay in Genealogy*. Princeton: Princeton University Press.

Williams, R. (1958) *Culture and Society 1780–1950*. London: Penguin.

Willmott, R. (2002) *Educational Policy and Realist Social Theory: Primary Teaching, Child-centred Philosophy and the New Managerialism*. London: Routledge.

Woods, P. (1995) *Creative Teachers in Primary Schools*. Buckingham: Open University Press.

Woods, P., Jeffrey, B., Troman, G. and Boyle, M. (1997) *Re-structuring schools, Re-structuring Teachers: Responding to Change in the Primary School*. Buckingham: Open University Press.

Zinoviev, A. (1979) *The Yawning Heights*. London: Penguin.

Index